GENDER ISSUES IN COOPERATIVES

GENDER ISSUES IN COOPERATIVES

By

Prof. S.Nakkiran

Professor
Department of Cooperatives
Institute of Cooperatives & Development Studies
Ambo University
Ambo, Ethiopia.
Email: doctorsnakkiran@gmail.com

&

Dr. M. Karthikeyan

Assistant Professor
Department of Cooperatives
Faculty of Business & Economics
Hawassa University
Hawassa
Email: mkeya2003@gmail.com
mkeya2003@yahoo.com

DISCOVERY PUBLISHING HOUSE PVT. LTD.
NEW DELHI-110 002

Published by:
Tilak Wasan
DISCOVERY PUBLISHING HOUSE PVT. LTD.
4383/4A, Ansari Road, Darya Ganj
New Delhi-110 002 (India)
Phone : +91-11-23279245, 43596064-65
Fax : +91-11-23253475
E-mail : parul.wasan@gmail.com
discoverypublishinghouse@gmail.com
web : www.discoverypublishinggroup.com

***First Edition:* 2012**
ISBN: 978-93-5056-085-3

Gender Issues in Cooperatives

Printed at:
Shree Balaji Art Press
Delhi

Preface

Dear Learners! It is our pleasure to introduce the textbook *Gender Issues in Cooperatives* to you. This book is designed in a detailed manner so as to help you to understand the gender concepts, roles and gender in development. This book covers the general concepts on gender issues and women participation in cooperatives and constraints.

Women all over the world are facing problems in societies to establish their will in discharging their duties. Discrimination and neglect take place in spite of number of legal measures taken to protect their rights and establish privileges. Unless an attitudinal change takes place in the minds and hearts of male population nothing could be done. Discrimination against women takes place even in developed societies in sharing resources and assigning positions, due to them, in administration, politics and utility areas. The present work deals with a review of women's position in societies, especially in developing societies, gender inequality in all walks of life, the degree of neglect of women by society and the role cooperatives play in alleviating the sufferings of women. Cooperatives as institutions of the poor and the deprived, have a notable role to uplift the social status and economic conditions of women.

This work is based on our experience as teachers, trainers and researchers in the field of cooperatives. The present work is based on Undergraduate programme and outcome of our teaching and research experience, articles published in reputed journals, and discussions with cooperative officials. This book will be very much useful to the students of undergraduate, and also to professionals involved in cooperative department, and the trainers who are working in various training establishments. We have drawn the inputs from various materials — papers, journals, books, websites and we have consulted several of our friends, colleagues and field experts. We are ever grateful and thankful to them for their immense support and healthy criticism. We hope that the readers of this book will get knowledge on gender issues in cooperatives. Any useful comments, suggestions to improve the present version are welcome and solicited from the readers. We are thankful and grateful to Parul Wasan, Discovery Publishing House Pvt. Ltd., New Delhi for publishing the book neatly under his renowned label for the cooperative knowledge community.

S. NAKKIRAN

M. KARTHIKEYAN

Contents

Part I — Gender Issues

Gender Concept

Agents

Ordinary people who create historical change through the activities and struggles of their everyday lives. Compare this with "change agent", an especially knowledgeable person or organization that brings change to others.

Androcentric

Male centred, a masculine point of view.

Androcentrism

A term developed by feminist theorists to describe the dominant worldview that, until recently, mostly excluded the experiences of women from its analyses. This term also refers to an approach taken to knowledge and the production of knowledge.

Assumption

A supposition that is taken to be true but might not be based on factual evidence.

Biological determinism

A view on which it is argued that human social behaviour is the result of factors inherent to the biological makeup of human beings. This is often contrasted with explanations of human behaviour based on social or socio-psychological factors.

Class

A social or economic division in society. Theorists sometimes differentiate between economic class (based on access to economic resources or material goods) and social class (based on status, prestige, family background, and other factors). One's class is defined largely by one's relationship to the means of production; the capitalist class owns the means of production.

Development

DAWN defined *development* as "socially responsible management and use of resources, the elimination of gender subordination and social inequality and the organizational restructuring that can bring these about" (Sen and Grown: 1987, p. 2). The indigenous-feminist theorizing informing this definition stresses the need for economic and social change, empowerment of women, and progressive changes in public-private relations to benefit women.

This is conceptually quite opposite to the definition of *development* held by other development theorists: "Economic development consists of the introduction of new combinations of production factors which increase labour productivity" (Hunt: 1989, p. 49). This definition locates development in the sphere of production and focuses only on changes in economic relations. To such theorists, economic development consists in introducing new combinations of factors of production to increase labour productivity. It is easy to recognize the bias against women in this definition. By emphasizing production factors, it focuses on formal economic activities, such as waged labour and large-scale production. In all these areas, women are under-represented and their contributions are devalued. More significantly, this definition ignores the critical connection between the reproductive work women do and how this underpins the formal, productive economy. It is a good example of how women are marginalized at the core of development theory.

The dictionary definition of *development*, referred to a process of unfolding, maturing, and evolving. When applied to plants and other organisms, the evolutionary implications of the term are unproblematic: a fully developed plant, an adult animal, or even a human animal has certain well-defined and fully predictable characteristics. If it lacks these characteristics, we are justified in saying that the organism is underdeveloped or undeveloped.

Equity

Within a modernization framework, *equity* refers to equal legal rights to participate in an ever-expanding global capitalist system (sustained growth). Equity does not, in this framework, imply equal effective opportunity to participate. The modernization framework does not recognize the systemic class, race, or gender barriers that negate the idea of an open society in which every individual makes progress according to his or her merits. Participation, here, does not imply making any choices about goals or lifestyles—it assumes that one can be modern in only one way. No ecological or temporal limits and no recognition of the uneven costs and benefits of the global economy accompany the idea of sustained growth.

Within the institutional framework of development agencies, these same terms have a different set of meanings and carry different assumptions. *Equity* becomes the equal right and obligation to participate in development programmes and projects determined by outside agencies (government, non-governmental, national, international). Non-participation is taken as evidence of backwardness, as these programmes and projects are designed by "experts" to "develop" local economic and political systems. Sustainability in this context is often associated with the ideas of efficiency and low cost. If the programmes have been well designed and participation is high, they are supposed to continue indefinitely, with minimal resources from government. Examples include centrally designed community health-care systems that are intended to reduce the need and demand for high-quality medical services or road improvements to be undertaken and maintained by villagers.

A third set of meanings for these same terms can be drawn from a more radical framework, with empowerment as its central objective. *Equity,* in this case, means equal effective power (overcoming race, class, and gender barriers) to participate in defining the goals and agenda of development processes that meet every human's need for a secure and decent livelihood, both for present and for future generations (sustainable development). The starting point for achieving these goals has to be the recognition of differences (along gender, race, and other dimensions). Sensitivity to difference (race, class, gender, region, history, etc.) is an essential component of attempts to develop new visions and plan for change: one group's liberation or "development" may otherwise cause another group to be neglected or, worse still, further oppressed. Third World feminists and those identifying with post-modernism have made major contributions to critique and new theorizing on questions of power and difference. Their work is examined in the next section ("Rethinking gender, race, and identity in a global context").

Empowerment of women

It refers to an act of building self-reliance for and among women, for promoting self-development which facilitates their decision-making on own ability as well as setting of goals or agendas, production and reproduction activities. It is a situation that enables women to have equal opportunities with men for participating in development process. It also involves collective efforts in minimizing or eradicating any discriminatory factors. Education plays an important role in empowering women as well as men.

Economic growth

The assumption that increased economic productivity and exchange constitute the basic requirement for development. It is measured by market output, GNP, per capita income, etc.

Egalitarianism

Relations based on more or less equal participation of all adults in the production of basic necessities, as well as in their distribution or exchange and in their consumption.

Equal opportunity

Conditions that must be created so that women have the same options as men and the same life chances.

Ethnicity

Group associations based on any combination of common characteristics, including culture, language, religion, phenotype, geographic region, and ancestry. It is recognized that historical and social factors shape the formation of ethnic groups and bestow on them a distinct identity.

Ethnocentric

Believing that one's own race, nation, or culture is superior to all others.

Feminist

An individual who is aware of the oppression, exploitation, or subordination of women within society and who consciously acts to change and transform this situation.

Flexibility

The ability of companies to quickly adapt to changes in markets, technology, and competition. Flexibility strategies include tying wages to productivity or profits, eliminating long-term commitments to workers by subcontracting and or offering part-time work, and finding cheaper sources of labour.

Gender

Gender is defined as the social meanings given to biological sex differences. It is an ideological and cultural construct but is also reproduced within the realm of material practices; in turn, it influences the outcomes of such practices. It affects the distribution of resources, wealth, work, decision-making and political power, and the enjoyment of rights and entitlements within the family as well as public life. Despite variations across cultures and over time, gender relations throughout the world entail asymmetry of power between men and women as a pervasive trait. Thus, gender is a social stratifier, and in this sense it is similar to other stratifiers such as race, class, ethnicity, sexuality and age. It helps us understand the social construction of gender identities and the unequal structure of power that underlies the relationship between the sexes. (UN. Report of the Secretary-General: 1999 *World Survey on the Role of Women in Development: Globalization, Gender and Work* (A/54/227)

Gender refers to the roles, behaviour, attitudes and activities that society assigns to men and women. It can also be the power relations between men and women in a given society. Sometimes there is a tendency to refers to women when dealing with gender without looking at there relationship with their male counterpart, one refers to gender issues as opposed to women's issues because the issues concern both men and women. We should therefore take care not to refer to women or men parse, but the relation between them, when we discuss about gender.

Gender equity

Gender equity refers to fairness in the treatment of both males and females in all aspects of life while recognizing differences between the two. It is believed that measures taken in the spirit of equity may eliminate some of the discriminatory practices, this is to mean that equal treatment of men and women may successfully remove gender disparities in some instances. Affirmative action is one stage in gender equity approach. Many people, who favour the Affirmative action, define it as a Compensation of the social and historical looses faced by the disadvantaged category of the society and the method of application has to be by including the disadvantaged group who need it.

Gender equality

Gender equality refers to equal opportunities, equal access to resources, equal rights and equal share of responsibilities regardless of sex of the individuals. This is the premise that women and men should be treated in the same way and implies the prevalence of some form of intentional or unintentional discrimination. Gender equality is therefore needed to eliminate discriminatory practices affecting women or men. Discrimination on the basis of gender is one of the main causes of poverty, and major obstacle to equitable and sustainable human development. The work of promoting gender equality starting from child treatment which concerns men as much as women is fundamental to development.

Gender discrimination

Gender discrimination is prejudicial treatment of an individual based on a gender stereotype. The act of denial of equal treatment, legal rights or fair opportunities because of their sex.

Gender stereotyping

Gender Stereotyping these refer to traditional, and in most cases false representation of a person based on his/her sex. Such stereotypes are often based on socially accepted gender roles and viewed as normal. A gender stereotype is a "psychological make-up" about male and female. Stereotype about female include: dependent, needful, passive, matronly nurturing, emotional, weak, delicate, affectionate, irrational, appreciative etc.

Stereotype about male is more or less opposite to this and include independent, aggressive, assertive strong, courage, ambitious, enterprising, adventurous, daring, self-confident, self-reliant, rational etc.

This implies that women are less intelligent, less competent and less able physically and psychologically and even spiritually.

Gender disparity

Gender disparity refers to the differences or imbalances in economic, political, social, and cultural status of men and women. These imbalances are sometimes referred to as gender gap or bias. They are developed right from childhood during which mothers train their daughters towards becoming good wives, cooks, house-keepers, mothers, livestock tenders, labourers etc. and father take the sons out for plowing, cattle rearing, outdoor games etc. Gender gaps are manifested in major socio-economic indicators such as employment, education, health, ownership of property, level of income and participation in decision-making at all levels.

Gender mainstreaming

Gender mainstreaming refers to the process where by attention to gender equality is integrated in to an organizations analysis, planning, performing etc thereby changing the content and direction of these practices at organizational and institutional level. Mainstreaming is the opposite of segregating gander issues in to separate women's projects.

Gender mainstreaming

Gender mainstreaming in a gender perspective is the process of assessing the implications for men and women of any planned action, including legislation, policies and programmes, in all areas and at all levels. It is a strategy for making women's as well as men's concerns and experiences an integral dimension of the design, implementation, monitoring and evaluation of policies and programmes in all political, economic and social spheres so that women and men benefit equally and inequality is not perpetuated. The ultimate goal is to achieve gender equality. (Economic and Social Council, agreed conclusions, 1997/2).

Gender awareness

Gender awareness refers to looking and understanding the men and women's common and specific needs. It is a understanding that women's have need, aspiration and vision distinct from men. Many projects fail to attain their aim due to lack of this gender awareness that help them to take women's need in to consideration. Socialization is a continuous process through which an individual learn the norm of the society and Gender socialization refers to the process through which individuals learn to become feminine and masculine, according to the expectation currents in their society. There are peoples who help us to internalize these gender norms and called as Agents. 'Socialization agents' include family, peers, mass media, day care centers, schools, community organizations etc.

Gender prejudice

This is a belief or disliking against an individual due to his/her sex or gender.

Gender barriers

Obstacles to equality that may exist in the laws, norms, and practices of a society and can be identified and removed.

Gender relations

A society's socially constructed relations between women and men.

Global feminism

The celebration of different feminisms, grounded in the specificities of women's multifarious experiences. This will not occur until women from all racial groups believe that feminism recognizes their lived realities and incorporates those realities into feminist theories.

Globalization

The idea that the world economy has reached a new level of integration. Heightened capital mobility with globalization means that companies operate worldwide, creating a "global assembly line"; goods, capital, and, to a lesser extent, people move around the globe.

Multiple jeopardies

Racism, sexism, and classism simultaneously experienced by women from marginalized groups, especially visible minorities. This simultaneous experience not only compounds these oppressions but reconstitutes them in specific ways.

Obstacles to growth

Barriers that distort the "natural" process of economic growth. If this growth does not occur, then the obstacles or barriers must be identified and removed.

Patriarchal ideology

A set of ideas defining women's roles as different from, and subordinate to, those of men.

Patriarchy

A system of male domination that is widespread but historically specific and can vary over tune and context. Originally, this term was used to describe societies characterized by "the rule of the father", that is, the power of the husband or father over his wives, children, and property. The term has now come to refer to the overall systemic character of oppressive and expioitative relations affecting women.

Personal is political

The view that male domination and women's resistance to male domination occur in both of the so-called public and private spheres. The concept is often associated with radical feminism.

Power

Personal, economical, political, or social ascendancy and control exercised by one individual or group over another. Often this is most clearly seen in relationships between people. Liberal and Marxist thinkers associate power with control over resources and institutions. Post-modernists see power not as something held only by the ruling class but as something diffused throughout society, exercised in many diverse ways by many diverse people, and closely tied to control over knowledge and discourse through attitudes, perceptions, and behaviour.

Race

Differentiation of human beings into various sub-species. This is usually based on outward physical (or phenotypical) features, such as skin colour, facial features, and hair type. Many social scientists today recognize that *race* is defined differently in different societies and at different tunes and so is largely socially determined. They prefer, therefore, to use the term *ethnicity*. Race is socially constructed and plays a crucial role in women's experiences and opportunities.

Representation

A term commonly used to refer to an aspect of democratic processes that permits individuals or groups to select those who will carry forward their ideas and agendas to higher authorities. The term is used in a different sense in current theoretical writings to question the power relations implied by having one group convey information about another group in authoritative ways that may deny the people being "represented" the opportunity to present their identity on their own terms.

Reproduction

The biological reproduction of children, that is, childbirth and lactation; the physical reproduction of the wage labour-force on a daily basis through domestic work; and the social reproduction of the patriarchal capitalist system through maintaining the ideological conditions that reproduce class and gender relations and the political and economic status quo.

Resistance

Action or inaction, talk or silence, often hidden or covert, through which members of oppressed groups indicate to themselves, each other, and, more rarely, outsiders that they reject the conditions of their oppression and the legitimations proffered by dominant groups.

Restructuring

The changes occurring in companies and economies as a result of the rapidly changing world economy and heightened global competition. Both economic forces and policy choices shape restructuring.

Sexual division of labour

The allocation of tasks and responsibilities in society to women and men. In most inegalitarian societies, the tasks allocated to women have a consistently lower value than those assigned to men.

Social capital

Anything, other than capital, that enhances economic performance.

Social construction of gender

The social definition and determination of ideas and practices. People socially define and determine and can therefore change the ideas and practices related to feminine and masculine characteristics, activities, and ways of relating to one another.

Stratification

Structured inequalities between groups in society, based on gender, class, ethnicity, or other distinguishing characteristics. Although systems of stratification have existed in virtually all societies, significant differences in wealth and power emerge within state-based systems.

Gender as a social construct

For centuries, it was believed that the different characteristic women and men exhibited were natural and immutable – determined by biological differences or divinely ordained. These characteristics included ideas and values about what was masculine and what was feminine (women are emotional/ men are rational) and sets of behaviour, attitudes or practices (women working with natural and simple objects/men working with machines).

Sexual division of labour

Every society assigns different tasks to men and women. This is called the sexual division of labour. In most cultures, both women and men do productive work, i.e., produce goods or services for income or subsistence, although in most specific situations, productive work is clearly divided into men's tasks such as ploughing, and working with machinery and women do planting, weeding, and teaching children. Women are mainly responsible for reproductive work like cooking, washing, cleaning, nursing, looking after children, building and maintaining shelter, and reproduce and maintain the labour force.

Gender and development – the linkage

Because women begin development from a position of subordination and relative disadvantage, special focus and support are necessary in order to enable them to fully participate and benefit from development. The empowerment of women requires changes in the behaviour and attitudes of men and women and the society at large. Thus the need to redesign development agendas from women's perspectives.

Gender analysis

Gender analysis seeks to extract and organize information pertaining to the differences between men and women in the allocation of their labour to production and routine domestic tasks and the difference in the distribution of resources and assets to which they have access or which they control.

Gender relations of production

An organizing construct encompasses both social and economic relations of production. It means socio-economic relations between women and men that are characterized often by asymmetrical power relations, different assignment of labour tasks, control over decision-making and differential access to and control over the allocation of resources including land and income. In making gender the focus, for example, we can learn most by concentrating on sets of relationships that affect land use and tenure. This concept therefore becomes a very important one for researchers, planners and programme implementers involved in agricultural development.

SEX AND GENDER

Sex is a natural attribute differentiating a male person from a female. A male person is biologically different from a female. This is evident in that while males have mustache, women do not; while women have big breasts that may produce milk, men do not; they also differ in their reproductive organs and their roles in child bearing. Being a male or female is, therefore, a natural phenomenon that we cannot change (except being through surgery) since the two sexes are born different.

Gender is a social attribute ascribing some characteristics or norms and modes of behaviour to the female and others to the male sex. The gender of a person is determined by the society and by its way of upbringing children. Gender is, therefore, the result of the interplay of cultural, religious, and similar factors of a society. It refers to historically defined identities, roles and behaviours or different groups such as men–women, girls–boys, old men–old women, mother-in-laws , daughter-in-laws, etc. The female and male sexes are socialized into being one of these groups. The differences among these groups brought about by socio-cultural factors are often mistaken for natural differences between the sexes or considered as God-given phenomena. Hence, as opposed to sex which is natural and biological differentiating a male person from a female, gender is the result of the socialization process.

Again the difference between sex and gender in that sex refers to the biological difference between male and female while gender is socially constructed. People born biologically female or male but they learn femininity and masculinity (i.e. they are brought up to act and behave to be girls and boys who grow in to women and men, as the result of sex role socialization.)

The learned characteristics are what make up gender identity and determine or govern gender roles in a given societal context.

What is clear evident here is that there is anatomical difference between the male and female, as female and male have different (reproductive) sex organs that we cannot change simply (except though high surgery). For example:

- Men impregnate and women bear children.
- Women breast feed and men do not.
- Women has big breast, men do not etc.

Why gender?

The concern with gender emerged as feminist theorists sought to understand the complexities of women's subordination. The word *gender* came into mainly academic use some 15 years after the reemergence of late-20th-century feminism, which has, unlike its earlier manifestations, made a significant dent in male-dominated (androcentric) scholarship.

Table 1.1 show the difference between gender and sex.

Table 1.1: Difference between Sex and Gender

Sex	Gender
❖ Fact of human biology	❖ The result of social construction
❖ What we born with	❖ Everything that happens after birth
❖ Is being born as male or female	❖ Gender is about the relations between male and female
❖ Universal	❖ Differ from culture to culture and over time
❖ Permanent (if not changed through surgery)	❖ Change over time due to social, economic or political change
❖ Naturally given	❖ Learned (result of socialization)
❖ Agent is "nature"	❖ Agents are parents, teachers peers, culture and tradition

Feminist scholars argued that the Western academic tradition, of which most universities and colleges in the world are part, has systematically ignored the experiences of women in its fields of learning, concepts, theories, and research methods. Additionally, although claiming to be scientific, it has really embodied mythical assumptions about women's and men's capabilities, the sexual division of labour in early human history, and, as a result, women's place in today's society. These assumptions were extended to non-Western societies, with the result that Western assumptions and values influenced relations between the sexes and between groups within each sex, relations that ranged from egalitarian to highly patriarchal and stratified.

The word *gender,* like *development,* had a specific usage before feminist theorists extended its meaning. One of the earliest uses of *gender* in feminist theory can be traced to the 1976 University of Sussex Workshop on the Subordination of Women and the school of thought that emerged from this workshop. Scholars such as Olivia Harris, Maureen Mackintosh, Felicity Odium, Ann Whitehead, and Kate Young argued that women, like men, are biological beings but that women's subordination was socially constructed and not biologically determined. They argued further that to conceptually differentiate between these two realities, it is necessary to identify "sex" as the biological differentiation between male and female, and "gender" as the differentiation between masculinity and femininity as constructed through socialization and education, among other factors. What is biological is fixed and unchangeable, but what is social is subject to change and should be the focus of attention for feminist theorists.

In its more recent use, *gender* has come to be used, like *class* and *ethnicity* or *race,* to designate an analytical social category, one that interacts with other social factors in influencing life experiences of groups and individuals.

Now this concept has gained widespread acceptance in a range of groups and often for different reasons. Some of these reasons are as follows:

- The need to include men in our analysis.
- To gain academic acceptance.

In its simplest recent usage, "gender" is a synonym for "women." Any number of books and articles, whose subject is women's history, have in the past few years substituted "gender" for "women" in their titles. In some cases this usage ... is about political acceptability in the field. In these instances, the use of "gender" is meant to denote scholarly seriousness of a work, for "gender" has a more neutral and objective sound than does "women".

Recently, the phrase "women in development" (WID) is also being replaced in some circles by "gender and development" (GAD) or "gender concerns in development" (GCID)

Today, however, two types of critiques have emerged in relation to the concept of gender. One of these comes from a movement perspective. As noted by Joan W. Scott: gender has become a useful and almost inescapable concept in women's studies and feminist theory (Scott 1989). Many people in the women's movement fear, however, that this is leading to a situation in which women are once more invisible. They note that the fields of WID, GAD, GCID, feminist theory, and women's studies all owe their origins to the women's movement and the struggles of women in the streets, towns, villages, and academies. Yet, today, with the growing acceptance of academic women's studies and gender specialists, the concern with the day-to-day problems and struggles of women and the movement is being marginalized and, indeed, no longer even acknowledged.

The other critique comes from a theoretical perspective. It is now being found that:

- The divisions between male and female are not as fixed and clear cut as once thought — the male-female dichotomy is seen as being just as problematic as other dichotomies in Western thought; and
- It is not so simple to extricate what is "sex" from what is "gender", as these two phenomena, as described, intertwine.

Although the concept of gender can never substitute for that of woman, it has added to our understanding of the complexities of human social relations in numerous ways. Clearly, it is a concept that is here to stay.

Gender and Society before the Development Era

It is important to recall the richness of the history of most developing countries before colonialism and the era of development. It is also important for us to understand the nature of social relations in the earlier periods of that history. The Third World, or the South, really comprises most of the world. It is a mistake to speak of this vast and varied area as if it were all the same.

Until recently, most of our history of this region was androcentric. It focused on the period after the encounter with Western Europe and emphasized male action or agency. In addition, it was often first written in Western languages by Western male scholars who, with few exceptions, were Eurocentric and intolerant of the people they studied. As a result, our historical records are laced with racism, sexism, and imperialist sentiments. The following 17th-century European male's description of matrilineality in West Africa is a clear example:

> The Right of Inheritance is very oddly adjusted; as far as I could observe, the Brother's and Sister's Children are the right and lawful Heirs, in the manner following. They do not jointly inherit, but the eldest Son of his Mother is Heir to his Mother's Brother or her Son, as the eldest Daughter is Heiress of her Mother's Sister or her Daughter: neither the Father himself or his Relations as Brothers, Sisters etc. have any claim to the Goods of the Defunct, for what Reason they can't tell: This Custom was introduced on account of the Whoredom of the Women, herein following the custom of some East-Indian Kings who educate their Sister's Son as their own, and appoint him to succeed in the Throne, because they are more sure that their Sister's Son is of their Blood than they can be of their own.

Although development theorists paid little attention to the complexities of these societies before the era of development, social anthropologists did. However, they also took with them androcentric and ethnocentric biases that clouded their view of these societies and of gender relations in these societies.

In the heyday of Third World nationalism, in the 1960s and 1970s, indigenous historians sought to correct this wrong. Most of these historians were male or trained in the androcentric worldview, so knowledge of women's experiences in precolonial society continued to be hidden. To counteract centuries of what Peter Worsley (1970) called "imperialist history," nationalist historians often distorted this history to highlight a great and glorious past, stressing the kings and queens, wealth and empire. In so doing, they often ignored the traditional *egalitarianism* of many precolonial societies, in which women had greater power and autonomy and life was more in tune with nature and the environment, not based on its destruction.

Today, as feminist activists and other concerned scholars reevaluate development and modernization, there is a renewed appreciation of the positive features of the ways of life in earlier societies, although we realize the limitations of those times. We also understand the need to preserve and protect the egalitarian and environmentally friendly practices that have survived in our societies and have been adapted to serve people's needs, often outside mainstream political and economic structures.

Gender Relations and Social Change

Since the late 18th century, social scientists have sought to develop a schema to explain the variety and differences in human experience. Early evolutionists incorporated the notion of progress: human development moving from primitive, backward forms to advanced and developed ones. Functionalist anthropologists in the mid-20th century concentrated on seeing each society as an integrated whole. They could not help interpreting what they observed through their biased perspectives and basing conclusions on their customary assumptions.

Today, although critical scholars no longer attribute value to societies in terms of progress or backwardness, they do recognize that pre-colonial societies may have been at different stages of social development. These stages are usually described in relation to the production systems that predominated at the time. Like all schemas, however, these descriptions provide only a partial understanding. Most societies cannot be neatly classified in one category or another. Many show signs of being at more than one "stage". In addition, it must be stressed that all societies do not necessarily pass through all the recognized stages.

Some anthropologists totally reject any theory of stages of social development because of their links to the notions of modernization and progress. They argue, instead, for a non-stage approach that examines each society on its own terms and sees movement (social change) taking place in any direction. Transitions from one stage to another, if these are thought to occur at all, are therefore the result of many factors that anthropologists are still exploring, including a society's environment and its historical relationships with other groups. The stages are usually identified as follows:

- Hunter-gatherer or foraging societies
- Horticultural societies
  - ⇒ Matrilineal descent
  - ⇒ Patrilineal descent

- Agricultural or agrarian societies
- Pastoral or herding societies
- Industrial societies
- Various combinations of the above

Feminist anthropologists have also argued that the organization of social and *production relations* — such as social *stratification,* the monogamous family, ownership of property, and forms of work and production — has greatly influenced the differences in gender relations around the world.

In some instances, as discussed earlier, societies were extremely stratified patriarchies before the arrival of European colonizers. This was sometimes the result of domination by other patriarchal and highly stratified groups or an existing system of social stratification. In many other instances, however, this was not the case, especially in matrilineal societies, as shown in Fatima Mernissi's description of Morocco before its Islamization:

> The panorama of female sexual rights in pre-Islamic culture reveals that women's sexuality was not bound by the concept of legitimacy. Children belonged to their mother's tribe. Women had sexual freedom to enter into and break off unions with more than one man, either simultaneously or successively. A woman could either reserve herself to one man at a time, on a more or less temporary basis, as in a *mut'a* marriage, or she could be visited by many husbands at different times whenever their nomadic tribe or trade caravan came through the woman's town or camping ground. The husband would come and go; the main unit was the mother and child with an entourage of kinfolk.

In all situations, women had been able to create spaces and possibilities for autonomy within the structures of subordination existing in their societies. However, these strategies were complicated or removed by the imposition of assumptions about a woman's or man's place in the new systems of stratification that were based on notions of class and racial or ethnic superiority.

Summary

- Different terms related to gender concepts and issues are discussed.
- The differences between gender and sex are tabulated.
- Although the concept of gender can never substitute for that of woman, it has added to our understanding of the complexities of human social relations in numerous ways. Clearly, it is a concept that is here to stay.

Self-Learning Activity

Try to answer the following questions on your own:

1. Define Gender.
2. Differentiate Gender and sex.
3. What do you understand from gender relations and social change?

Place of Women in Society

STATUS OF WOMEN

General information

During the UN Decade for Women (1975-85) focus was directed on women's issues and a favourable legal and institutional climate for women was created. Many governments established special offices for women's issues, and efforts were made to increase women's representation in decision-making and to involve them as key components in development policies. Since then progress has been made in the promotion of equality issues in most countries of the world but there is still often a discrepancy between principle and practice, and many policy approaches still treat women as a marginal minority group.

Regarding the status of women today, there have been some improvements but generally the situation appears to have deteriorated. On the one hand, there are more literate women today than few years ago and more women can be found in higher positions in political and economic spheres of life. But, on the other hand, according to a UN report many women are poorer than ever before. The number of women living in poverty nearly doubled over the past 20 years, and women today constitute at least 60 per cent of the world's one billion poor. Studies also suggest that a deterioration of the living conditions of women from low-income sectors often results in violence, a breakdown of the family and mental health disorders. A situation that affects not only the family but the whole of society.

Undoubtedly the most disconcerting development is the widening gap between the North and South, the rich and poor and the rural and urban populations. The conditions of the rural poor in developing countries, have deteriorated drastically over the past years, often due to structural adjustment programmes which have increased the hardship of rural women in particular. Rural women are the first to suffer from reductions in public sector services such as education and health.

In the field of education there are, however, signs of a positive trend worldwide. There has been a decline in illiteracy amongst women from 46.6 per cent in 1970 to 33.6 per cent in 1990, and this trend looks like continuing according to UNESCO. But, nevertheless, girls and women still represent two-thirds of the world's illiterates. With regard to rural women, their access to education and training facilities is much more limited than for women in the urban areas.

Direct gender discrimination still exists and discriminatory attitudes and practices are widespread. In many parts of the world, girl children often deliberately receive less education, less food and less health care than boys. According to the WHO, one-sixth of all female infant deaths in India, Pakistan and Bangladesh were, for example, due to neglect and discrimination.

Illiteracy Rates (UNESCO)

Illiteracy rate are falling for young women but still much higher than men. Over 40 per cent of young women are still illiterate in Africa and Southern and Western Asia.

In the economic sphere inequality is also prevalent. Women today represent 34 per cent of the workers in the formal labour sector worldwide and, although the wage gap between men and women has decreased, women still earn 30-40 per cent less than men for comparable work and more women are still found in traditionally low-paid jobs. Most women, however, work in the informal sector. The number of women in this insecure sector, unprotected by unions or employment legislation, far exceeds that of men.

Another issue that affects women throughout the world is their heavy workload. Due to the double burden of productive/economic activities and family responsibilities, women work much longer hours than men and do not have much time to spare for other activities (such as participating in meetings or community and training activities). In addition to this much of the work carried out by women is unrecorded and undervalued, or not valued at all since it often does not appear in a country's official statistics. Furthermore, when national surveys are carried out in the agricultural sector, they invariably underestimate the agricultural work carried out by women. For example, the national figures in Egypt showed that 3.6 per cent of the women were involved in agricultural work whereas a local study showed that between 35-50 per cent women were involved. In Peru the national figures estimated 2.6 per cent women involvement and the local figures estimated 86 per cent (FAO).

For women in poorer rural and urban areas in developing countries the workload is particularly heavy. Women are often engaged in activities such as subsistence crop production, family cash crop production (planting and weeding and harvesting), market gardening, or informal commerce, small-scale manufacturing etc., in addition to their household and family care responsibilities.

Women in many parts of the world are regarded as successful traders and entrepreneurs. However small-scale enterprises are difficult to establish and many women are hampered by lack of access to credit and other resources such as training and education. Traditional practices and customs can also often impede women's entrepreneurial aptitudes and potentials.

Poverty, low status and lack of participation and integration into the mainstream have resulted in the marginalization of women. To integrate women into the mainstream is not an easy task, but the first step is to change attitudes and overcome the existing resistance to the change in women's roles. Society must recognize and value women's productive and reproductive roles and their contribution to sustainable economic development.

There has been a growing awareness among governments, policy and decision-makers in recent years that women are indeed important, although under-utilized, contributors to economic growth and development rather than just passive beneficiaries. There is also a growing understanding of the fact that whatever happens to women will have significant consequences for the well-being of future generations in all parts of the world.

Place of Women in Society

Women play an important role in developing the family and society by means of advancing the culture of the society and upbringing the values. The development of a family and children is mainly in the hands of women. They play the role of mother, wife, and other important roles. The place of women is discussed as follows:

Household worker

All the routine working in the family like cooking, washing, cleaning, etc are undertaken by women. Though in modern society, due to education and equality, men have come forward to share the burden of women, the ultimate responsibility for the household work lie with the women.

Upbringing children

From time immemorial it is the duty of the mother to upbringing the children. In all societies the children are brought up by mother up to a stage, say teenage. Even after that stage the mother would like to take care of her children by means of taking interest in their welfare, health and growth.

Bring good habits

Women as mother and responsible citizen bring good habits to the family and the society. The good name of a family is pronounced only by the hard work and good habits shown by women apart from men, who may play a very minor role.

Ethics and religion

Women inculcate good habits, virtues and ethics to their children and society. Such virtues form as ethics, which are the basis for a cultured society. Likewise, women play an important role in practicing religion, taking the message of God to their children. Any religion cannot get purity without the involvement of women in the sacred affaires of religion.

Public administration

Women play a significant role in public administration in modern days. They actively participate in the civic and political administration as corporate, council members, legislators, ministers and administrators.

Labor force

Women form a major labor force in agriculture and related activities. In the organized sector women labor force has become very precious in the fields of education, health, social welfare, etc.

Women in decision-making

Decision making affairs relating to family, corporate sector and government are looked after well by women. Ethiopian women are still under-represented in leadership and decision-making roles in community affairs. They are under-represented in traditional structures. They hardly serve as elders or religious leaders in their community. In the field of education also the role of Ethiopian women is very negligible. Due to financial problems girls are often obliged to work as maids and street vendors. Cultural and social norms such as early marriage, abduction are major constraints, which hinder the capacity of the girl child to perceive education. Social norms, cultural factors and lack of education tend to contribute towards the lower status of women.

Agriculture

In many of the African countries, women play the major role in the field of agriculture. Though they lack title to the land they do all sorts of agriculture work and make agriculture a success.

Discrimination and Underdevelopment

It is relevant to consider some aspects of the marginalisation of the status of women in the world by having a look at the figures which are based on the documents of the United Nations. Some of the findings are:

- *Unemployment Rate:* Male unemployment rate decreased by 11 per cent from 1984 to 1988 while that of women, unemployment rate increased by 0.5 per cent during the same period.
- *Women in the Informal Sector:* Without legal protection or security, women depend on informal trade for their survival. In Third World countries, a high percentage of food vendors were women: in Nigeria 94 per cent, Thailand 80 per cent, 63 per cent in the Philippines.
- *Inequality in Pay:* All over the world women earn only two-thirds of men's pay and earn less than three-quarters of the wages of men doing similar jobs. Women form a third of the world's official labour force, but are concentrated in the lowest-paid jobs and are more vulnerable to unemployment than men.
- *Domestic Work:* Women do almost all the world's domestic work and coupled with their additional work in the productive spheres. This means most women work a double day. Unpaid domestic work is regarded as women's work. Though it is vital work, it is invisible work, unpaid, undervalued and unrecognised. Yet, the women's contribution to society in this regard is enormous.
- *Agriculture:* Women grow about half of the world's food, but own hardly any land, have difficulty in obtaining credit and are overlooked by agricultural advisors and projects. In Africa, three-quarters of the agricultural work is done by women while in Asia, Latin America and the Middle-East, women comprise half of the agricultural labour force.
- *Health:* Women provide more health care than all health services combined and have been major beneficiaries of a new global shift in priorities towards prevention of disease and promotion of good health.
- *Education:* Women continue to outnumber. The men among the world's illiterates by about 3:2 ratio, but school enrollment boom is closing the education gap between boys and girls.
- *Political Affairs:* Due to poorer education, lack of confidence and greater workload, women are still under-represented in the decision-making bodies of their countries.

The effects of the long-term cumulative process of discrimination against women have been accentuated by under-development. Graphically, while women represent nearly 50 per cent of the world's adult population and one-third of the total labour force, they labour nearly two-thirds of the total working hours but receive only one-tenth of world income and own less than one per cent of property. The story of overworked women in the rural areas of the developing and underdeveloped countries of the world is too well known. The type of agricultural activities generally expected of women is highly labour-intensive and the rural women generally do not enjoy the benefits of new technologies. Their wages are generally less because it is assumed that the efficiency of women's labour is poor compared to that of men.

Regarding ownership of land, women do not enjoy equal rights, particularly in the developing countries where most of the production, processing, storage and preparation of food is carried out by the women. These account for 50 per cent of the total labour required for food production. Many of these tasks are performed by children, especially the girls. Besides helping the menfolk in many farm operations, women have to shoulder the entire responsibilities for household chores. Bringing water from far-off wells and rivers and gathering fuel-wood from forests are also part of their daily duties. Such enormous waste of human energy is unnecessary in this technological age.

Gender Equality and Sharing of Opportunities

The Universal Declaration of Human Rights recognised several dimensions of human rights for all people. Some are tangible and quantifiable, such as access to education, health and a decent standard of living and ability to take part in the government of the country. Others are intangible, such as freedom, dignity, and security of person and participation in the cultural life of the community.

The goals of gender equality differ from one country to another, depending on the social, cultural and economic contexts. So, in the struggle for equality, different countries may set different priorities, ranging from more education for girls, to better maternal health, to equal pay for equal work, to more seats in parliament, to removal of disrimination in employment, to protection against violence in the home, to changes in family law, to having men take more responsibility for family life. Equality is not a technocratic goal – it is a wholesale political commitment. Achieving it requires a long-term process in which all cultural, social, political and economic norms undergo fundamental change.

CRITICAL AREAS OF CONCERN

A review of progress since the Nairobi Women's Conference held in 1995 highlights the areas of particular urgency that stand as priorities for action. The twelve critical areas of concern are summarized as follows:

- The persistent and increasing burden of poverty on women.
- Inequalities and inadequacies in and equal access to education and training.

- Inequalities and inadequacies in and unequal access to health care and related services.
- Violence against women.
- The effects of armed or other kinds of conflict on women, including those living under foreign occupation.
- Inequality in economic structures and policies, in all forms of productive activities and in access to and control over resources.
- Inequality between men and women in the sharing of power and decision making at all levels.
- Insufficient mechanisms at all levels to promote the advancement of women.
- Lack of respect for and inadequate promotion and protection of the human rights of women.
- Stereotyping of women's role and inequality in women's access to and participation in all communication system especially in media.
- Gender inequalities in the management of natural resources and in the safeguarding of the environment.
- Persistent discrimination against and violation of the rights of the girl child.

UNDP HUMAN DEVELOPMENT REPORT, 1995

The UNDP Human Development Report, 1995 outlines a vision for the 21st century that should build a world order that:

- Embraces full equality of opportunity between women and men as a fundamental concept.
- Eliminates the prevailing disparities between men and women and creates an enabling environment for the full flowering of the productive and creative potential of both sexes.
- Promotes more sharing of work and experience between women and men in the workplace as well as in the household.
- Regarding women as essential agents of change and development and opens many more doors to women to participate more equally in economic and political opportunities.
- Values the work and contribution of women in all fields on par with those of men, solely on merit, without making any distinction.
- Puts people – both women and men – clearly at the centre of all development processes.

The UNDP Report, 1995 also states that the GDI [Gender-related Development Index] ranking can be different in different situations, as is shown by the following conclusions of a recent survey:

- No society treats its women equal to its men. Substantial progress on gender equality has been made in only a few societies.
- Gender equality does not depend on the income level of a society. What it requires a firm political commitment, not enormous financial wealth.
- Significant progress has been achieved over the past two decades, though there is still a long way to go. Not a single country has slipped back in the march towards greater gender equality at higher levels of capabilities, though the pace of progress has been extremely uneven and slow.

Much progress remains to be made in gender equality in almost every country. And in equality of choice in economic and political participation, industrial countries are not necessarily taking the lead. The areas showing the least progress are parliamentary representation and percentage share of administrators and managers. The clear policy message from this simple exercise is this: "In most countries, industrial or developing, women are not yet allowed into the corridors of economic and political power. In exercising real power or decision-making authority, women are a distinct minority throughout the world".

Summary

- Women play an important role in developing the family and society by means of advancing the culture of the society and upbringing the values. The development of a family and children is mainly in the hands of women.
- The effects of the long-term cumulative process of discrimination against women have been accentuated by under-development. Graphically, while women represent nearly 50 per cent of the world's adult population and one-third of the total labour force, they labour nearly two-thirds of the total working hours but receive only one-tenth of world income and own less than one per cent of property.
- The goals of gender equality differ from one country to another, depending on the social, cultural and economic contexts.
- There are twelve critical areas of concern.

Self-Learning Activity

Try to answer the following questions on your own:

1. Write about women in decision making.
2. Discuss gender discrimination.
3. What are the critical areas of concern?

3 Women in Agriculture

Introduction

Personal observations and some surveys indicate that a female farmer is commonly perceived by the society in developing countries as follows:

- As a co-farmer;
- It is a taboo for a female farmer to plow and sow;
- It is physically far demanding for a female farmer to plow, thus she is considered as unable to farm and manage. Though various studies in the northern part of Ethiopia indicate that female farmers plowed their land during the struggle to overthrow the then military regime.
- Not as a key but marginal players in agricultural development particularly by those individuals with significant influence in research, extension, peasant association and rural development positions.
- As there is no as such a "female farmer" and a "male farmer"; and hence do not need separate extension advice/service for the farmer's wife.
- Since female farmers are not considered, their agricultural activities and/ or issues concerning them have been the least priorities in the country's agricultural research agenda, and so lacked improved extension packages that assist them to improve their productivity.
- So far the extension system in Ethiopia is unable to address the cultural taboo against the participation of female farmers in plowing and sowing, which subsequently reduce the rigid division of labour of both at the household and field levels.
- There is lack of acknowledging the multiple roles of female farmers in doing research on identifying their priority problems and developing extension systems that are appropriate to the farm family's life cycle stages.

So very little efforts have been made to address and reduce the heavy burden of work female farmers face.

- Often it is observed that major emphasis in agriculture is given to men's activities, while the role of women and children in the Ethiopian farming systems have been ignored.
- Married-women in particular are bypassed in the transfer of improved agricultural technologies assuming that they will get the information through their husbands and this has proven wrong.

Women play an indispensable role in farming and in improving the quality of life in rural areas. However, their contributions often remain concealed due to some social barriers and gender bias. Even government programmes often fail to focus on women in agriculture. This undermines the potential benefits from programmes, especially those related to food production, household income improvements, nutrition, literacy, poverty alleviation and population control. Equitable access for rural women to educational facilities would certainly improve their performance and liberate them from their marginalised status in the society. Other areas where women's potential could be effectively harnessed are agricultural extension, farming systems development, land reform and rural welfare. Landmark improvements have been recorded in such cases as the extension of institutional credit and domestic water supplies where women's potential have been consciously tapped.

Socio-economic goals of productivity, equity and environment stability are closely woven around the agriculture sector policies and new dimensions in programmes implemented are already emerging as new values. Regardless of the level of development achieved by the respective economies, women play a pivotal role in agriculture and in rural development in most countries of the Asia-Pacific region.

Asia-Pacific region had witnessed spectacular development in crop yields which even surpassed the population growth rate in the past decade. However, pockets of hunger remain when landless or small farm holding rural population lack economic access to food because of a lack of remunerative non-farm employment in rural areas, where 80 per cent of Asia-Pacific's 400 million poor live. It has also been suggested that with the acceleration of crop-diversification programmes and the transformation of agriculture to commercial production levels, women's lot had been even further worsened by the addition of new burdens which they have to shoulder in order to realise profits in farm operations.

Rural women, who are obliged to attend to all the household chores, children's welfare, nutrition and family cohesion along with farm work, are desperately driven to adopt a survival strategy to save the family food security from total collapse. Rural poverty has increased in the region particularly for farmers, as priority has been accorded to the industrial and service sectors: this is both the cause and an effect of rural-urban migration leading to the "feminisation of farming". Thus the numbers and the proportion of rural women among the absolutely poor and destitute.

In spite of social, political and economic constraints, women farmers have proved extremely resourceful and hardworking in their attempt to ensure household food security. Social constraints place barriers around their access to scientific and technological information. Lack of collateral denies them access to agricultural credit. Culture or traditions accord membership of cooperatives only to heads of households — usually a man. Many rural women, even in highly mechanised farming systems such as the Republic of Korea and Japan would have agriculture for work in other sectors if choices were available.

After some decades of development, global problems and issues concerning environment, women in development, and poverty have reappeared. All these have emerged in rural communities and threatening their sustainability. Rural communities with norms developed for managing resources are important for the stability of community life. Gender-oriented rural development programmes which focus on role of women to guarantee the stability of life provide a sound basis for integrated development of the quality of life.

In progressive economies like Japan, rural women have shown anxieties over several concerns affecting their livelihood. Some of the priority items include measures for success in agricultural enterprises, expansion of periodic farming resulting in reduced holidays, the need to reduce agricultural work, changes in awareness of rural societies and reduction in the work connected with caring for elderly people. In order to redress these problems, five tasks have been identified for promotion which will result in making rural living more pleasant and comfortable. These tasks include:

1. Creating awareness of changes and measures pursued to change the status of women by their active participation in agricultural and fisheries cooperatives.
2. Improving working conditions and environment.
3. Appreciating the positive aspects of living in rural areas and creating a conducive environment which will contribute towards better rural life.
4. Acquiring skills to diversify areas of involvement supporting women in entrepreneurial roles.
5. Adopt a structured approach to execute the vision to improve rural conditions.

Gender Gap in Agriculture

Agriculture is thought to be the domain of men's activity. Particularly plowing and sowing are in most places assumed to be done only by men. However, women are also predominantly engaged in agricultural activities. Though farming is believed to be male's domain of activity, women take part in it except plowing. Soil preparation, weeding, harvesting, winnowing and marketing are shared by both men and women.

In many parts of developing countries, women are equally involved with men in livestock raising which is another form of agricultural activity. In fact, women assume additional work of making butter and preparing dung cake for fuel as these activities are taken as part of housework. On the other hand, their labour in livestock raising has an indirect contribution for farming through providing farm animals and also through manuring.

The point here is that though women are involved in agriculture, their contribution in this sphere has not been given due consideration. Especially married women involved in agricultural activities are considered as helpers (of men), and therefore their economic contribution is not acknowledged. One of the implications is that since women are not seen as farmers, they cannot be admitted to peasant associations where decisions regarding land redistribution and resource allocation are made unless they are female household heads. This may mean that resources/inputs and appropriate extension and other services in agriculture are not directed to men in male headed households due to this bias.

Gender Bias in Land Ownership and Resource Allocation

Most of the rural women and women of the lower class have little control over the different resources of the country. Almost all resources are under the control of their husbands, fathers, brothers, brother-in-laws, etc. Female heads of households are even worse off as a result of some structural problems related to their gender.

In the case of divorce, the couples are entitled to equal share of the land as per the legal provision. In practice, however, this legal provision is not always adequately enforced as a result of customary procedures in many parts of developing countries.

Constraints faced by Rural Farm Women

Based on the experiences of farm extension workers, field advisors and rural farm women in the Asia-Pacific region, the following are the general constraints faced by them:

- High illiteracy rates and poor living conditions among rural women.

- Lack of leadership and inadequate participation in the organisational and economic affairs of their agricultural cooperatives.
- Absence of property inheritance rights, restriction on acquiring membership of agricultural cooperatives consequently being deprived of farm credit etc.
- Inadequate health care services in rural areas.
- Inadequate water supply for household and farm operations.
- Lack of appropriate agricultural technology aimed at reducing the physical burden of farm women.
- Inadequate access to credit and agricultural inputs and other services.
- Lack of female farm extension workers.
- Lack of marketing facilities and opportunities;
- Traditional, religious, social and cultural obstacles.
- Less participation in decision-making – even within the household.
- Male migration/urban drift which increases pressure on women.
- Lack of opportunities to improve socio-economic status of farm women.
- Lack of skills and attitudes in leadership and management development.
- Lack of secretariat supporting functions for women's organisations and allocation of funds for them in cooperative organisations.

MAJOR TRENDS IN FEMINIZATION OF AGRICULTURE

Rural women have been involved in agricultural production since the invention of agriculture. The type and depth of participation has varied widely over regions and culturally differentiated areas. Women's work in agriculture has become more visible over the last few decades. In part, this is due to research and data collection that has attempted to more accurately measure women's activities in rural areas. Yet, there has also been a tendency over the last few decades for women to broaden and deepen their involvement in agricultural production as they increasingly shoulder the responsibility for household survival and respond to economic opportunities in commercial agriculture. An FAO document (1999: 12-13) shows that while the proportion of the labour force working in agricultural declined over the 1990s, the proportion of women working in agriculture increased, particularly in developing countries. In some regions such as Africa and Asia, almost half of the labour force is women. This trend has been called the feminization of agriculture.

Much of the literature that examines recent changes in women's work in agriculture links these changes to the neo-liberal policies put into place by most countries since the early 1980s. Fiscal stabilization policy sought to correct balance of payments problems, reduce inflation rates, and increase exports. Accompanying stabilization, structural adjustment policy included import liberalization, privatization of government sector resources and services, and liberalizing the labour, land, and capital markets. These policies have changed the type of export agriculture practiced (high-value agricultural exports have replaced traditional lower-value exports), the type of wage labour demanded by commercial agriculture (a seasonal and temporary labour force rather than permanent labour force), and the viability of smallholder agriculture. In broad terms, the feminization of agriculture refers to women's increasing participation in the agricultural labour force, whether as independent producers, as unremunerated family workers, or as agricultural wage workers. Women work not only in the fields and pastures, but also in agricultural processing and packaging plants. Katz and Deere provide more specific definitions for the feminization of agriculture:

1. An increase in women's participation rates in the agricultural sector, either as self employed or as agricultural wage workers; in other words, an increase in the percentage of women who are economically active in rural areas.
2. An increase in the percentage of women in the agricultural labour force relative to men, either because more women are working and/or because fewer men are working in agriculture.

This review of relevant literature will consider both definitions and be limited to changes occurring since the early 1980s, in the agricultural sector of the developing regions, within the broader context of neo-liberal policies and an increasing global economy. By examining the literature for Latin America and sub-Saharan Africa, we will attempt to determine whether women have been increasing their participation in the agricultural labour force in these developing areas, what forces have been driving this tendency, and the implications for development policies.

To understand recent tendencies in women's work in agriculture, it is useful to locate them within the broader agricultural context. In broad terms, export agriculture in developing countries has shifted from traditional export crops grown on plantations, such as coffee, sugar, and cocoa to labour-intensive horticulture crops such as vegetables, fruits, and flowers. In Kenya, for example, the IMF and the World Bank recommended production of high-value niche crops, such as flowers, fruits, vegetables, and spices, taking comparative advantages of Kenya's climate, land, and cheap labour.

Vegetable production experienced dramatic growth during the 1980s as the principal traditional export crops earned declining revenue. The value of fresh horticultural exports grew in value from 9.7 to 71.6 thousand Kenya pounds. At the same time, smallholder agriculture in Latin America and Africa, producing mainly food crops and animal products for its own consumption and for local and national markets, is becoming an increasingly unviable activity.

In Latin America, increasing relative rural poverty and the economic crises of the 1970s, 80s, and 90s encouraged family members to seek wage labour; it is not clear, however, how much total wage labour and total labour in agriculture (agricultural EAP) has increased. Both traditional export and peasant agriculture have declined, but there is no adequate information on the size and distribution of the agricultural labour force across agricultural sectors (smallholder production, as well as traditional and non-traditional exports). What is known is that in Latin America, as well as in Africa, women have been employed in increasing numbers for the production and processing of many non-traditional agricultural exports such as fruits, flowers, and vegetables. Women make up a significant proportion of field workers and a majority of process plant workers. Yet, since women's participation in traditional cash cropping and in smallholder agriculture is not well known, it is difficult to determine whether women's work across all sectors of agriculture today represents a feminization of agriculture.

As part of these changes in agriculture, women and gender relations play an important role. Whitehead maintains that gender relations condition the operation of the economy, are a basic determining factor in the division of labour (between what is considered productive and reproductive), and provide one of the differentiating elements in the distribution and allocation of work, income, wealth and assets, and productive inputs.

As we examine women's work in agriculture, the role of gender relations becomes quite evident. The data and national statistics for women's participation in agriculture are stronger for Latin America than for Africa. Thus, most of the discussion will center on that region. There are, of course, important differences between the two regions. One of the most relevant is the stronger gender division of labour in African cultures; for this reason one could hypothesize that gender has more impact on the economy, and particularly on agriculture, in Africa than in Latin America. Another important difference is that African rural households, as compared to Latin America rural households, are less likely to share and pool resources, assets, and income. This has implications for small household production, income allocation, and household welfare. This paper will not attempt to examine these differences and their implications in depth; rather, we suggest that research on and policy recommendations for rural economies and populations need to take these gender differences into consideration.

Examining national statistics spanning the last two decades from the majority of Latin American countries, Katz considers women's participation in the agricultural sector as compared to other rural occupations and women's share of agricultural employment. With regard to the former tendency, Katz calculates that across the region, less than one-third of economically active women are employed in agriculture compared to over two-thirds of men. This overall number, however, conceals large differences across countries: only 10 per cent of economically active rural women in the Central American countries work in agriculture while 86 per cent in Bolivia, 70 per cent in Brazil, and 43 per cent in Paraguay work in agriculture. Data also show that trends with regard to women's participation in agricultural employment vary considerably across the region. In some countries, women's participation has been decreasing, in others it has been increasing, particularly since the 1980s. Katz concludes, nevertheless, that increasingly larger percentages of women are working in agriculture, in both wage work and unremunerated family labour.

Katz and Deere, by looking at national data and local case studies, indicate two different agricultural labour force sectors that have become feminized in many Latin American countries. Women have increased their participation in the agricultural wage labour force, particularly in non-traditional export agriculture. In the smallholder sector, women are assuming more responsibility in agricultural production either as principal farmers or as unremunerated family workers. Case studies in sub-Saharan Africa indicate similar trends in that region.

Change in the Nature of Agricultural Labour Force

The dramatic growth of non-traditional or high-value agricultural exports, dominated by agri-business and export firms, during the last few decades has dramatically changed the agricultural labour force. Where formerly plantations hired a largely permanent and male labour force supplemented by temporary male and female labour force for the peak harvest period, agri-business and agricultural export firms now hire mostly temporary labour force with a small cadre of permanent workers. Very few products (fresh flowers in Colombia and Uganda, for example) employ mostly permanent workers all year.

In Latin America, women's percentage of the agricultural wage labour force was small during the 1970s and 80s—mostly harvest workers on traditional export crops. Rural women were more likely to work on their own family farm, as unremunerated family labour. In the beginning 1980s, non-traditional export agriculture increased significantly, spurred by liberalization policies. Non-traditional agricultural exports grew from 10 per cent of total exports in 1970 to 23 per cent in 1990, creating a demand for a wage labour force.

A study of the fruit export industry in Chile exemplifies these changes. Chile has had the highest rate of non-traditional agricultural export growth in Latin America over the last few decades. While in early 1970s two-thirds of the agricultural labour force was permanent and one-third was temporary, by late 1980s one-third was permanent and two-thirds temporary; 60 per cent of the temporary workers were employed in the export fruit industry. Between 1986 and 1994, female agricultural workers increased by more than 20 per cent, while male agricultural workers declined by 20 per cent. Between 52 to 70 per cent of temporary workers in the fruit export labour market are women and permanent workers are mostly male.

Studies from various countries in Latin America reveal that as the vegetable, fruit, and flower agri-businesses have grown dramatically in the last few decades, women make up a large proportion of the labour force. In the fruit production of Chile's central valley, women made up over 50 per cent of the temporary workers. In Sinaloa's (Mexico) vegetable industry, women comprised 40 per cent of the field workers and 90 per cent of the packinghouse workers by the early 1990s. In the northeast of Brazil, over 65 per cent of the field workers in the vineyards were women (Collins: 1993). And in the flower industry in Colombia and Mexico, women comprise between 60 to 80 per cent of the workers (various studies cited by Dolan and Sorby: 2003). These studies also revealed that the small proportion of permanent jobs in these industries is overwhelmingly held by men.

As in Latin America, economic liberalization policies have opened new work opportunities for rural women in sub-Saharan Africa. Dolan and Sorby (2003), citing a number of studies across different export crops and countries, found that women comprised between 53 and 85 per cent of employed labour force in high-value agricultural export production such as flowers, fruit, and vegetables. In Kenya's fruit and vegetable exports, for example, women work in the field and in processing and packing plants. By the late 1990s, they comprised between 70 and 80 per cent of workers in certain tasks such as packing, labeling, and bar-coding of produce. Horticultural export firms prefer young, single women who were seen as appropriate for this type of work and flexible in their willingness to work at many tasks and without security of employment. Many of these women are also migrants.

Gender Segregated and Segmented Labour Force

The non-traditional and high-value agricultural export labour force is highly segmented and gender segregated. It is evident that employers prefer women workers for the labour-intensive tasks associated with non-traditional and high-value agricultural export production. Women are regarded as submissive and docile, having greater dexterity for tasks that require care and patience, and flexibility with regard to work conditions (work hours, wages, contracts). Agri-business enterprises have gender-differentiated occupations: women do the labour intensive tasks such as weeding and pruning in the fields, selection and cutting in processing, and sorting and wrapping in packing. Men do the tasks that entail strength such as lifting crates and construction of greenhouses, or that involve machinery such as driving tractors and trucks, applying pesticides, and maintaining equipment. Women's work is more likely to be considered unskilled and women are less likely to receive training and acquire skills that make them eligible for higher-paid work.

Flexible Labour Force

The defining characteristic of the new female wage labour in Latin America and Africa is its "flexible" labour force—seasonal, temporary, or casual women workers—with an underpinning of a small permanent labour, largely male, labour force. Because the world market for vegetables, fruit, and other fresh products, such as flowers, is very competitive, agri-business seeks a flexible labour force that works long hours, only part of the year, for low wages and no social benefits.

The most critical groups of temporary workers are casual and migrant labour. In the casual agricultural labour market in Africa, for example, women's casual wages (whether in cash or in kind) are usually half of men's wages. Increasingly, the casual labour force is made up of women and in some countries they make up over 50 per cent of casual labour force. While wage labour seems to significantly increase household income, bringing in higher returns than farming and self-employment, casual labour often indicates extreme poverty of smallholder agriculture particularly for women who are overwhelmingly clustered in low-entry, unskilled, and low-return activities. Women's reserve price of labour is likely to be low where the income potential of their own production is low, where off-farm income generating opportunities are few or give low returns to labour, and where there is urgent need. There are few local opportunities and an excess of women needing work. When food supplies run out or they face other emergencies such as debt or illness, women seek casual labour, sometimes migrating to agri-business sites. Because of their urgent need and lack of assets, women will accept lower wages; often they are paid in kind (food) rather than in cash. Men are in a position to command better wages because they have assets and have better farming opportunities.

Deere mentions the increased number of women in the migrant worker labour force (2005: 30). This characteristic is also found in sub-Saharan Africa such as Kenya where 100 per cent of workers in packinghouses and 86 per cent of farm workers are migrants. In some cases, wage work on cash crops often conflicts with own-farm production in that it may be taking family labour away at crucial times of the agricultural cycle. In this case, wage labour does not provide rural families with secure income and employment that provides adequate support for rural households. Rural families and women cannot live on the products and income they get from their land and resources, but then neither can they live off rural wage labour because of its very informal nature.

Wages and Benefits

Agro-industry tends to label female tasks and skills as feminine qualities that do not warrant skilled wage levels or wages equal to men's. On the other hand, many tasks undertaken by men are considered worthy of higher wages because they involve strength or operating machinery. As a consequence, women are concentrated in what are considered women's (unskilled) work and remunerated at lower levels than men's work. For example, in Brazil women who graft grapevines are paid at a lower rate than men who operate tilling machinery (Collins: 2000). While wage rates continue to be biased against women, the wage gap between women and men is often smaller than in other rural activities.

Because of labour laws, permanent workers enjoy minimum wage rates and social benefits (such as sick leave, paid vacation, health insurance, pension). By hiring seasonal, temporary or casual labour (and mostly women), agro-industry avoids labour market regulation for the majority of its labour force. For women, who often have children and other dependents to support, lack of social benefits represents a particular hardship. Deere (2005: 28) notes that what is different in Latin American wage labour practices of non-traditional agricultural export production from those in traditional export agriculture is that women are working as independent wage workers, in other words, not represented by a family male member who collects wages for all family wage workers—women are now more likely to be independent and visible workers.

Training and Skills

There are also gender differences in opportunities to acquire skills. Agro-industry generally offers formal training (for example, in management or the operation of machinery) to its permanent workers who tend to be men. The skills that women do acquire are generally acquired on the job through repetitive task performance. This means that most women do not have the opportunity to increase the wage level and to move into supervisory and managerial positions. After reviewing numerous case studies in Latin America and Africa, Katz, Deere and Dolan Sorby draw following conclusions regarding non-traditional or high-value export agriculture:

- women are employed for the labour-intensive tasks;
- women are generally earn lower wages than men and are more likely to be paid at piece rate;
- workers, including women workers, in packaging and processing plants earn more than field workers and have better working conditions; work is nonetheless hard, often involving long hours of standing, and long work days during peak seasons;
- women are the major supplier of temporary, seasonal, and casual labour and men occupy the majority of permanent jobs as well as administrative and supervisory positions; and
- women are a labour reserve for this type of production.

In summary, although demand for labour in non-traditional or high-value agricultural export production has created new economic opportunities for women, their working conditions are characterized by insecurity, long working hours, environmental health hazards, low wages, and limited opportunities for training and skill development. The competition among agri-business firms, particularly horticultural export firms, pressures them to reduce costs by hiring unskilled women as informal workers (i.e., temporary, seasonal, and casual) at low wages and without social benefits. Little or no advance notice is given when workers are laid off.

Women Working in Smallholder Agriculture

In differing degrees, smallholder agriculture has been declining for at least the last several decades across regions. Land concentration in Latin America and land scarcity in Africa, together with national policies that privilege agri-business production and marketing, has made smallholder agriculture less viable, increasing relative rural poverty. Rural families respond to these deteriorating conditions by diversifying livelihoods; often this includes migration of some household members to secure wage work. In some cases, these policies have allowed peasant producers to participate in the non-traditional agricultural export market. As a result, some women are increasing their participation in smallholder agriculture, either as principal farmers or as unremunerated family workers.

Women as Principal Farmers

Women are increasingly taking charge of farms as men either migrate for extended periods or engage in off-farm employment. Although national-level data are lacking with regard to women as independent producers, this type of feminization of agriculture has resulted in women's increased visibility as farmers. Most agricultural censuses do not collect data on who exactly owns owner-operated farms, the assumption being that the principal farmer (assumed to be the male head of household) owns the land. Only one country in Latin America has gender disaggregated census data for 2 points in time: Peru showed an increase in women farmers from 13.3 per cent in 1972 to 20.3 per cent in 1994

As smallholder production has become less viable and land ownership concentration has increased over the last half century, household members seek off-farm work, often through migration. In addition, male abandonment and death of husbands from HIV/AIDS is increasing. Women left on the farm undertake more and more of the agricultural fieldwork and tasks, work longer hours on the farm, and make most of the decisions. Regional statistics show that in Southern Africa female-headed households represent 42 per cent of the total and in the Caribbean they represent 35 per cent (United Nations 2000: pp 42, 46-50).

Katz examining demographic trends for Latin America, reports increasing rates of rural female headship. The proportion of rural female-headed households for the late 1990s across 13 countries in Latin America reached nearly 23 per cent. In sub-Saharan Africa, women's traditional role has been independent farmer on land her husband has made available to her for the production of food for the household and for sale. This role as provider of food for the household does not appear to have changed over the last several decades. The major change has been the increasing difficulty by smallholder households and its women farmers in providing enough food for the household.

Across communities, women's direct participation in the production of food for their households has increased; this increased participation has followed different paths. A case study of an indigenous community with high male out-migration, in Mexico's central highlands where the key staple crop is maize, has shown that in spite of high input costs, low prices for maize, and withdrawal of support for peasant agriculture, rural households continue to grow the local maize variety. Wage rates have dropped in real terms and community members began migrating, particularly to the United States in the late 1990s. Women have taken over production of maize (and other foods) for home consumption rather than for the market. Because they face constraints such as less access to land, credit, and technical assistance, women producers use less fertilizer and herbicides and do more weeding by hand.

Brazil offers a different process. State policy in Brazil, since the mid-20th century did not support peasant food production for the local market; state support such as subsidized credit and technology was targeted to large producers of mechanized agriculture. Thus, neo-liberal policies did not significantly affect an already pauperized peasant sector. In fact, the peasant sector was successfully able to mobilize and organize and demand land reform and other support programs for family agriculture. Women have assumed responsibility for agricultural production in the northeast, the poorest region of Brazil, where men migrate to long distances and the number of female-headed households is high. In KwaZulu Natal (South Africa), Mtshali (2002: 87) reports that women have to take on more activities and tasks because of social changes such as male migration and education of children. Women who want their children to go to school take on the work children traditionally did such as caring for small and large livestock. When men migrate, women are also clearing the land for planting.

There is also evidence that in some areas, women are being pushed out of smallholder agriculture. In southern Niger where land shortages have become critical over the last 20 years, women and young unmarried men are no longer receiving a parcel of land from the household head as used to be the custom. Previously, the household head would give out land to his wife (or wives) for them to cultivate; the production from this parcel was theirs to sell, allocate, or use as they wished. With the increasing shortage of land, wives are no longer given their own parcels. This is being culturally justified by instituting a type of female seclusion—women are not supposed to work in the fields. Women have taken up non-farm income-producing activities (such as extracting oil from groundnuts) in order to cover household food needs not provided by ever-smaller land.

Women in Smallholder Production of Agro-Exports

The production of non-traditional agricultural exports is dominated by medium- and large-sized commercial farms and agri-business. Nevertheless, smallholders with a certain level of assets are able to engage in contract farming of some agricultural exports, particularly those crops where human labour is not easily replaced by mechanization, such as vegetables. The comparative advantage of smallholder families for labour-intensive production is unremunerated family labour. Agro-industry out-sources production of these crops to the smallholder sector, often under contract farming. Smallholder farms producing cash crops, particularly non-traditional or high-value agricultural exports, are highly dependent on their women's labour. For example, Vanilla production by smallholders in Uganda found that the levels of female and male family labour were the same, and that family adult labour was ten times that of hired labour. A 1999-2000 study in the central highland of Kenya, where both food and cash crops are grown, revealed that while women and men invest their labour in both food and cash crops (coffee and tea), women put in significantly more labour on food and cash crops with the exception of coffee. Njuki et al. contend that the traditional division of crop labour between genders—men on cash crops and women on food crops—is changing as more men migrate to urban areas in search of wage labour.

Women find themselves managing all crops on the farm and doing tasks, such as land preparation, that were traditionally male tasks. In Guatemala, smallholder vegetable production for export began in the 1980s. Household members, including women and children, work in almost all agricultural tasks throughout the year. Wage workers, mostly women, are brought in for the harvest. A study undertaken in the late 1980s revealed that 40 per cent of the women working in the fields were unremunerated family workers and 7.5 per cent were independent women producers. Most of these vegetable farms producing snow peas, broccoli, and cauliflower are year-round, work-intensive enterprises. Smallholder production of non-traditional agricultural exports is not always viable. In Chile, for example, a sizeable number of peasant households attempted to participate in the early years of fruit export market, particularly land reform beneficiaries. Household women worked in the fields doing traditionally male tasks, particularly during peak seasons. By the late 1990s, most of these peasant producers had lost their land because they did not have access to the credit and product markets that larger commercial farms had, and were unable to support the levels of debt needed for export of fruit production. Many of these peasant households, particularly the women, now work as wage labourers for the agri-businesses and medium-sized producers that purchased their land.

A similar process occurred in Kenya, one of the strong producers of non-traditional agricultural exports, where exports expanded from Asian vegetables to luxury fruits and vegetables (such as dwarf carrots, baby corn, snowpeas, and courgettes). Contract farming was promoted in the 1980s as the way to connect Kenya's smallholder sector to the global market and capital. Since state expenditures for credit, input subsidies, and agricultural extension were cut because of austerity measures, contract farming offered an alternative to smallholders. In central Kenya, for example, smallholders on ¼ acre plots grew winter vegetable for export firms. These vegetables require high levels of labour to ensure quality, which is supplied mostly by smallholder farm households. Export firms have controlled the production process in order to achieve certain quality standards, without any risks since they neither own nor manage the farms. The smallholder family assumes all the risks of agricultural production and is compensated by how much it sells, not the amount of labour invested.

Between 1993 and 1999, fresh vegetable exports grew in volume by 53 per cent and over 206 per cent in value to become Kenya's third largest source of foreign exchange by 2000. Most of the export vegetables went to Europe, particularly to the United Kingdom. As marketing of these fruits and vegetables was taken over by big supermarket chains, corporate farms and processing facilities took over the production and processing of these products. Contract farming by smallholders was no longer viable and they in general lost their comparative advantage to the corporate farms and plants. Because women are responsible for supplying food to the household, they may be unwilling to switch production on their own plots from food crops to cash crops. Whitehead cites a 1997 study by Wold who concluded that women are more risk averse and do not respond to price incentives for certain crops with volatile prices such as high-value agricultural exports.

A study by Chavas and Smith concluded that because men and women in African households have different preferences for their labour and other resources, households did not respond efficiently to market opportunities for certain commercial crops. This has implications for women's participation on men's cash crop production. Cotton production, a cash crop, was controlled by men and women were expected to work in the cotton fields. Women, however, obtained minimal income from their household's cotton and they preferred to invest their labour and other resources in food crops for their households. This preference for (non-cash) food crops decreased the amount of labour they put into the household's cash crop. Whitehead offers other reasons for women's non-participation in direct production of commercial crops in sub-Saharan Africa. Based on a study in Tanzania, Whitehead argues that the private sector provides inadequate factor and product markets for smallholder farmers and that exposure to world markets increases vulnerability of smallholders, particularly because of the volatility of agricultural commodity prices. Even women who produce food crops find sometimes that their crops are overpriced when cheap food is imported.

Gender Relations in Agriculture

The role that gender relation plays in society is quite evident when examining how social and cultural norms and practices are often based on gender differences. The point here is that gender also "influences the division of labour, and the distribution of work, income, wealth, productivity of inputs, and economic behaviour of agents".

The level of influence of the different drivers vary by region and sub-region. For example, the HIV-AIDs epidemic has a much stronger impact in southern Africa than in Latin America. Migration patterns also differ with more women migrating in Latin America than in Africa. The same would be true for diversification of the rural economy, which may be more advanced in some areas of Latin America than in many areas of Africa. While the end-result may appear to be similar, the causes and implications may differ, and hence policy responses should also be different. Broad regional and country differences argue for the need to have differentiated policies and strategies, as opposed to a one-size-fits-all strategy.

Economic Policies

The adoption of neo-liberal economic policies and economic re-structuring became widespread in Latin America in the early beginning of 1980s and in sub-Saharan Africa in the late 1980s. These policies, particularly trade liberalization policies together with agricultural policies that favor export products, stoked the growth of agri-business, particularly in the production of high-value horticultural crops, and agricultural exports, provided a growing demand for wage labour. At the same time, liberalization policies have resulted in higher input costs, lower farm gate prices, and significant cuts in access to credit and extension services for the smallholder sector that produces mostly food for local and regional markets. Increasing land concentration in Latin America and the beginning of land scarcity in Africa compounds the impact of these policies The decline in the profitability of food production and in food security has forced low-income and low-asset rural households to seek other income sources (off-farm employment) in order to maintain the household. Livelihood diversification included out-migration of both women and men and employment in the agri-business industry. The labour-intensive nature of horticultural production motivated the industry to hire women workers who command lower wages, particularly in the rural sector. The global market and international competition drives product prices down, keeping wages low, but more importantly, keeping the labour market flexible.

Gender Relations

Gender relations and the gender division of labour that justify lower wage rates and flexible (read temporary) employment conditions for women have contributed to the growth of agri-business's production and export of high-value agricultural crops. Other gender dynamics, such as the greater mobility of men and their out-migration, leaves women farming the land in order to provide food for their families. This, together with the increase in female-headed households results in an increase in rural households that depend solely on women's work and income. In some regions, such as Africa, men's greater access to education and ability to leave the farm results in off-farm employment. Again, women are left on the farm to work the land. Gendered access to assets and resources may also have impact on women's bargaining position in the household and in the wage labour market. Agricultural producers with assets and access to resources such as credit, technology, and product markets have been in a position to benefit from liberalized markets. Women, with decreased access to resources, are not able to participate equitably in these liberalized markets, except as wage labour and unremunerated family labour.

The intersection between economic policy and gender relations is also found within the household. Women's responsibilities to reproduce the household result in much of their labour falling into the reproductive and unpaid sector. Neo-liberal policies have intensified and extended reproductive (and unpaid) labour. Since the gender division of labour assigns reproductive and domestic work to women, their workday has been extended because of the decline of social services and the rise in costs of food and other household basic needs. Where the gender division of labour is stronger, such as in Africa, the increasing labour burden on women may be greater than in other regions. This is not to say that gender relations are not constantly shifting. Men and women negotiate access to and control over income, assets, labour, and other productive resources.

Access to Land and Women

Throughout history, land has been recognized as a primary source of wealth, social status, and power. It is the basis for shelter, food, and economic activities; it is the most significant provider of employment opportunities in rural areas and is an increasingly scarce resource in urban areas. Access to water and other resources, as well as to basic services such as sanitation and electricity, is often conditioned by access to rights in land. The willingness and ability to make long term investments in arable land and in housing is directly dependent on the protection that society affords the holders of rights. Thus, any concept of sustainable development relies heavily on both access to property rights in land and the security of those rights.

Land also has great cultural, religious, and legal significance. There is a strong correlation in many societies between the decision-making powers that a person enjoys and the quantity and quality of land rights held by that person. In rural areas social inclusion or exclusion often depends solely on a person's landholding status. Even in urban areas, the right to participate in municipal planning, in community decisions, and sometimes elections, can depend on the status of an individual as a "resident" or "home owner". This is not a new phenomenon, since for many centuries only "land owners" could participate in elections in most western democracies. Access to land then is an important aspect of household, community, and national decision-making powers.

Access to land is governed through land tenure systems. Land tenure is the relationship, whether legally or customarily defined, among people, as individuals or groups, with respect to land. (For convenience, "land" is used here to include other natural resources such as water and trees.) Rules of tenure define how property rights in land are to be distributed within societies, along with associated responsibilities and restraints. In simple terms, land tenure systems determine who can use what resources, for how long, and under what conditions.

The manner in which rights to land are actually distributed and used can be very complex. Land tenure is often categorised as:

Private

The assignment of rights to a private party who may be an individual, a married couple, a group of people, or a corporate body such as a commercial entity or non-profit organization. For example, within a community, individual families may have exclusive rights to residential parcels, agricultural parcels and certain trees. Other members of the community can be excluded from using these resources without the consent of those who hold the rights.

Communal

A right of commons may exist within a community where each member has a right to use independently the holdings of the community. For example, members of a community may have the right to graze cattle on a common pasture.

Open access

Specific rights are not assigned to anyone and no-one can be excluded. This typically includes marine tenure where access to the high seas is generally open to anyone; it may include rangelands, forests, etc, where there may be free access to the resources for all. (An important difference between open access and communal systems is that under a communal system non-members of the community are excluded from using the common areas.)

State

Property rights are assigned to some authority in the public sector. For example, in some countries, forest lands may fall under the mandate of the state, whether at a central or decentralised level of government.

In practice, most forms of holdings may be found within a given society, for example, common grazing rights, private residential and agricultural holdings, and state ownership of forests.

Rights to land are diverse and, in practice, multiple rights to an object can be held by several persons or groups. This has given rise to the concept of the "bundle of rights". Different rights to the same parcel of land, such as rights to sell the land, rights to use the land through a lease, or rights to travel across the land, may be pictured as "sticks in the bundle", each of which may be held by a different party. Although a large and varied number of rights may exist, it is sometimes useful to illustrate that rights of access to land can take the form of:

- *Use rights:* The right to use the land for grazing, growing subsistence crops, gathering minor forestry products, etc.

- *Control rights:* The right to make decisions on how the land should be used and to benefit financially from the sale of crops, etc.
- *Transfer rights:* The right to sell or mortgage the land, to convey the land to others through intra-community reallocations or to heirs, and to reallocate use and control rights.

Very often, the poor in a community have only use rights. A woman, for example, may have the right to use land to grow crops to feed the family, while her husband may collect the profits from selling any crops at the market. While such simplifications can be useful, it should be noted that the exact manner in which rights to land are actually distributed and enjoyed can be very complex.

The rules of land tenure are applied and made operational through land administration. Land administration, whether formal or informal, comprises an extensive range of systems and processes to administer:

- *Land rights:* The allocation of rights in land; the delimitation of boundaries of parcels for which the rights are allocated; the transfer from one party to another through sale, lease, loan, gift or inheritance; the registration of land rights; and the adjudication of doubts and disputes regarding rights and parcel boundaries.
- *Land-use regulation:* Land-use planning and enforcement and the adjudication of land use conflicts.
- *Land valuation and taxation:* The gathering of revenues through forms of land valuation and taxation, and the adjudication of land valuation and taxation disputes.

In many communities, access to land resources is governed by both statutory and customary laws. Conflicts can exist between traditional norms and national laws, as is often the case when land rights are considered. Local norms as enforced by community members are most likely to prevail, particularly in rural areas. National constitutions and laws granting equal access to productive resources are essential for gender equity. However, for these rights to appear legitimate and be enforced, they need to be accepted by the local community. Such acceptance is primarily enhanced through local community involvement in the process of the design and implementation, as well as the approach used during information and education campaigns. Understanding the local situation, as well as the national legal structure, is therefore essential in land-related programmes.

Increasingly, the dramatic demographic, economic and social changes affecting urban and rural communities in developing economies is marginalising those who are least equipped to cope with these shifts. Whether the issue is growth of informal settlements in urban areas, the decreasing role of men in the community due to labour migration, or the need to readjust household relations to accommodate the elderly, the orphaned, and the sick, people need to be able to access land and shelter efficiently and equitably.

As non-traditional household arrangements emerge, and as rural lands become engulfed in the urban fringe, the greatest risks of losing access to land fall generally to the most disadvantaged segments of society. Nations and communities need to rethink how overstressed land resources will be accessed and allocated in order to adjust to the changing demands and opportunities at the local level. The economic and social well-being of households are at increased risk when maintenance and decision-making roles are altered by, for example, death, divorce, abandonment or disability. When the heads of households do not or cannot exercise their traditional responsibilities, there is a need to ensure that remaining household members have appropriate access to the land that supports them.

The changing dynamics of households and communities must be considered in land administration if it is to be effective and equitable. Improving gender inclusive access to land, and the benefits from land, may be one way to overcome economic and social disadvantages. Men as well as women can suffer discrimination in society through, for example, age, health, or education and they should also be seen as "an untapped resource"

WHY IS GENDER AN ISSUE IN ACCESS TO LAND

Gender differences in land tenure should be recognized if land objectives, such as increasing land productivity, providing affordable housing, or promoting sustainable resource management, are to be met. There is a need for land tenure policy frameworks that explicitly address gender inclusive access to land. Without specific attention to gender inclusiveness, important segments of society may be excluded from the benefits of land administration, management, and development schemes. This is underscored by the findings of the Women's Summit that, in most of today's societies, there are great gender inequities in access to land, housing and basic infrastructure. Finally, but not least of all, equitable access to land is a human rights issue and, as the UN Economic and Social Council Commission on the Status of Women states, "land rights discrimination is a violation of human rights."

In many countries, there is still a lack of adequate provisions for women to hold land rights independently of their husbands or male relatives. Statutory law often does not provide for women's independent rights and when such legislation does exist, mechanisms to enforce it are often absent. In traditional or "customary" societies, women's direct access to land through purchase or inheritance is often limited, yet they may have greater management and use rights than men. Since women are frequently the major household food producers, there are usually customary provisions for indirect access to land in terms of use rights acquired through kinship relationships and their status as wives, mothers, sisters, or daughters.

These use rights, however, may not grant enough security for women and other dependants when traditional family structures dissolve. Through labour mobility, divorce, separation, or death, an increasing number of women are becoming the heads of households. They are thus making many of the day-to-day decisions affecting shelter, food production, and household economics. Yet only a small proportion of these women hold secure land rights. Similarly, there are societies where access to land stems from the female line, and in this case male partners and children may be disadvantaged as societies change.

Urbanisation is a major factor in such societal changes. The Second United Nations Conference on Human Settlements (Habitat II) noted that people and investments are being attracted to cities and this trend is expected to accelerate in the future. Friedmann estimates that about 30-40 per cent of urban populations are female-maintained, i.e., responsible for food and other household matters. That number can be expected to be larger in many developing countries where more people may comprise a household and thus be the responsibility of women. On the other hand, there are increasing numbers of men and children who are homeless. Such gender-related changes in household and community maintenance need to be addressed in housing and economic development projects which target groups, for example, through special credit or rental arrangements.

Migration to urban centres has resulted in a rapid rise in the number of rural families that have women as the heads of households. Many of these women are those with the least social power (i.e., single parents, widows, divorcees, wives of migrant workers, the aged and the infirm). They are largely without effective decision-making powers, often without a voice in community governance, and increasingly without security as individuals under traditional law. Attempts to assert their rights can cause conflicts at the community or even national levels. Too often, women are left holding whatever rights they have at the will of male relatives. Single, divorced or widowed women can end up dependent on the goodwill of distant family members.

At the same time female-headed households are faced with the responsibility for food production for growing populations. Even in male-headed households, women often have prime responsibility for food production while men commonly concentrate on cash crops. Rural women in particular are responsible for half the world's food production and produce between 60 and 80 per cent of the food in most developing countries. In sub-Saharan Africa and the Caribbean, women produce up to 80 per cent of basic foodstuffs. In Asia, between 50 and 90 per cent of work in the rice fields is done by women. After the harvest, rural women in developing countries are almost entirely responsible for storage, handling, stocking, marketing and processing.

Making access to land more equitable does not mean addressing only the quantity of rights allocated. To make use of the rights and opportunities, access to land must also be enforceable or secure (for example, against seizure by force or by law). Equitable access to land must also be effective, i.e., by including equitable access to transportation, credit, markets, etc. The support of legal, customary and family institutions are fundamental if more effective access to land is to be improved for men and women.

To create gender equity, whether on the basis of human rights or for reasons of economic efficiency, then the principal challenges for land administration are:

- to understand and acknowledge the complexity of property rights regimes as they relate to the dynamic roles of both men and women in today's societies; and
- to provide effective institutional structures that can protect and strengthen equitable access to land within the framework of a society's particular land policy goals.

This is important given that land is the main source of income and food security for the majority of rural households in many countries.

These are not easy challenges because land tenure arrangements are dynamic and can vary greatly within and among countries. There may not even be any clear consensus, nationally or regionally, on what land policy goals are or should be. Despite these limitations, land administrators need to understand how land reform, land management and land development schemes may impact on access to land from a gender perspective.

There is increasing evidence that outcomes of land reform and land administration activities have different implications for men and women. Traditionally, the involvement of men as the *de jure* heads of households as primary beneficiaries in such programmes was viewed as sufficient to ensure that other household members would equally enjoy the benefits of the projects as dependents. Today, it is increasingly being recognized that such assumptions cannot be made.

With significant demographic shifts in rural and urban areas, development organisations and professionals have had to seek new strategies to tackle gender issues. In the land sector, this may mean giving women and men, directly or through co-ownership, greater security of tenure and better access to land resources. Greater security of rights to land increases the holder's ability to make decisions regarding appropriate economic strategies that may include diversification from subsistence farming. Security of tenure is a key to enabling individuals and households to participate effectively in economic development.

The timeliness of this new vision is underscored by some experience from the past. As Rocheleau and Edmunds (1997) comment:

> "Women who enjoy access to a variety of tree, forest and rangeland resources across the rural landscape may find their access restricted after formal land titling or land tenure reforms have invested greater powers of exclusion in land owners, whether male or female. Even where formal title is given jointly to a husband and wife, a woman may lose decision-making authority over her former domains on and off farm as the household 'heads' take on the full and exclusive responsibility for the management of household land and all the plants and animals upon it."

Another example is given by Lastarria-Cornhiel (1997):

> "Among the Mandinka ... of Gambia both common and individual property rights are recognized: family-cleared land designated *maruo* collectively farmed by the family but under the control of the male household head; and individually cleared land designated *kamanyango* which if cleared by a woman gives her access to land with partial autonomy, controlling the profits and able to transfer land to daughters. In the late 1940s and early 1950s women sought to establish *kamanyango* rights of new rice lands by clearing former mangrove swamps. In 1984, the Jahaly Pacharr irrigation project, designed to increase productivity of the rice paddies by enabling year-round cultivation, recognizing that women were the key farmers on this land, sought to title the land to women. Household heads (generally male) registered the land in women's names but then designated it as *maruo* land."

The "Toolkit on Gender in Agriculture" prepared by the World Bank includes the following observation:

> "Land title and tenure tend to be vested in men, either by legal condition or by socio-cultural norms. Land reform and resettlement have tended to reinforce this bias against tenure for women. Land shortage is common among women. Compared to men, women farm smaller and more dispersed plots and are less likely to hold title, secure tenure, or the same rights to use, improve or dispose of land."

Statistical information is far from complete and, where it exists, lack of uniformity makes comparison difficult. For example, in some cases the definition of "ownership" does not take into account "co-ownership". Some researchers put land ownership by women at less than 10 per cent worldwide. Others argue that women may actually have more direct use and management of land than men through lesser rights than ownership. However, the discrepancy between decision-making powers and labour input is compelling in many situations.

As the percentage of population living in households that can be considered *de facto* or *de jure* female-headed household is on the rise, there is a need to re-examine how property rights are allocated and secured. There is also a need to better understand the complex relationships between use, control and ownership of land resources. A simple certificate of title could certainly not reflect the diversity of land rights found in many cultures.

Documenting Customary Tenure

There is increasing interest in several African countries in documenting customary rights (e.g., Uganda's Land Act of 1998). The arguments for registering these certificates of customary tenure are that the processes will:

- provide greater security of tenure on customary lands.
- provide a document that can be used as collateral for credit.
- provide more information for planning and land management.

Despite the merits or limitations of the processes, there could be significant impacts on some land rights. A major difficulty is the fact that such documentation can effectively freeze customary rules that are in place at the time. No account is made, for example, of such future rights as the right of a child to return home and receive a parcel of family land after a divorce. Limited rights such as the right to pick fruit or gather wood on another's property may be eliminated by the documentation. And then there is the question of whose name(s) the certificates or registers will record. For example, will the name be the *de facto* head of household, who may be a woman whose husband works away from home, or the *de jure* head of household according to customary law? There are limitations with both of these approaches, including the problem of whether the documents have priority over customary law in cases of inheritance when both names are recorded. In this regard, polygamy is a significant complicating factor when issuing land titles. Unregistered marriages, divorces and polygamy can have a major impact on women's security of tenure.

Dynamic Cultural and Religious Values

Traditional laws and religious laws often protected women and provided for wives, widows, and female children through other means than, for instance, equal land shares on inheritance. Under Islamic law, for example, daughters may receive half the land that sons receive on the death of their father. This is in effect their dowry to bring to a marriage. The sons on the other hand have the responsibility to provide for unmarried sisters and their mother and in theory require more land. Other cultures have had similar traditional laws.

Traditional societies and religious based communities are not immune to the influence of social changes around them. Education of women and greater opportunities for employment and self-sufficiency are affecting many traditional communities. Divorce, desertion, and urban migration may also challenge the traditional safety nets. The devastation of HIV/AIDS and war have further fragmented the extended and traditional family arrangements. At the same time, in the midst of obvious need for changes, who has the right to demand that these changes be made or to force another community to adopt its values? This raises ethical dilemmas for the land professional.

Gender-targeted Development Projects

International aid organisations have been targeting particular groups such as women and children for special assistance for decades. More recently the protection and enhancement of women's rights to land have become a focus for some land reform projects. One difficulty is that these projects often enhance the economic value of the land which may change how that land is viewed within the community. For example, part of a community may have used parcels of marginal land to raise personal crops. After a land development project, this marginal land may have access to irrigation and to a new road, thus enhancing its value. Will local authorities allow the original land users to maintain their land rights after the project is over? Experience in housing projects has also shown that making improvements to a house may lead to "expropriation" of rights to the house by more powerful members of the community.

The intention of this discussion is not to discourage gender-related projects and programmes. Instead, it is to demonstrate that making changes does not always result in the benefits originally intended. The situation is complex and requires looking at the existing constraints at the macro-level (legislation and policies), institutional arrangements (mechanisms and procedures for land administration), and local dynamics (prevalent social organizations and related factors in social beliefs, rules, and customary practices).

Summary

- Women play an indispensable role in farming and in improving the quality of life in rural areas. However, their contributions often remain concealed due to some social barriers and gender bias.

- Women are increasingly taking charge of farms as men either migrate for extended periods or engage in off-farm employment. There is also evidence that in some areas, women are being pushed out of smallholder agriculture.
- The role that gender relation plays in society is quite evident when examining how social and cultural norms and practices are often based on gender differences. The point here is that gender also "influences the division of labour, and the distribution of work, income, wealth, productivity of inputs, and economic behaviour of agents"
- There are gender issues like access to land, employment, distribution wealth, etc.

Self-Learning Activity

Try to answer the following questions on your own:

1. What is gender gap in agriculture?
2. Describe gender segregated and segmented labour force.
3. Why is gender an issue in access to land?

4 Gender Issues, Roles and Analysis

Gender issue is problem and concern brought up in the distinction and roles of women and men. When we put line to divide males and females based on activities they do, resource they have and so on, problems happen, which can be best explained as problem of inequality and gender issue is nothing but this problem that concern every body as member of society. Women's are always part and parcel of male as Plato describe them, they are our Mother, wife or Sister. Institutional factors reinforce this problem of inequality since gender issue is related to political, economic and social issues.

Gender issue can be developmental issue; but why is Gender a development issue? As we all know human potential is a huge resource that is underused everywhere, partly for reasons linked to Gender, so considering gender issue is integrating this half part of the society in to development activity.

Gender issue is also justice and human right issue, the Ethiopian constitutions say, "All persons are equal before the law" which is to mean that everybody should be treated equally without any discrimination on grounds of race, colour, sex gender, language, political opinion, national origin, wealth etc. If half of the worlds or Ethiopian population receives fewer resources than the other half, it shows that there is a problem and it is violation of human right.

GENDER ANALYSIS

Gender Analysis and Planning

The aim of gender analysis is to analyse the position of men and women in a society or community and to identify the specific needs and strengths of each. This method is applied in the planning, management, implementation and evaluation of programmes in order to ensure the equal participation of men and women according to their identified needs, special skills and potentials.

The gender relation analysis is also called as gender analysis and we have important tools and techniques to analyze gender relations in the household community and development activities.

These tools are believed to, provide qualitative information on Gender relations, and create understanding and awareness of the existing gender issues at the level of development workers, community and planners. They also increase our understanding of the implications of different development activities or projects for male and female.

Now a day's a number of Gender relation analysis tools are available for Gender analysis. The relative nature of Gender as a concept by itself invites scholars to develop different and very many forms of this Gender analysis tools and techniques.

Some writers even define Gender analysis as:

"Seeing what our eyes have been trained not to see"

Women's and Men's roles can be better understood with qualitative and quantitative information about their activities, resources and constraints and challenges, benefits and incentives and roles in decision-making.

Gender Analysis	
Gender Based	*Qualitative and Quantitative Information*
Activities	• What are men and women's role? • What are the daily and seasonal variations in labour availability?
Resource and constraints	• Who has access to and control over resources • Which decisions are made by male and by female? • What made them different?
Benefits and Incentives	• Who control production/service/who earns • What wages or benefits from production? • Who controls income/resources? • Which expenditures are men and women responsible for?

Components of Gender Analysis

The key components of Gender relations analysis are Gender roles, Gender division of labour (GDOL), Access to and control over resources/benefits, Decision making (power relation) and Gender needs (practical and strategic needs).

These components of Gender analysis influence one another in one way or another and form a kind of vicious–circle. (*See Fig. 4.1*)

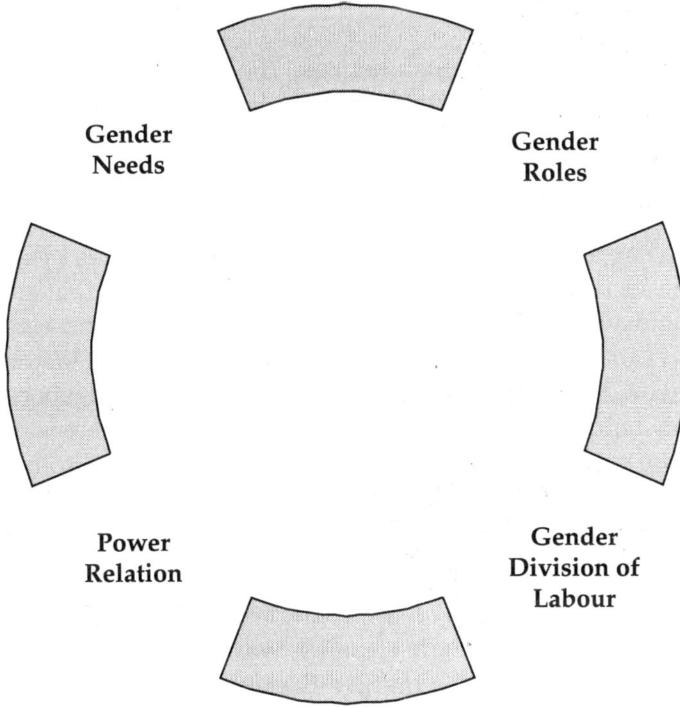

Fig. 4.1: **Components of Gender Analysis**

GENDER ROLES

Gender roles are roles that are played by both women and men which are not determined by biological factors, but by the socio-economic and cultural environment or situation. For example, in parts of Africa and Latin America unskilled construction work is regarded as 'men's work', whereas in India it is regarded as 'women's work.'

Women's Productive and Reproductive Roles

Women are in most societies responsible for all domestic activities such as housework, food preparation and child rearing (reproductive role), in addition to their involvement in economic/income-generating activities (productive role).

This "double day" results in general in a heavier workload on women than on men (although this also depends on social class, age or ethnic group). In the poorer rural and urban areas, for example, women are often engaged in activities such as food crop production, assisting in family cash crop production (planting and weeding), market gardening, informal commerce, small-scale manufacturing etc. in addition to their household and family care responsibilities.

It is important to distinguish between the productive and reproductive roles when planning women's programmes as women spend a lot of time on reproductive activities and productive work. It should also be noted that women's work in both areas is often not remunerated and therefore does not appear in official (or national) economic statistics.

Roles are expected behaviour of an individual, which is assigned to him or her by the society. Based on this, Gender Roles are Roles that are played by both men and women, which are determined by the socio-economic and cultural environment or situation but not by Biological factors. Starting from childhood, both boys and girls are taught about their respective Gender Roles. For instance, Girls are expected to be feminine whereas on the other hand boys are expected to be masculine. Boys are expected to be aggressive and courageous and help their fathers hunting, farming, cattle herding etc, in this case they enjoy their rights fully and more family resources are devoted towards their welfare.

Girls are expected to play an important role in supporting their mothers in the household tasks, especially cleaning, washing, cooking, fetching water and firewood and going to the market. Because of expectations of feminine personality, girls are thought to be shy, soft-spoken, submissive, obedient, honest, care-givers etc. For these reasons girls do not have opportunities to speak about their feelings in public.

Gender roles are systematically constructed, maintained, justified and perpetuated in a systematic process from the household, the church, the workplace, and the media. Gender roles vary widely from one culture to the other and within the same culture. To mention an example, in parts of Africa and Latin America unskilled construction work is regarded as men's work, whereas in India it is regarded as women's work. Because of the different gender roles, opportunities and expectations, there is a preference for one sex over the other.

For instance, in south Ethiopia there is a preference for girls over boy child because of dowry. In northern Ethiopia male childs are preferred because, first they are considered as an important Agricultural labour resource and are entitled to inheritance and second, boys are considered an important safeguard against enemies.

As culture is dynamic and socio-economic conditions change over time so do gender patterns and gender role, for example, twenty years ago women were not allowed to go to the market, and those who did were severely beaten by their husbands. But this has changed, because of economic problems and women's participation in income generating activities, as well as the impact of feeding and caring for their children.

ISSUES OF SEX AND VIOLENCE

Sexual Violence against Women and Girls

Sexual violence is a term used for describing sexual exploitation or rape against women and girls by men. It always comes up as a result of low socio-economic status of the former. The vulnerable categories of women are the housewives, street girls, students, widows and working women. There is also an indication (without empirical evidence) that violence against women is rampant within households where husbands batter (beat) wives and force them to have sexual relations against their wish. Cases of this type are not reported in police stations because they are regarded as 'domestic or family affairs'.

Wife battering is common among house-wives due to their poor economic situation. The wives' financial dependence on their husbands have subjected them to submissiveness, even in matters relating to reproduction and family planning practices. Most women have little or no power to take decisions on their desired number of children, hence rely on the decisions of their husbands and continue to have as many children as the husbands' wish or as 'God provides'.

Abduction is — illegal taking away or kidnapping of girls into forceful marriage. This action is more prevalent in the rural areas especially among the poor men who are not capable of paying bride price. The victim girls are deceived or lured with a token amount of money or sometimes ambushed and rushed away to the prospective husband's home. If the victim is resistant, she is subjected to rape.

Desired Family Size

Desired family size is the number of children a man or woman desires in his or her life time. Many poor people, particularly those on subsistence farming desire numerous children for assistance on their farmland. Such people strive to get as many children as God provides. In certain cases, men might desire more number of children than their wives or that the wives cannot bear their husbands' desired number of children. In such cases, the husbands might marry additional wives to get additional children.

Gender Factors in Sexually Transmitted Diseases

Sexually transmitted diseases (STD), Human Immuno-deficiency Virus and the Acquired Immune Deficiency Syndrome (HIV/AIDS) are found to be common in Africa. They are more common among the heterosexually active adults and intra-venous drug users than any other group of the society. These adults are mostly the ones who have sexual relations with several partners. In Ethiopia, at least sex distinct vulnerable groups of people have been identified. They are commercial sex workers, their children sexually active teenagers, drivers and solders, traditional medical practitioners and clients, health staff and blood transfusion recipients. Among all the groups, women have much greater risk of contacting AIDS infection than men due to their helpless poor status. The commercial sex workers, mostly found in urban areas, have the highest risk. Most of them engage in commercial sex as the last resort in the absence of safe wage employment. The 1989 AIDS survey indicated that 2.4 per cent of blood donors, 50 per cent of antenatal patients and 3.6 per cent of females in low economic class had HIV positive. This topic is discussed in detail in another chapter of this handbook.

Infant and Maternal Death

Infant death is the death among babies whose age is below one year. Infant death rate, also known as infant mortality rate (IMR), is an indication of the level of death event during a year among the infants. There are various methods of calculating the rate. The simplest and conventional method among them is done by dividing the number of infant deaths during a year by the total number of births in that year and then multiply by 1,000. Infant death rate for male births is generally greater than that of female births due to differences in their physiological make-up.

Maternal death is the death associated with complications of pregnancy and childbirth. This implies that this type of death occurs only among the women in the childbearing age group. Maternal death is caused by complications of induced abortion, obstructed labour, haemorrhage (heavy bleeding), pregnancy-induced hypertension and infection. Other causes of maternal death are under-nutrition, inadequate sanitation, impure water, traditional harmful practices, such as female genital mutilation and massaging of the womb, lack of or limited access to immunisation services, antenatal and postnatal care, etc.

Explanation of Domestic Role and Responsibility

Men's and women's domestic roles and responsibilities are determined by the gender-based division of labour. The gender-based division of labour, which is also known as the sexual division of labour specific, which activities and roles should be performed by women and which by men. This division is not uniform in all places. There may be slightest difference in what men and women do in different areas. Nevertheless, we can safely say that women all over the place are primarily responsible for household or domestic activities while men predominate in activities that are performed outside home and that are economically rewarding. However, men are primarily responsible for 'disciplining' household members, major decisions concerning the household, shopping major household items like furniture, etc.

Gender Role Stereotyping in the Family

The society portray women as inferior suited only for domestic labour as opposed to men to whom courage, vigor, and all dispositions of value are attached. Men's disposition is highly appreciated and taken as the standard according to which that of women is judged. However, women are not also encouraged to have men's disposition. On the contrary, 'good natured' women is expected to be submissive, obedient, cool, shy, tolerant, 'ignorant', etc. Male aggressiveness is taken as virtue. Womanhood on the other hand is associated with docility; and this in turn is the source of contempt for 'feminine traits'.

Gender role stereotyping works against both boys and girls, men and women and society at large. It prevents girls and women from aspiring for professions that are considered appropriate only for men such as engineering, medicine, etc. Boys and men also could not enjoy the satisfaction of cooking and doing housework in general.

Traditional Harmful Practices

There are many traditional practices in African countries. Some are good practices while others are harmful. The good ones include breast-feeding, extended family system, communal activities for child-naming, wedding and funeral ceremonies. The harmful ones include female genital mutilation, early marriage and tattooing. The harmful practices are discussed in order to stress the importance of their eradication.

Female Genital Mutilation

Female genital mutilation (FGM) is the collective name given to several traditional practices that involve the cutting of female genitals. It is, to a large extent, a ritual performed by elders in communities. It is one of the harmful traditional practices prevalent in Ethiopia and many other countries in Africa, Asia and Middle-East.

Female genital mutilation is regarded as female circumcision in certain areas. Whereas the female circumcision involves the cutting out of the clitoris which is the sensitive little soft knob at the front end of the vagina, genital mutilation involves more severe operation.

Female genital mutilation is of different types which are classified into three main categories: clitoridectomy, excision and infibulation.

Clitoridectomy: Clitoridectomy is the operation which involves partial or total removal of clitoris and some other part of external genitals.

Excision: Excision is the removal of part of clitoris and/or part of the labia minora.

Infibulation (also known as or Sudanese circumcision): Infibulation is the cutting of the clitoris, the labia minora and part of the labia major and afterwards stitching the resulting wound with acacia thorns or silk, leaving a small opening for urine and menstruation.

Reasons for FGM

(a) *Religion*

FGM is practiced among Moslems, Christians, Animists, traditional believers and adherents of other religions. The fact that the practice is done by most members of the society regardless of the religion, implies that it is more traditional than religious.

(b) *Tradition*

FGM is regarded in many societies as a traditional practice and women particularly agitate to maintain it. It has been practiced for a long time and very common in African societies. Many women in north Sudan, part of Kenya, Nigeria, Mali, Cote d'Ivoire, for examples, celebrate the operation with feast. They believe that cutting of the clitoris would prevent hurting male partner during coital activity and also protect a baby from dying during childbirth. They also believe that it reduces the sexual sensitivity in women and protect against temptations or immoral behaviour. At least 98 per cent of adult female population of Africa has undergone such an operation.

In Ethiopia, about nine out of ten females, whether Muslims or Christians, have undergone the operation. Clitoridectomy is common among the Amhara and Tigray, excision among the Oromos, Kunana, Shankila and Tigray people and infibulation among Muslims in general.

(c) *Cleanliness*

People who practice FGM believe that it makes the genitals clean and beautiful.

Impact of FGM

Most of the genital operation take place within traditional homes under unsterilized conditions and with unsterilized equipment. The cutting off or around the genital organ causes a log of complications which include painful scar, excessive bleeding, physical dislocation, small vagina opening and infectious urinary tracts.

The adverse effects of the complications are numerous. When the females, whose genital organs have been mutilated, become adults, they are likely to have gynecological-related problems such as:

1. Irregular flow of menstrual blood due to the accumulation of blood in the vaginal wall or uterus.
2. Difficulty in urinating due to the damaged urethral opening.
3. Difficult and unsatisfied sexual intercourse.
4. Delay in getting pregnant (infertility) due to the chronic pelvic infection and blocking of fallopian tubes.
5. Prolonged child labour due to stiff vaginal wall.
6. Birth (delivery) to still-birth or babies with damaged heads or mental handicap a result of prolonged child labour and lack of oxygen in the vagina and womb.
7. Repeated miscarriages or prolapsed uterus as a result of prolonged labour.

They also have social and psychological problems. They usually lose their genital sensitivity and do not enjoy sexual relations. This situation subject them to rejection by their male partners or spouses.

Early Marriage

Marriage is the union between a man and a woman as husband and wife. Early marriage is relative term depending on the society. However, marriage is said to be early when the person getting married is immature in age and in physiological development. For instance, any marriage taking place at age earlier than 15 is early. Early marriage is one the traditional practices, especially in Africa.

For example in Ethiopia, about one-third of female population was found to be married at age earlier than 15 years and the average age at first marriage was 15.6 years. The ideal age for marriage was 16.1 years for females and 21.1 years for males. Some studies indicate that majority of respondents supported age 10-15 years as ideal age at first marriage while 2 per cent supported age 9 as ideal.

Early marriage has adverse effects on socio-economic and health status of the persons involved. Girls who marry at early ages, say between 10 and 15 years, would lose the opportunity of formal education. They also have little or no opportunity for wage employment and hence mostly in informal type of job or fully engage in house work and childcare. Their standard of living is generally low because of their insecure type of income-generating venture. They have little money for good quality food, thereby having poor nutrition (malnutrition) which in turn adversely affects their health. In addition, the children of the persons who marry at young ages also suffer from severe malnutrition, under-nutrition and poor health.

ACCESS TO AND CONTROL OVER RESOURCES/BENEFITS

Access to and control over resources and benefits make a difference in the economic, social and political life of men and women. It is important to know who has access to and control over resources. Resources include training, credit, capital, technology, markets, technical assistance information and local knowledge. Project interventions should take into consideration the realities of who has access to and control over resources.

Women and men have different levels of access to and control over natural or community, human and financial resources as well as to public services and facilities. For example, if we take income profile, male earned income from the sale of farm products, livestock and fuel wood, on the other hand women's sources of income were casual work related to Agriculture, collecting fuel wood, sale of hay and animal products such as milk, butter etc, they have limited access to income opportunities and do not therefore generate enough income for survival for this reason, they have to seek alternative means to satisfy their many needs.

Given the patriarchical system of society women by large are deprived of direct ownership of resources such as land, most women in Ethiopia, especially most rural women and women of the caucus class have little control over the different resources of the country. Almost all resources are under the control of their husbands, fathers, brother-in-laws etc.

Female heads of households are even worse off because of some structural problems related to their gender.

Decision Making (Power Relation)

The political role and decision-making activities are obviously dominated by the male sector of the society even in developed society until recently. The best concept that shows irregularity in power relationship is patriarchy, which is a hierarchical social system and way of thinking where 'fathers' or ' patriarchs' rule which has become a model for every form of domination and subordination. As a term 'patriarchal' refers to power relations, in which women's interests are subordinated to the interests of men. These power relations take many forms, from sexual division of labour and the social organization of procreation to the internalized norms of femininity by which we live.

Dear reader, you can answer this question in different ways and that is wonderful if you have included the following. Patriarchy is a gender ideology or system of belief that accords male dominance over the values, processes and decisions that define how society should be organized, how it should function and what is the roles of its members.

Power relation in gender analysis is the concept that meant from inequalities emerging from division of labour and equal/differential access to resources control over benefits and decision making.

Increasing the power of disadvantaged groups and changing systematic subordination is the necessary steps to address the practical needs of deprived society. Studies show that 80 per cent of the decision in Ethiopia is made by males and it is only around 15 per cent of the decisions on very simple activities like sending children to school are undertaken by females. This shows that women's are less decisive or they have very limited chance to decide on all matters of the livelihood activities.

Strategic and Practical Gender Needs

Men and women in a given society have different needs and interests. The needs and interests of women and men with respect to their gender relations could be summarized as practical gender needs and strategic gender needs.

Practical gender needs refer to those needs, which arise from concrete conditions of women's positions, the gender division of labour. Practical gender needs are usually a response to an immediate perceived necessity which is identified by women within specific context. This includes access to health services, water supply and grinding mills etc.

Strategic gender needs are needs, which basically arise from the subordination of women by men. Women's subordination is the outcome of the destiny—social and institutional discrimination against women in a given country or culture. The overall goal of strategic gender needs therefore is to abolish women's subordination.

Examples are legal reforms, equal decision making power, reproductive health rights etc.

Addressing gender inequalities can be the best tool and framework in gender integration and it is possible through the understanding and addressing of practical and strategic gender needs and interests.

Addressing Gender Inequality, PGNs and SGNs

Addressing PGNs facilitate existing gender roles by:

- Enabling women to do existing work better.
- Reducing work burdens within their multiple roles, and
- Overcoming practical problems in all roles (e.g. health food, tool, training income).

Practical Gender Needs and Strategic Gender Needs

Practical Gender Needs (PGNs)	Strategic Gender Needs (SGNs)
❖ Represents what people require in order to carry out their gender roles more easily and effectively ❖ Do not require a change in gender roles, only coherence between roles and culture patterns. For example in order to fulfill the role of a good mother, a women must have access to resources (e.g. food, shelter) ❖ Tend to be easily identified due to the direct demand of society to fulfill gender roles. For example, PGN for women is to respond to the need to care for children. Fulfillment of this need is demanded by other members of the household, the community and children themselves. Thus PGNs are felt with urgency. ❖ Addressing PGNs does not ensure that other needs will be met nor that access to meeting those needs will be sustained	❖ Represents what women or men require in order to improve their position or status in regard to each other. ❖ Place people in greater control of themselves and their own context, instead of limiting them to the restrictions imposed by socially defined roles. ❖ Tend to refer to social relation between groups of people. ❖ SGNs are less visible and obvious than PGNs. ❖ Satisfaction of SGNs requires actions over the long term because they demand changes in attitudes, behaviour and power structures. ❖ Addressing SGNs is conducive to greater satisfaction of practical needs. ❖ Addressing or drawing attention to SGNs might create resistance.

Addressing PGNs and SGNs

Actions that Address PGNs	Action that Address SGNs
❖ Reducing women's workload. Provision of grinding mills improved stones, access to daycare confer. etc. ❖ Improving health, primary health care centers, family planning/child spacing/clean water supply. ❖ Increasing access to enterprise services such as skills training, credit, access to market. ❖ Improving services, such as schools, transport facilities housing and so on.	❖ Ensuring rights to productive assets such as legal status on land ownership, rights to use common property, inheritance, financial services. ❖ Enabling women to take part in Decision-Making through local committee membership, participation in elections/politics, and advocacy for their rights. ❖ Supporting equal opportunity for employment through access to jobs, traditionally done by men, equal pay for comparative jobs. ❖ Improving educational systems. Neutral textbooks, for instance through curricula by including moment's contribute on in history, science and society.

Addressing SGNs changes existing gender roles by:

- Achieving greater equality for women with men
- Raising women's status, power and choice
- Closing access gaps (provide equal wages, access to services, legal rights, asset ownership, non-traditional jobs, control of fertility, life style).

Addressing SGNs is assumed to be harder to achieve in short period and with simple methodology, because it needs the change of this institutional factors and it can be taken as transition, addressing this need can improve the position of women in society and empower them and change (transform) the existing gender relation to achieve greater equality.

In case of addressing practical needs of women, it can be improving the conditions of their lives but does not change (alter) traditional roles and relationships of gender. The Women in Development (WID) approach mainly focuses on this need (PGNs) of women while the Gender in Development (GAD) approach to development focuses on both the Practical and the Strategic needs of women.

GENDER GAP IN VARIOUS AREAS

Agriculture

Agriculture is thought to be the domain of men's activity. Particularly plowing and sowing are, in most places, assumed to be done only by men. However, women are also predominantly engaged in agricultural activities. Though farming is believed to be male's domain of activity, women take part in it except plowing. Soil preparation, weeding, harvesting, winnowing and marketing are shared by both men and women.

The point here is that though women are involved in agriculture, their contribution in this sphere has not been given due consideration. Especially married women involved in agricultural activities are considered as helpers (of men), and therefore their economic contribution is not acknowledged. One of the implications is that since women are not seen as farmers, they cannot be admitted to peasant associations where decisions regarding land redistribution and resource allocation are made unless they are female household heads. This may mean that resources/inputs and appropriate extension and other services in agriculture are not directed to women in male headed households due to this bias.

Wage Employment

Wage employment is another area where the gender imbalance between men and women is manifested.

Female employees are concentrated in low paying, requiring lower skill and less prestigious jobs, or in areas that are traditionally considered women's. Male employees, on the other hand, predominate in the managerial and prestigious jobs.

Only 6.5 per cent of the managerial positions in public establishments are occupied by women. Women are more represented among less educated and unskilled labourers.

For all educational levels, women's participation in employment is very low ranging between 9.5 per cent – 26.8 per cent of the total employment rate. They are highly represented among those who have a lower educational level, i.e., unskilled labourers. Obviously, gender disparities in employment are partially attributed to the unequal access women have to education.

Education

In traditional societies preference in education is given to boys; for this reason more boys have access to educational opportunities than girls. This fact holds true more for rural areas where majority of the population lives.

Reasons for female lower rate of participation and drop-out include values/attitudes towards girls' education, economic cost, opportunity cost, location of schools, gender blind school atmosphere, lack of role models, early marriage, etc.

- Though there is no open discrimination that prevents girls from coming to school, girls' education is not encouraged. This is mainly because of the widely held belief that girls have to be given for marriage early in the ages.
- The second factor is the economic cost. As most families are economically weak, if they afford to send their children to schools, they give preference to their boys.
- Girls are expected to help out their mothers with domestic chores that are often time-taking and tedious. This forces girls either to stay at home, or if they have already been enrolled in schools, to weakly perform.
- Another reason for low participation of girls in education is early marriage. In most rural areas, girls are given to marriage at a very early age which is found to be the major reason why girls are forced to drop-out of school or not to be enrolled in the first place.

Health

While the right to health is a basic human right, most men and women in developing countries could not meet their health needs. This is even worse in the case of women because of their vulnerability which emanates mainly from the unequal gender relations between men and women. This is manifested in that:

- Women constitute the majority of the poorest of the poor due to the unequal access to resources and social services which makes them unable to meet their health needs.
- Women are often overworked especially in the rural context where facilities such as provision of water, substitute for fuel-wood, and grinding mill are not available.
- Some backward practices such as early marriage that cause health complications like fistula, circumcision which is also known as female genital mutilation, domestic violence, rape and similar practices exacerbate women's ill health.
- Absence of easy access to family planning facilities, high fertility rate, abortion induced by their weak economic status also have adverse effects on their health.
- The fact that women care for all household members forces them to ignore their own health. As a result, they seldom seek health services for themselves.

Workload

We find most relegated to the informal sector performing activities that are less rewarding, time consuming and arduous. The activities which women are involved in from dawn to dusk include unpaid activities in the family business, small-scale production of goods and services, housework as domestics, etc. which are performed at their own home. These and other similar activities of women are not valued or taken into according of the GNP. As a result, little effort has been made to mechanize these activities.

Men predominate in decision making and remunerated activities. Their men's involvement in housework is negligible. However, some men of the poorest families may occasionally help women, in some housework activities which are considered less feminine. In general men are engaged in occupation which are properly remunerated and prestigious. In most cased, these require higher level of skill and they take place outside their home

Household Security

It is important to consider gender divisions in making decisions about how to spend household income. In addition, women often suffer more than men from policy decisions about natural-resource management in which they have no say. *Markets*. Do men and women have equal access to markets? How will constraints related to transport, getting information about markets, and being able to leave home to go to market, affect the success of out-scaling a new option?

Management of Natural Resources

How would gender differences related to natural-resource management (at local through to national levels) affect the uptake of a new option? Overall, women take little part in policy-making processes. Women can be helped to take part by making sure both men and women have skills to do this—teaching them to read, giving them information, teaching them leadership skills. All members of the community need to be involved otherwise there is no guarantee that women's voices will be heard even though they might sit on committees that influence management and policies. However, more women taking part can be seen by men as a threat.

Ownership of Assets

We must also consider gender differences in control over and access to assets, including user rights, animals and technologies. Loans taken out by women are often commandeered by men. Although goats, poultry, vegetables and self-recruiting fish species are often considered to be household assets and fall to women to look after, the extent to which women control these assets—selling, spending the money earned—is not clear. In Nepal women and men make decisions about selling goats equally, whereas in Zimbabwe women cannot make decisions about selling their own livestock.

Summary

- The aim of gender analysis is to analyse the position of men and women in a society or community and to identify the specific needs and strengths of each. This method is applied in the planning, management, implementation and evaluation of programmes in order to ensure the equal participation of men and women according to their identified needs, special skills and potentials.
- Gender roles are roles that are played by both women and men which are not determined by biological factors, but by the socio-economic and cultural environment or situation.
- Access to and control over resources and benefits make a difference in the economic, social and political life of men and women. It is important to know who has access to and control over resources. Moreover, we find gender gap in all aspects of our life.

Self-Learning Activity

Try to answer the following questions on your own:

1. Why is gender a development issue?
2. What is FGM?
3. Discuss gender disparity in workload?

5 Theories Regarding Gender Roles

Talcott Parson's Views of Gender Roles

Talcott Parson is an American sociologist who is the current proponent of functionalisms, one known theory in sociology. He developed a model of the nuclear family in 1955 and compared a strictly traditional view of gender roles to more liberal views of Gender role in modern society.

Parsons believed that the feminine role was an expressive one, whereas the masculine role, in his view, was instrumental. He believed that expressive activities of the woman fulfill 'internal' functions, for example to strengthen the ties between members of the family. The man, on the other hand, performed the 'external' functions of a family, such as providing monetary support.

The Parsons' model (Chart 5.1) was used to contrast and illustrate extreme positions on gender roles. Model A describes total separation of male and female roles, while B describes the complete dissolution of barriers between gender roles.

Both extreme positions are rarely found in reality. Actual behaviour of individuals is usually somewhere between these poles. The most common 'model' followed in real life is the 'model of double burden'.

According to the interaction's approach, roles (including gender roles) are not fixed, but are constantly negotiated between individuals (males and females).

Gender roles can influence all kinds of behaviour, such as choice of clothing, choice of work and personal relationships.

Culture and Gender Roles

Gender role is composed of several elements. A person's gender role can expressed through clothing, behaviour, choice of work, personal relationships and other factors. Gender roles were traditionally divided into strictly feminine

Chart 5.1: Talcott Parson's Model of Gender Roles

	Model A - Total role segregation	**Model B- Total disintegration of roles**
Education	Gender-specific education; high professional qualification is important only for the man	Co-educative schools, same content of classes for girls and boys, same qualification for men and women.
Profession	The workplace is not the primary area of women; career and professional advancement is deemed unimportant for women	For women, career is just as important as for men; therefore equal professional opportunities for men and women are necessary.
Housework	Housekeeping and child care are the primary functions of the woman; participation of the man in these functions is only partially wanted.	All housework is done by both parties to the marriage in equal shares.
Decision making	In case of conflict, man has the last say, for example, in choosing the place to live, choice of school for children, buying decisions.	Man cannot dominate over woman; solutions do not always follow the principle of finding a concerted decision; this may lead to separate vacations or living in different apartments.
Child care and education	Woman takes care of the largest part of these functions; she educates children and cares for them in every way.	Man and woman share these functions equally.

and masculine gender roles, though these roles have diversified today into many different acceptable male or female gender roles. However, gender role norms for women and men can vary significantly from one country or culture to another, even within a country or culture people express their gender role somewhat uniquely.

Gender role can vary according to the social group to which a person belongs or the subculture with which he or she chooses to identify.

Androgyny - a term denoting the display of both male and female behaviour also exists. Many terms have been developed to portray sets of behaviours arising in this context. The masculine gender role has become more malleable since the 1950's, one example is the "sensitive new age guy", which could be described as a traditional male gender role with a more typically "female" empathy and associated emotional responses. Another is the *metro-sexual,* a male who adopts or claims to be born with similarly "female" grooming habits. Some have argued that such new roles are merely rebelling against tradition more so than forming a distinct role.

According to sociological research, traditional feminine gender roles have become less relevant and hollowed in Western societies since industrialization started. For example, the cliché that women do not follow a career is obsolete in many western societies. On the other hand, in the media there are attempts to portray women who adopt an extremely classical role as a subculture.

Ideas of appropriate behaviour according to gender vary among cultures and era, although some aspects receive more widespread attention than others. An interesting case is described by R.W. Connell in Men, Masculinities:

> "There are cultures where it has been normal, not exceptional, for men to have homosexual relations. There have been periods in 'western' history when the modern convention that men suppress displays of emotion did not apply at all, when men were demonstrative about their feeling for their friends. Mateship in the Australian outback last century is a case in point."

Other aspects, however, may differ markedly with time and place. In pre-industrial Europe, for example, the practice of medicine (other than mid-wifery) was generally seen as a male prerogative. However, in Russia, health care was more often seen as a feminine role. The results of these views can still be seen in modern society, where European medicine is most often practiced by men, while the majority of Russian doctors are women.

In many other cases, the elements of convention or tradition seem to play a dominant role in deciding which occupations fit in with which gender roles. In the United States, physicians have traditionally been men, and the few people who defied that expectation received a special job description:

"woman doctor". Similarly, there are special terms like "male nurse", "woman lawyer", "lady barber", "male Secretary," etc. But in China and the former Soviet Union, medical doctors were predominantly women, and in the United Kingdom, Germany and Taiwan it is very common for all of the barbers in a barber shop to be women.

For example, in the western society, people whose gender appears masculine and whose inferred and/or verified external genitalia are male are often criticized and ridiculed for exhibiting what the society regards as a woman's gender role. For instance, someone with a masculine voice, a five o'clock shadow (or a fuller beard), an Adam's apple, etc., wearing a woman's dress and high heels, carrying a purse, etc., would most likely draw ridicule or other unfriendly attention in ordinary social contexts (the stage and screen expected). It is seen by some in that society that such a gender role for a man is not acceptable. This, and other societies, imposes expectations on the behaviour of the members of society, and specifically on the gender roles of individuals, resulting in prescriptions regarding gender roles.

It should be noted that some societies are comparatively rigid in their expectations, and other societies are comparatively permissive. Some of the gender signals that form part of a gender role and indicate one's gender identity to others are quite obvious, and others are so subtle that they are transmitted and received out of ordinary conscious awareness.

Summary

- Talcott Parson is an American sociologist who is the current proponent of functionalisms, one known theory in sociology. He developed a model of the nuclear family in 1955 and compared a strictly traditional view of gender roles to more liberal views of Gender role in modern society.
- Gender role can vary according to the social group to which a person belongs or the subculture with which he or she chooses to identify.

Self-Learning Activity

Try to answer the following questions on your own:

1. Describe Model A of total role segregation.
2. Discuss about culture and gender roles.

6 Gender and Development

Gender and Development Defined

Different scholars defined development in different ways. Dudely Seers says the main aim of development is the realization of the potential of human personality. We need to ask three basic question that say "What happen to poverty, what happen to unemployment and what happen to inequality" this condition in turn lead us to the expansion of the necessities for human life specifically the expansion of the different forms of capital. So development can be defined as a means of enabling some one to attain what they need.

Gender and Development (GAD) is a concept that evolved from the analysis and lessons from the Women in Development (WID) approach developed in the sixties and sixties and seventies. It is based on the recent recognition that women and men play different roles in society and within their communities, because of their different role they have different needs. It reflects a change in focus from women's exclusion from development to the gender relation between men and women — the position of women has to be seen in relation to men instead of being seen as opposed to men.

Gender and development is an approach, which considers the gender relations in development and seeks to empower women and the disadvantaged group of the society. The approach seeks to transform unequal relations between women and men. GAD also addresses the practical needs that are determined by women and men to improve their conditions and the strategic interests. Hence, GAD recognizes the need to work with men and women on gender in order to change the existing relations. Gender and development challenges the notion of an equal distribution of resources, opportunities, and benefits to different population groups served by a particular intervention. It challenges the gender division of labour and the unequal relation of power that prevent equitable and sustainable development and women's full participation in development. Furthermore, GAD recognizes that women are not a homogenous group, they are divided in many ways such as class, ethnicity and age, hence, the need to consider these distinctions in research and development planning.

GAD is people-centered development process, but *what do we mean when we say people centered*? aiming to achieve sustainable development where men and women themselves participate as development agents. It emphasizes the need for people's participation at the various levels of policy formulation and implementation. It recognizes the cardinal point about gender and development that both men and women are potential agents for social transformation.

Three important questions are asked to understand the differences between female and male roles, responsibilities, opportunities and rewards. These are, *first,* the division of labour, who is doing what? *Second,* access to and control over resources, which has access and control over resources, benefits and opportunities? *Third,* what are the social economic, environment, religious and political factors that influence the division of labour and the division of resources? The Gender and Development approach helps project planners to pinpoint important differences in female and male responsibilities and thus to use this information to plan development programmes and projects more effectively.

This approach emphasizes the importance of using the gender tools of analysis such as the Harvard Analytical Framework to explore and analyze the differences, between the kinds of work performed by women and men and resources accessed and controlled by women and men. Further, it focuses on the need to sue the analysis tools to identify and explore factors influencing gender roles such as social, cultural and economic circumstances. The tools of analysis enable planners to find out how an intervention would affect the different groups in the community. These tools enable planners, development workers and all concerned to take corrective measures and ensure that the project will meet the needs of all identified groups equality.

Why Gender in Development?

Women play a crucial role in food security and food production. According to various sources, women produce 60-80 per cent of the food in most developing countries and are responsible for half of world food production. However, their ability to produce enough food and earn adequate income which would ensure food security is hindered by unequal resource allocation, i.e. access to input, credit, fertilizers, extension services, and access to technology. Gender-biased planning and unequal resource allocation have left women little room, if any, to increase their in production. In this regard, development activities have to be geared towards increasing the capability of both men and women and thereby to satisfy their basic need and aspirations as a basis for a healthy society.

Because of gender-biased planning women have not benefited from the development process. They have limited access to productive resources, higher education and training, and they have little employment opportunities. The majority of women earn their meager incomes from the informal sector. The informal sector does not offer adequate job opportunities to all women and those who are already engaged in this sector have little income for survival. In many of the developing countries, women are over-represented among the poor, with inadequate basic services and facilities. The number of female-headed households shouldering family responsibilities is increasing rapidly. In the Beijing Platform for Action the feminization of poverty has been emphasized. Moreover the number of women living in absolute poverty is increasing disproportionately to the number of men.

Similarly, women are the health agents of the household and they have a key role in household maintenance, family nutrition and education. In many of the developing countries women work longer hours than men, and child care and family responsibilities take a large part of women's time and energy. Women's dual role as contributors and beneficiaries in the development process has been constrained by their heavy workload in reproductive activities. In addition, due to gender discrimination in development programming and planning, the different needs and opportunities available to men and women are not taken into consideration.

Because of the problems mentioned above women are not available to participate in development planning. Thus the need for an affirmative action programme that would give women new skills or resources so that they can participate on an equal basis with men. A gender programme mean the relationships between women and men would be explored and understood and changes in social roles would be negotiated between men and women. This would ensure that women are equally available, while men are equally burdened in reproductive responsibilities to allow them both to participate in development.

At present, women see some advantages in being ignored because then they are not given more responsibilities or duties on full-time basis without having the benefits of development. Women and men are the main actors of development, and each constitutes half of the population. Therefore, if development has to succeed the untapped potential of women has to be fully exploited in the process.

The gap between men and women in terms of opportunity for participation, access and control over resources, gender division of labour, etc. is widening rapidly. Women are excluded from decision-making including crop production and decision-making. Yet, programmes and projects might continue overlooking women unless they take affirmative action to improve and incorporate their positions and conditions in programmes and operational plans. According to Sarah Longwe development is defined as enabling people to take charge of their own lives and escape from poverty. Empowering women enabling them to participate equally in the development process is one of the prerequisites of development.

To sum-up, removing inequality and embracing gender integration are pre-requisites to sustainable development. These need to be recognized, addressed and mobilized at programme and planning levels. Working with women and men in development thus requires special effort and commitment. Any development planning has to efficiently target resources and benefits to both men and women while at the same time ensuring that the fruits of development are shared equitably. Gender planning ensures women's participation right from the beginning including the issue of how they will benefit from the development process.

Gender and development:

The focus	– is on the relations between men and women.
The problem	– is the unequal relations of power between men and women on the same socio-economic level. This results in the unequal distribution of the benefits of development and hinders women's full participation in the development process.
The solution	– is to empower the disadvantaged and women, and to transform unequal relations.
The aim	– is to attain equitable and sustainable development with both men and women in decision-making and leadership positions.
How?	– enhance the democratization and de officialization process of cooperatives. – identify the (practical and strategic) needs and interests of men and women which can improve their condition. – enhance women's access resources including credit and education and training facilities etc. – involve women in decision-making. – enhance women's access to leadership positions, e.g. through quotas or "affirmative action", which is action taken to correct the already existing imbalances.

Women in Development

Between the 50's and 70's development issues in the so-called Third World focused on modernization and technological innovation. The assumption was that it would be possible to benefit the poor and remove poverty. However, the benefits of development were not able to reach the needy people. More specifically, the status and the traditional rights of women have deteriorated more than ever, mainly due to planners' failure to address the roles and needs of women as distinct from men, and women's limited access and control over resources and benefits. Easter Boserup is credited with bringing onto the international agenda the issue of women and their marginalization in the 1970s. In particular, she highlighted the impact of technological innovation on women—the displacement of women from their productive labour and the entrenching of the sexual division of labour.

There are three additional factors that contributed to bring the Women in Development (WID) issue onto the international agenda. *First,* it was believed that because of their central role in productive and reproductive tasks, women in the Third World could play a crucial role in the population control programme. *Second,* women's crucial role in subsistence farming and social reproductive tasks were thought to be an important channel for the provision of basic needs for the family. *Third,* following Easter Boserup, concern about the Third World women grew and the need to study the lives of poor women as a way of getting to the bottom of poverty became clear. Moreover, the UN Decade for Women, UN conferences, the proliferation of women in development agencies and bureaus within governments of developing countries also played a significant role in highlighting the issue of women in development.

In order to adjust the imbalance between men and women and integrate women in the development process, the transfer of technology, provision of extension services and credit facilities were taken as major intervention strategies. This strategy saw women as producers, but it did not address the root causes of women's poverty, and the gender division of labour. The WID approach focused mainly on addressing the practical needs of women.

The WID approach served as a major instrument in influencing development policies aimed at integrating women into the development process. The result was evident in improved women's organization and networking. It played a significant role in bringing the whole question of women's marginalization in the development process onto the international agenda and national development policies of many countries as well as within multilateral and bilateral agencies.

The Women in Development (WID) approach, aiming mainly to address women's issues, passed through five different development stages: welfare, equity, anti-poverty, efficiency, and empowerment.

Welfare Approach

The welfare approach recognizes only the reproductive role of women and their practical needs, its main purpose to upgrade women to be better mothers. It does not challenge the existing gender relations. The main method of implementation is through the free distribution of goods and services. Women have a passive role in development and are excluded from the larger part of development programmes.

Equity Approach

The equity approach was developed in response to the negative impact of modernization of women. It recognizes women's active participation in development. It advocates the equitable redistribution of resources, equitable participation and political and economic autonomy of women and men, by means of different levels of interventions. These interventions include policy, top-down legislation, and state interventions. The equity approach has been politically unpopular with many governments, as well as multilateral agencies, because the notion of redistribution is highly threatening. One of the criticisms of the equity approach is that it considers women as a homogeneous group and ignores differences between women of different castes and classes.

Anti-poverty Approach

It revealed that often women bear the greater burden of poverty at the household level compared to men. Women's poverty is seen as a problem of under-development. This approach focuses on specific anti-poverty programmes for women, skill building and provision of credit to relieve women from the burden of poverty. The criticism leveled against this approach is that it does not challenge the sexual division of labour and structural problems of women's poverty. Proponents of the anti-poverty approach favor interventions that address women's reproductive tasks. It is criticized for perpetuating the gender division of labour. The anti-poverty approach is designed to meet the practical needs of women, without attempting to increase women's autonomy. In practice, participatory procedures are rarely employed thereby limiting sustainability.

Efficiency Approach

This approach begun with concern about the result of global economic crises and the need to cut back expenditures in the service sector, and achieve efficient development through women's economic contribution by channeling women's labour into the productive sector. It meets practical gender need relying on women's triple role, but at the cost of long working hours and an increased workload for women. The underlying idea is to tap women's economic potential for development and thereby increase equity. This approach is popular with governments and multilateral agencies who are anxious to overcome economic problems and achieve development with little or limited resources.

Empowerment Approach

The empowerment approach, the most recent approach, tried to integrate women into pre-existing structures. (Empowerment is the process of generating and building capacities to exercise control over one's life.) It was initiated by DASN (Development Alternatives for Women in the New Era) a Third World women grassroots organization and feminist activists. It raised questions about the causes of women's subordination and incorporated new insight and a critique of the overall development process. It sought to clarify the mechanisms of women's marginalization. It advocated participatory approaches involving women and women's organizations as the focal point of development. The empowerment approach acknowledges the need for women to come together to understand their diverse experiences of oppression and challenge the roots of such oppression. It explicitly includes participatory planning and bottom-up mobilization and conscientisation.

The empowerment approach highlights the need to incorporate three critical conceptual tools that focus on the household, gender division of labour and social relations of gender. Details are as follows:

Household

Experiences of the gender neutral and the gender biased development approaches that introduced the use of the household at the basic unit of development analysis and intervention has resulted in the invisibilisation of women. The relations among family members within the household are mainly based on power that is determined by sex and age. The empowerment approach, therefore, highlights the need to investigate and understand the status of women within the household, and the conflicting processes that determine decision-making patterns.

Gender division of labour

It is evident that because of the gender division of labour, women's and men's working hours, workloads, roles and responsibilities are distinct. Women work longer hours than men and are given sole responsibility of the domestic tasks. Unless development policy recognizes the need for equal responsibility for reproductive tasks, women will be restricted to their marginalized position in society. Women, therefore, should be accorded the opportunity to enter into non-traditional tasks and more lucrative sectors of the economy.

Social relations of gender

There is lack of understanding on how the unequal relations between men and women are constructed and perpetuated. Where men have socially-constructed roles and responsibilities, they inform and perpetuate the socially-constructed unequal power relations between men and women in all social institutions – the household, state, bureaucracy, and so on. Until this inequality of power is addressed, any effort to improve the condition and power of women will be incomplete.

Feminist development theories: applying WID and GAD

This section provides tools and exercises to help you become familiar with, and operationalize, the two major feminist development theories. The tools are drawn from *Two Halves Make a Whole: Balancing Gender Relations in Development* (Moffat et al., 1991) but are somewhat revised. This section also provides three case studies that highlight the significance of the WID and GAD frameworks. These case studies show that when you approach a problem from a particular framework, you identify a certain set of problems and arrive at certain types of strategies and solutions. WID tends to focus on practical needs, whereas GAD focuses on both practical needs and strategic interests (Tables 6.2 and 6.3). In addition to focusing on everyday problems, GAD is concerned with addressing the root inequalities (of both gender and class) that create many of the practical problems women experience in their daily lives.

GAD Perspective

Women may need to modify their behaviour in the short term to avoid further injury, but in the long term the major modification required is in men, as they are the perpetrators of this violence. The cultural values and social institutions that give men power over women in their households, on the streets, and in the workplace need to be changed. This will require massive and long-term public education. It will probably involve new legislation or the enforcement of existing legislation to ensure zero tolerance of domestic violence so that assaults in the home are prosecuted in the same way as assaults between strangers would be; sexual-harassment regulations are actively implemented through workplace committees; and women and men each regard the effective maintenance of safe streets as a public priority. Occupational segregation should also be eliminated so that women can have economic power and can, if necessary, be financially independent and women are no longer viewed as inferior workers doing inferior jobs.

Table 6.1: Development of the Women's & Gender Issue from WID to GAD

	Women in Development (WID)	Gender in Development (GAD)
Approach	• Seeks to integrate women into the development process	• Seeks to empower women and transform unequal relations between women and men
Focus	• Women	• The relation between men and women
Problem	• The exclusion of women from the development process	• Unequal relations of power that prevent equitable development and women's full participation
Goal	• More efficient, effective development	• Equitable, sustainable development • Women and men sharing decision-making and power
Strategy	• Implement women's project, women's components, integrating projects Increase women's productivity and income Improve women's ability to manage their household	• Identify and address short term needs determined by women and men to improve their conditions • Identify and address women's and men's long-term interests

Table 6.2: Comparison of WID and GAD

	WID	GAD
Approach	• An approach that views the absence of women in development plans and policies as the problem	• An approach to development that focuses on global and gender inequalities
Focus	• Women	• Socially constructed relations between women and men, with special focus on the subordination of women
Problem	• The exclusion of women (half of productive resources) from the development process participation	• Unequal power relations (rich *vs.* poor; women *vs.* men), which prevents equitable development and women's full
Goal	• More efficient, effective development that includes women	• Equitable, sustainable development, with women and men as decision-makers
Solution	• Integrate women into the existing development process	• Empower the disadvantaged and women and transform unequal relations
Strategies	• Focus on women's projects, on women's components of projects, and on integrated projects	• Reconceptualize the development process, taking gender and global inequalities into account
	• Increase women's productivity and income Increase women's ability to look after the household	• Identify and address practical needs, as determined by women and men, to improve their condition; at the same time, address women's strategic interests • Address strategic interests of the poor through people-centred development

Note: GAD — gender and development; WID — women in development.

Table 6.3: Practical needs and strategic interests

Practical needs	Strategic interests
• Tend to be immediate, short-term	• Tend to be long-term
• Are unique to particular women, according to the roles assigned to them in the gender division of labour in their society	• May be viewed as being relevant to all women (e.g., all women experience some inequality relative to men, but the degree varies by class, race, religion, age, etc.)
• Relate to daily needs: food, housing, income, health, children, safety	• Relate to disadvantaged position: subordination, lack of resources and education, vulnerability to poverty and violence, etc.
• Are easily identifiable by women	• Are not always identifiable by women (e.g., women may be unaware of the basis of disadvantage or potential for change)
• Can be addressed by providing specific inputs: food, handpumps, clinics, etc.	• Can be addressed by consciousness-raising, increasing self-confidence, providing education, strengthening women's organizations, fostering political mobilization, etc.
Addressing practical needs	**Addressing strategic interests**
• Tends to involve women as beneficiaries and perhaps as participants	• Involves women as agents or enables women to become agents
• Can improve the condition of women's lives	• Can improve the position of women in society
• Generally, does not alter traditional roles and relationships	• Can empower women and transform gender relations and attitudes

Tools of GAD analysis

Tool 1

Gender Division of Labour: Most societies allocate different roles, responsibilities, and activities to women and men, according to what is considered appropriate in a particular culture. This is called the gender division of labour. An examination of the gender division of labour usually shows that although both women and men work to maintain themselves and their households, there tends to be differences in the nature of their work and in the ways it is valued. These differences are a central aspect of gender relations.

Tool 2

Types of Work: Women and men, and to some extent boys and girls, are likely to be involved in three main areas of work: productive, reproductive, and community work. In many societies, however, women do almost all of the reproductive and much of the productive work. Any intervention in one area will affect the others.

Tool 3

Access to and Control over Resources and Benefits: Women's subordinate position can limit their access to, and control over, resources and benefits. In some cases, women may have access (the opportunity to make use of something) to resources and benefits, but no control (the ability to define its use and impose that definition on others). For example, women may have access to land but no control over its long-term use or ownership.

Tool 4

Influencing Factors: Gender relations (including the division of labour, the type of work women and men do, and their respective levels of access and control) change to some degree over time in any society. Many factors influence, shape, and change these relations. For example, gender relations are affected by such factors as changes in the economy, environment, religion, culture, and political situation.

Tool 5

Condition and Position: A distinction can be drawn between the day-to-day condition of women and their position in society. As noted, women's "condition" refers to their material state — their immediate sphere of experience. A woman would describe her condition in terms of the work she does, where she lives, what she needs for herself and her children (clean water, food, education), etc. "Position" refers to women's social and economic standing relative to that of men. It is measured, by male-female disparities in wages and employment opportunities, participation in legislative bodies, vulnerability to poverty and violence, etc. Development activities tend to focus on women's condition, aiming to improve their ability to carry out traditional roles and responsibilities. Little attention has been paid to enhancing women's position or promoting their ability to participate fully with men as agents of development and change.

Tool 6

Practical Needs and Strategic Interests: Practical needs are linked to women's condition. They can be readily identified and usually relate to unsatisfactory living conditions and lack of resources. For example, practical needs are usually related to immediate needs, such as those for food and water, the health and education of children, and increased income. Practical needs and family survival are always priorities. The satisfaction of these needs is a prerequisite for women's ability to promote their strategic interests. Strategic interests for women arise from their position in society (disadvantaged) relative to that of men. Strategic interests are long-term, related to improving women's position. For example, empowering women to have more opportunities, greater access to resources, and more equal participation with men in decision-making would be in the long-term strategic interest of the majority of the world's men and women alike.

Tool 7

Levels of Participation: The formulation of more gender-aware policies requires women's (and men's) involvement as participants, beneficiaries, and agents. Women benefit significantly if their decision-making capacity and status are increased through a process of consultation. Passive recipients of assistance they become agents of change when they organize themselves to address their own needs and plan solutions and when their voices are heard and taken into account.

Tool 8

Potential for Transformation: Women's subordinate position is not a static state, nor is it experienced the same way by all women. Throughout history and around the world, women have challenged gender inequality and the limitations it imposes on their potential as human beings. Significant gains have been and will continue to be made everywhere through the struggle of women, sometimes with men's support. In all societies, transformatory processes are creating a better life, addressing inequalities, and improving the position of women. Women's movements have a long history in most countries, and an awareness of these movements should be part of our gender analysis.

WID Perspective

Women may need to modify their behaviour to reduce their exposure to violence. This might involve the development of more home-based work opportunities to avoid going to an outside workplace; improved financial-management skills to make cash stretch farther and reduce tensions over money; and training in avoiding violence on the streets (through such tactics as walking in groups, refusing night shifts, not wearing sexually provocative clothing, and asking men from their household to accompany them at all times). Shelters should also be provided to assist women in urgent need. While they are in the shelter they should have access to the above types of training and counseling. A governmental or non-governmental agency should provide this training, along with other services for women. Laws should be passed to strengthen penalties for violence against women.

Tools of WID Analysis

Tool 1

Gender Division of Labour: Definitely part of the problem in Case Study 1 is that women's and men's work in different spheres allocates them differential financial and social power.

Tool 2

Types of Work: Women's involvement in productive work seems to be little recognized, as they are punished by their husbands for leaving the home; and they shoulder the burden of domestic budgeting (as part of their reproductive work), leaving them vulnerable to accusations of mismanaging income. To make up the shortfall of cash from an inadequate income, they seek paid productive work outside. The demands placed on women in these two spheres are contradictory. This probably lowers their self-esteem, as they feel they are failing to meet expectations. All this contributes, directly and indirectly, to the cycle of violence in which they are trapped.

Tool 3

Access to and Control over Resources and Benefits: Men have access to better jobs than women do, although some men may be unemployed or paid low wages, which possibly increases domestic stress. Women have access to household income but do not really control it in the sense of being free to decide on spending priorities. It seems they must meet their husbands' expectations and requirements above all else.

Tool 4

Influencing Factors: Violence in this case is increasing, not static, so something must be changing in the environment to explain it. Research should focus on factors such as changing patterns of work, prices, and ideas about appropriate behaviour for women and men.

Tool 5

Condition and Position: Women's condition is a problem: they experience violence in their daily lives. Their position relative to that of men seems to be the cause of the problem.

Tool 6

Practical Needs and Strategic Interests: Immediate practical needs include those for shelters, jobs, housing, medical care, and counselling. Strategic interests include measures to improve women's position relative to that of men; these measures should focus on both empowering women and bringing about long-term societal change in men's attitudes and behaviour.

Tool 7

Levels of Participation: Women need to organize to empower themselves and to bring about long-term change. They should participate in efforts to provide many of the practical services needed by women experiencing violence, but they should not take sole responsibility for providing these: getting male-dominated governmental and non-governmental agencies to acknowledge these problems and take some responsibility for solving them would be an essential part of long-term change. Women who have been the victims of violence should be involved in solving the short-and long-term problems, thereby moving from the status of passive victim to that of active decision-maker.

Tool 8

Potential for Transformation: A mixed strategy of meeting practical needs while bringing about long-term changes has good potential to transform society. As the problem in this case study has ramifications in the areas of law, policing, economics, welfare, health, education, and media, its solution might involve a great number of agencies and individuals and thereby transform institutions and personal styles of life.

Summary

- Gender and Development (GAD) is a concept that evolved from the analysis and lessons from the Women in Development (WID) approach developed in the sixties and sixties and seventies.
- Gender and development is an approach, which considers the gender relations in development and seeks to empower women and the disadvantaged group of the society.

- The Women in Development (WID) approach, aiming mainly to address women's issues, passed through five different development stages: welfare, equity, anti-poverty, efficiency, and empowerment.
- There are differences between WID and GAD. Number of tools are available to analyze GAD and WID.

Self-Learning Activity

Try to answer the following questions on your own:

1. Define GAD.
2. Explain the stages involved in addressing women's issues.
3. Write short note on: Level of participation as a tool of WID analysis.

7 Gender Inequality

Rationale for Gender Equality

- Moral and ethical issue - basic human rights of women and men
- Promotion of economic growth based on the full use of human resources

– "gender equality is good for business" and thus brings added value to its membership and community - valuing differences for social and economic benefits.

Gender equality as a base for reducing gender-based poverty

- There are hard facts to show that gender equality is the basis for reducing poverty in general, and women's poverty in particular.
- The struggle for gender equality is a key instrument for lifting hundreds of millions of people out of poverty.

Key conclusion drawn for the UNDP analysis is that progress towards gender equality is not dependent on the income level of a society, but more on political will.

Recent years have seen a broadening of the debate around poverty, which has led to a more pluralistic approach to measuring or assessing poverty and deprivation. There is increasing emphasis on self-assessment of poverty, leading to issues such as domestic violence and social support networks becoming part of the mainstream poverty debate.

From a gender perspective, this opens up the possibility for highlighting the gender–specific dimensions of deprivation, using concepts of vulnerability, shocks, fluctuation, powerlessness and so on.

Actors to Meet Challenges

There are different actors that can play a role in reducing poverty, among which are government, civil society, the private sector, donors, trade unions and so on.

Government

The fundamental responsibility for the achievement of gender equality rests with governments. They also command the public resources needed to deliver basic services in an equitable way and to set the 'rules of the game' for actors at the civil society and private sector levels.

Civil society

Can lobby governments and the private sector to ensure that policy commitments are delivered and, where necessary, appropriate changes to policies and laws are made. Civil Society also provides innovative solutions based on cultural and social realities that can be scaled up to improve the impact of programmers.

Private sector

The private sector, which includes the business community, is the engine of economic growth and development as well as a standard setter in relation to the rights of both workers and consumers.

Donors

Donors can make an important contribution within a framework of collaboration with key actors in governments, civil society and the private sector, and through experience sharing and developing of new ideas. More importantly, improved coordination and cooperation will be needed if good governance and maximum progress must be achieved.

Local and International Organization

Such types of organization can play a key role in addressing timely issues for target groups. By working in collaboration with communities at the grassroots level they can easily identify and take measures to solve different developmental problems.

Key Areas of Gender Inequality

Since the 1970s four world conferences on women was held at different time and place to discuss about the position of women in the world in relation to their male counterparts. If we take the latest and most recent conference, it took place that Beijing, the capital of China, from September 4-15, 1995, members of the conference were representatives of women all over the world from both governmental and non-governmental bodies.

The aim of that conference was to evaluate the progress in the status of women over the past quarter century before the 1995, i.e. (1970-95). The conference pointed out that only modest progress was achieved by then and to overcome the main obstacles, the conference adopted 12 areas of concern on women world wide called the Beijing Platform For Action (PFA). These areas of concern are:

Poverty

Studies have shown that women, especially in rural areas are more impoverished than their men counterpart. They constitute 70 per cent of the world poor. This is because of absence of economic opportunities due to their lower position in the gender relationship/lack of land ownership and in heritance, education etc). From the conference it is concluded that Gender Equality is a base for reducing poverty in general and women's poverty in particular. The struggle for gender equality is a key instrument for lifting hundreds of millions of people out of poverty.

Education and Training

Almost two-thirds of all illiterate people in the world are women, the majority being from rural areas. Moreover dropout rates among girls are much higher than boys due to problems including preference of boy's education at the household level. Research of the World Bank has shown that education for girls is the single most effective way of tackling poverty. Women with even few years of basic education have smaller, healthier families. Child and maternal mortality is lower with higher number of years of education of the mothers. Each additional year of female education is estimated (taught) to reduce child mortality by 5-10 per cent.

Health care

Mortality rate of women is high due to inadequate attention given to reproductive health. For example, in Ethiopia it is estimated that 8 per cent of every mother die due to course related to pregnancy.

Violence against women

Violence of women could be domestic at home or outside (at school, on the road and workplace so on). It includes beating, rape, and sexual abuse (harassment) causing physical or physiological damage on women. The participant of the conference noted that violence is a global problem yet no preventive laws exist to protect women and even if laws exist, there is reluctance from the part of authorities to enforce them.

In part of Africa, South and East Asia, some traditions see girls as a burden rather than an asset. Infanticide, sex-selective abortion and preferential care for and feeding of boys, particularly in early childhood appear to lie behind demographic data which show alarming evidence of "missing" women in some populations.

Effect of war on women

Women are affected in many areas during war. Women are left to maintain families when economic and social life is disrupted, women are also victims of disappearance and rape as a weapon of war. Moreover 75 per cent of the world's 23 million refugees are women and children which show the devastated position women hold/face in society.

Inequality in economic structures and access to resources

Though women do produce food and contribute significantly to economic life every where, they are excluded from economic decision makings in most societies, they lack equal access to and control over various means of production/land, capital, technology, moreover their work is underpaid and undervalued.

Inequality in sharing power and decision-making

Not enough women participate fully as top-level diplomats or leadership positions though there have been noticeable progress over the years. Yet to attain the goals of equality and development the participants of the conference passed some recommendations in order to create rooms for women at top levels. Figures published in 1999 on women's participation in politics show, women hold only 12. 7 per cent of the world's parliamentary seats and only 8.7 per cent of those in the least developed countries.

Women focused institution

A number of institutions like national ministries, NGOS, Women Associations which analyses the needs and problem and women research units have been created in most countries for the advancement of women's right, but they didn't hit the nail on the head until today because some of them are infant, some suffer from lack of financial and human resources to perform adequately.

Human rights of women

Women may have rights guaranteed by law, but do not exercise them because they might not be aware of them and because governmental bodies fail to promote and protect those rights. Women with disabilities suffer multiple disadvantages severe challenges with regard to the achievement of their human rights.

Women and media

Although more women work in the media, few make policy decisions still in most countries mass media provides a distorted picture of women, their role and contribution to communities and countries.

Women and environment

In most developing countries women are responsible for fetching water and fuel wood and management of household consumption. Yet, because they are mostly absent from decision-making, environment policies do not take in to account the close links between women's daily lives and the quality and sustainability of the environment.

Girl child

In many countries of the world. Girls are often treated as inferior to boys. Girls are subjected to detrimental customary practices as genital mutilation and early marriage. The International Labour Organization approximated that 95 per cent of child prostitutes are girls. As many as 800,000 children in Thailand, 400,000 in Brazil and 100,000 in the Philippines and countless thousands elsewhere have been forced in to prostitution.

The UNDP conclude that progress towards gender equality is not dependent on the income level of a society but more on political will so the government, the civil society, private sector, donors, and national and International organizations are central actors to meet the challenges and to contribute for speeding up of gender equality in the history of human kind.

Measures and Strategies to Eliminate Gender Disparities

Education

- Equal access to education imply that boys and girls need differential treatment. The needs of girls should be looked into.
- Teachers also need to give extra attention to girls in view of encouraging them in their studies.
- An attempt should be made to have more female teachers that may serve as role models for girls. Bringing more women into the profession of teaching will have a positive influence on girls education.
- Another major step that may improve the education of girls is having schools in easily accessible distance. This will minimize their exposure to risks such as rape and other form of violence on their way to and from schools.
- The school atmosphere also needs to be gender responsive on matters such as the provision of toilets, i.e., toilets for girls need to be built farther than those for male's.
- An equally important measure that needs to be taken is creating awareness among the community on the value of educating girls. Here we need to emphasize the need to revisit the gender-based division of labour so as to alleviate some of the workload girls bear.
- As it is often said, educating a man is educating a person, whereas educating a woman is educating a family. The multiplier effect of girls education should be made known for everyone.

Traditional harmful practices

In order to prevent the adverse consequences of harmful practices:

- Policy makers or law enforcement agents should mobilize the support of religious and community leaders who encourage the practices.
- Mother should also be encouraged to avoid genital mutilation and early marriage of their daughters.
- Efforts should be made towards encouraging parents, religious and traditional leaders to involve girls in gainful activities such as formal or informal schooling, vocational and handicraft occupations.
- Factors that promote postponement of marriage such as full participation in labour force should be encouraged.
- Health workers should discourage further practice of tattooing by enlightening people about the hazards it does to the skin.

Family planning

Family planning practices can increase through the following strategies:

- Mobilising men to participate in contraception.
- Mobilising men to give consent to their wives to use contraception when necessary.
- Promoting user-friendly services for men and adolescents.
- Improving the quality and increasing the quantity of the contraceptive devices.

Infant and maternal death

Mortality of infants, children and reproductive women can be minimized if the following measures are taken:

- Health workers should encourage pregnant women to utilize the available ante-natal and post-natal services in order to avoid complications.
- Partners of pregnant women and nursing mothers should assist in household chores.
- Adolescents should be enlightened regarding the adverse consequences of too many and too frequent childbirths.

Legal provision

In many countries constitutions have granted women equal rights with men. Some of the provisions in the constitution include:

- Prohibiting of gender based discrimination.
- Granting the right to vote, to run for and hold political offices.

- Removing restrictions which prohibit women from entering into commercial transactions in their own capacity.
- Granting equal right to property, inheritance and succession.
- Recognizing women's rights to maintenance and to have custody of minor children.
- Requiring the consent of women in marriage arrangements.
- Granting the right for women to institute legal action in courts in their own name, including filing for separation of divorce.

Challenges

Achieving gender equality is a difficult task, but one that must be addressed at all levels. The lack of understanding of what gender equality really means is perhaps the greatest hindrance. The simplistic interpretation is that equality means treating people in the same way and thus applying existing policies and practices in the same way. Equal treatment of persons in unequal situations will simply perpetuate inequalities. The challenge is how to identify barriers and change institutional cultures so as to create a level playing field for equal opportunities for women and men. This is different than simply integrating women into existing policies and practices, as it requires an approach based on gender mainstreaming or assessing the implications for both women and men. Gender therefore is not a women's issue but an issue that must be tackled by both men and women together. However, once gender sensitive policies and strategies are in place, there is no assurance that organizational, much less individual behavioural change will be forthcoming. For despite the fact formal legislation, regulations and policies are not discriminatory and therefore seem to provide equal opportunity, there are still other invisible barriers which bar women from fully participating in decision-making and/or make it undesirable to them. Achieving gender equality will involve redefining power relationships, overcoming non-legal barriers to equality, and confronting gender stereotypes. Recent analysis of progress has also identified a number of other issues indicating that actions taken to date remain insufficient.

- Despite the emerging focus on issues of masculinity and gender identities, traditional gender stereotypes and discriminatory attitudes towards women continued to pose a barrier to gender equality.
- The growing political rhetoric in support of gender equality was not matched by policies and programmes to make this a reality.
- The absence of a critical mass of women in decision-making was a major obstacle to moving the agenda forward.

Summary

- There are hard facts to show that gender equality is the basis for reducing poverty in general, and women's poverty in particular.
- Achieving gender equality is a difficult task, but one that must be addressed at all levels. The lack of understanding of what gender equality really means is perhaps the greatest hindrance. The simplistic interpretation is that equality means treating people in the same way and thus applying existing policies and practices in the same way. Equal treatment of persons in unequal situations will simply perpetuate inequalities.

Self-Learning Activity

Try to answer the following questions on your own:

1. What are the key areas of gender inequality?
2. How can we eliminate gender disparities?

8 Women's Participation in Decision-Making and Leadership

Current Levels of Women's Participation

Women's share of decision-making and leadership is small and, in most parts of the world, shows no clear trend toward improvement. Only in the Nordic countries women are approaching equality in the political sphere, and even in those countries the picture in the private sector and such key institutions as universities is often much less satisfactory. For example, almost no women are managing directors in the 100 largest private enterprises in the Nordic countries.

By 1995, only 24 women had ever been elected as heads of State of Government in modern times. In this case the trend appears more encouraging: half had been elected to office since 1990. Between 1987 and 1995, the number of countries where women held no ministerial posts fell from 93 to 59. However, less than 6 per cent of cabinet ministers were women in 1994 and women held more than 15 per cent of ministerial positions in only 16 countries.

Changes in women's participation in government show no clear trend. For example, most countries where women hold top ministerial positions do not have comparable representation at the sub-ministerial, suggesting that women senior ministers are not pioneering a new trend. Women's membership in parliaments has declined in eastern and western Asia and fell sharply in eastern Europe after 1987, although women seem to have increased their share of seats in recent elections. However, measures such as the 33.3 per cent reservation for women introduced by the Government of India at the local level and now being considered for other levels of decision-making can be expected to create a pool of experienced potential women leaders. These women may begin to move into political decision making in increasing numbers of future.

Table 8.1: Women's Participation in National and International Leadership, 1995

Heads of State or Government	• By 1995, only 24 women had been elected as heads of State or Government, half since 1990
Government and Cabinet	• 1994, women were 5.7 per cent of cabinet ministers (3.3 per cent in 1987) • 1994 women held no ministerial position in 59 countries (93 countries in 1987) • 1994 women held more than 15 per cent of ministerial positions in only 16 countries (8 countries in 1987) • Sweden 1994, 52 per cent of ministers were women
Sub-ministerial level	• 1994, women held more than 15 per cent of positions in 23 countries (only 14 countries in 1987)
Parliamentary representation	• Wide variation 1987-1994, proportion of women declined in eastern and western Asia • Strongest in northern Europe (Nordic countries)
Overall	• Women's representation at highest levels of government weakest in Asia • In southern Asia, women hold 5-6 per cent of senior positions, but in other regions of Asia women hold not more than 2 per cent • Women most represented in social, law and justice ministries • 1991 formation of International Association of Women Judges
United Nations	• First Woman Assistant Secretary General 1972 • 1993/94, 12 women at this level • 1985 General Assembly first set goals for women staff • 30 per cent women in the Secretariat achieved 1990 • By end of 1993, only 13 per cent of women in senior management • No women ever elected to the International Court of Justice (89 male judges elected since 1945) • No woman ever appointed executive head of a UN autonomous or specialized agency
Private sector	• 1993, women comprise only 1 per cent of CEOs and 2 per cent of senior managers in the largest US corporations. Outside the US, there was no woman at the top level, 1 per cent in the second level and only 2 per cent at the third.

Source: United Nations, 1995, *The World's Women 1995, Trends and Statistics*. United Nations: New York.

Table 8.2: Women's Participation in Decision-Making 1990 and 1995

Country	HDI Rank	Women in Government 1995			Administrators and Managers 1990 [Per cent female]	Professional and Technical 1990 [Per cent female]
		Ministerial	Sub-ministerial	Total		
1	2	3	4	5	6	7
Japan	3	6.7	8.8	8.3	9	42
Australia	11	13.3	26.7	23.7	43	25
New Zealand	14	7.4	20	16.8	32	48
Thailand	52	3.8	4.5	4.4	22	52
Korea, Rep. of	29	3.4	1.2	1.5	4	45
Singapore	34	0	7.1	5.1	34	16
Fiji	47	8.7	10.7	9.8	10	45
Malaysia	53	7.7	4.7	5.8	12	45
Iran, Islamic Rep. of	66	0	0.5	0.4	4	33
Philippines	95	8.3	26.3	23.9	34	63
Lao PDR	138	0	4.1	2.7	...	...
Vietnam	121	6.5	2.4	3.9	...	...
Myanmar	133	0	0	0	...	...
Pakistan	134	3.7	1	1.6	3	20
India	135	4.2	6.3	6.1	2	21
Bangladesh	143	4.5	3	3.4	5	23

(Contd...)

1	2	3	4	5	6	7
Nepal	151	0	0	0	...	...
Papua New Guinea	126	0	3.1	1.6	12	30
Indonesia	102	3.6	1.4	1.8	7	41
China	108	11.1	21.1	16.2	13	48
Samoa (Western)	88	6.7	7.4	7.1	12	47
Mongolia	113	0	8.7	4.7	...	...
Korea, DP. Rep. of	83	1.2	0.6	0.6	...	...
Sri Lanka	89	12.5	7.9	8.7	17	25
Cambodia	156	0	6.6	5.1	...	...
Developing	...	7.7	8.5	7.6	10	36
Industrial countries	...	12.6	11.3	10.8	27	48

Source: UNDP, 1996, *UNDP Human Development Report, 1996.*

Table 8.2 suggests that women are excluded from decision-making by more than just lack of education. Women's position in the labour force as a significant source of highly skilled and qualified labour as professional and technical workers is not matched by an equivalent contribution as administrative and managerial workers. In the world as a whole, women provide almost 40 per cent of professional and technical workers but less than 15 per cent of administrators and managers. Even in the industrial countries, the proportions are quite unbalanced: almost half of the professional and technical workers but just over one quarter of the administrators and managers. As the experience of the United Nations suggests (Table 8.1), the imbalance becomes more pronounced in the higher levels of decision-making. The UN experience also shows how fragile improvement may be: in 1949 there were more women in the UN, although heavily concentrated at the lowest levels, than a quarter of a century later in 1975.

Why should women share decision-making and leadership?

The Beijing Platform for Action includes a strong statement calling for governments to ensure women's equal access to and full participation in power structures and decision-making. It also called for government to increase women's capacity to participate in decision-making and leadership. Why is it necessary or desirable for women to share in decision-making and leadership? Two kinds of argument may be advanced, a human rights argument and a more pragmatic, efficiency-based argument, although there is considerable overlap between the two.

In democratic countries, rights-based arguments are difficult to deny (although the Beijing Platform merely noted that women's participation in decision-making is needed in order to "strengthen democracy and promote its regular functioning"). It is a basic principle of democracy that adult citizens from all walks of life should have equal access to participation in decision-making and leadership. Ideally, representatives of groups with specific interests and perspectives should participate directly in decision-making processes and leadership to ensure that both the agenda of issues to be considered and the decisions subsequently made incorporate their views. It is untenable that any specific interest group, say a particular ethnic or religious group, could be systematically excluded from direct participation in decision-making on the grounds that others can "speak" for them. Since women and men play different roles in society and therefore have different needs, interests and priorities, it follows that women also cannot be adequately represented in decision-making by men.

The pragmatic, efficiency-based argument for women's participation in decision-making and leadership also starts from recognition that women and men have different needs, interests and priorities arising from their specific roles and situations. Even when men are aware of and seek to represent this difference, they lack information in the same way that mainstream decision-makers are unable to capture the perspectives and needs of minority cultures or the poor. This failure to incorporate women's concerns in decision-making represents a major loss for society as a whole. Women's needs, interests and concerns are not just those of women themselves, but reflect their primary roles as mothers, wives and caregivers. Therefore, incorporating a woman's perspective in decision-making should result in better decisions that more adequately reflect the needs and interests of children and families (including the male members).

Finally, the Beijing Platform recognizes that women's equal participation in decision-making and political life is vital for the advancement of women. Women remain in a position of inequality compared with men partly because their situation, needs and concerns are not even considered in current decision-making: they do not even reach the mainstream agenda. Much of the discussion at the NGO Forum focused on women's need to become involved in "setting the agenda". The advancement of women demands that women participate actively in setting the agenda and determining issues on which decisions are to be made. An Australian woman politician recently pointed out that it was only when women entered the Australian parliament in significant numbers that issues such as child care, violence against women and the valuation of unpaid labour were even considered by policy-makers. As a result of these issues entering the agenda, Australia now promotes family-friendly employment policies, including work-based child care. It also recently undertook a nationally representative survey of violence against women, collects time allocation data and is now using that data to try to incorporate the value of unpaid work in national policy making.

Why women are marginalized in leadership?

Women are marginalized in decision-making and leadership by a variety of processes that begin in infancy. In most societies, women lack experience of decision-making and leadership in the public arena because girls, in contrast to boys, are socialized to play passive roles and given little opportunity to make decisions or develop leadership skills outside the family context. In most traditional societies girls are kept largely within the confines of the household and family where they are protected and taught to accept the decisions that others, parents, teachers, brothers make on their behalf. As a result of this lack of experience in a public context, girls tend to lack self-confidence and skills needed to function effectively in positions of formal leadership. An added handicap for many is their lack of capacity due to discrimination in access to education and training: in most countries, women have higher levels of illiteracy and fewer years of schooling than men.

Even women when succeed in gaining education and enter the decision-making mainstream, they are often marginalized by an institutional setting that reflects men's needs and situation and ignores women's different needs and experience. Modern work patterns and practices are designed for men who have a supportive wife to take care of their essential domestic needs and family responsibilities at home, hence the saying that every career woman needs a good wife! Because it is designed to fit the needs and expectations of men, the modern work environment is not family friendly. The hours and inflexibility of the working day, overtime, the location of work and commuting times make it difficult for working women to meet the dual expectations of their family and work roles, giving rise to role conflict.

Most men do not face such role conflict because society regards their family and personal roles as discretionary, meaning that they are subsidiary to and have to be fitted in with the primary work role. Thus, although men play important roles as husbands and fathers, these generally do not interfere with their primary work role as family breadwinner. For example, if a man's wife or child falls ill or is otherwise in need of his assistance, he is not expected (nor, in most cases, permitted) to leave his work in order to attend to them. Nor will he be considered a "bad" father or husband as a consequence. By contrast, women's primary roles as wife and mother require their attention 24 hours and thus, for working women, must be carried out simultaneously with the work role. Even where a working woman has domestic assistance, she is still held responsible for managing her family. If her child or husband is ill, she is expected (and grudgingly permitted) to interrupt her work in order to ensure that their needs are met. If she fails to do so, society tends to judge her as a "bad" wife or mother.

In addition to role conflict, women often find themselves isolated and marginalized in unfriendly, if not hostile, male-dominated institutional cultures. A colleague recently described the situation of women in her office in the following terms: women must continually prove themselves to be capable, but the men are assumed to be competent even when they are demonstrably not. Women must provide strong arguments to support their views; men are simply believed on the basis of their professional qualifications and personal relationships.

In the workplace, women are often judged by two quite different and conflicting standards, as women and as workers, placing them in a classic no-win situation. For example, good employees at the management level are usually expected to be decisive, articulate, assertive and clear about their goals and objectives. However, in most cultures women *as women* are expected to be submissive, passive and demure. Thus, a woman who displays the characteristics of a good manager may find that her supervisors are not appreciative because they are actually and probably unconsciously judging her as a woman, as well as a worker. Some women also find that there is no "space" for them to perform effectively as decision-makers because men dominate debate, male networks determine promotions and sexist stereotypes (for example, assumptions such as "women cannot work in the field", "will not take transfers away from their families", made without actually consulting the women concerned) bar them from gaining the experience required for senior decision-making positions.

What can be done?

This analysis of the reasons for women's exclusion from decision-making and leadership suggests a number of strategies to work toward equal access for women to decision-making and leadership. The Beijing Platform for Action also identifies several specific issues that need to be addressed, including socialization and negative stereotyping, which have kept decision-making the domain of men. The Platform calls on actors to: create a gender balance in government and administration; integrate women into political parties; recognize that shared work and parental responsibilities promote women's increased participation in public life; promote gender balance within the UN system; work toward equality between women and men in the private sector; establish equal access for women to training; increase women's capacity to participate in decision-making and leadership; and increase women's participation in the electoral process and political activities.

At the personal level, perhaps the first thing that needs to be done is to change the way we rear our children. We must provide our daughters with opportunities to develop their decision-making skills and leadership capacities, and we must train our sons to respect their sisters as equals. In particular, we must ensure that daughters have equal access to the same quantity, quality and type of education as sons. Since this is a long-term objective, we must also take immediate steps to place more women in decision-making and leadership positions and, at the same time, provide them with the necessary catch-up training and experience in order to be effective.

However, as the experience of capable women decision-makers has demonstrated, these measures alone will not be sufficient. We also need to address the institutional context of decision-making and leadership to create more women- and family-friendly institutions and organizational cultures. Some industrial countries have already begun slowly to move in this direction, reducing working hours, introducing flexi time and career structures for part-time workers (most of whom are women) and providing government-subsidized or work-based child care, maternity and parental leave and emergency leave for caregivers. In addition, institutions need to reexamine their organizational culture and work practices. An interesting example of this may be found in a study of organizational culture in the Bangladesh NGO BRAC in the most recent issue of the Oxfam Journal *Gender and Development* (Volume 5, No. 1, February 1997). We also need to ensure that there are women in senior positions able to act as role models and mentors for young women and to establish women's networks that can support women in the same way that conventional male-dominated networks support the career development and promotions of men.

An essential step toward the more equal participation of women in decision-making and leadership is awareness-raising for men. Institutional cultures that are unfriendly to women are not usually the result of deliberate policies but the consequences of their development over time to meet the needs and situations of men, who have for so long dominated the public domain and who have different needs, priorities and concerns from women. Men need to become aware of the ways in which their assumptions, attitudes and behaviour are gendered to reflect their own situation, exclude a woman's perspective and thus obstruct women's equal participation. Women and men together must then negotiate a new institutional setting that provides space for both groups.

What is being done?

As noted, a number of countries have introduced measures designed to promote women's equal access to decision-making and leadership. Some of these, particularly in the industrial countries, are ongoing activities that are part of a long-standing drive toward equality. Others are more recent and seem to be specifically related to commitments made at the Beijing Fourth World Conference on Women or to the equally important awareness-raising processes that preceded it. An exciting example of these is the introduction of a 33.3 per cent quota for women in the local *panchayat* elections in India. This has resulted in a sharp increase in the number of women decision-makers at the local level and provided an important training ground for women to move on to higher levels of decision-making and leadership. The Government of India is now considering introducing a similar quota at higher levels of government.

Over the last two decades, most interventions have been directed toward strengthening women's leadership through women's organizations and national machineries. While this is clearly essential, perhaps the time has come to pay more attention to complementing these measures with programmes to strengthen the capacities of individual women. In the private and public sectors, mentoring and other leadership programmes for women are being introduced in a number of countries. Although most of these activities have been in the industrial countries, some developing countries, particularly the Philippines, are now exploring the potential for such programmes.

One area of decision-making in which developing countries in the Asia-Pacific region have been particularly active is politics and the electoral process. As part of the preparatory activities for the Beijing Conference, most regions of the world held national and regional meetings seeking a more active role for women in political decision-making at all levels. These culminated in Regional Conferences and the First Global Congress on Women in Politics held at the NGO Forum in Huairou. The Second Global Congress on Women in Politics was held in New Delhi in February 1998. The Secretariat was the Center for Asia-Pacific Women in Politics (CAPWIP), a regional network of national and sub-regional bodies, has set up a regional training programme to support women who are already in or who are considering entering politics at any level. A number of countries also held training programmes to prepare women for participation in specific elections. For example, in Thailand a number of training programmes were set up to assist women participate in local elections in 1996. In the Pacific, a sub-regional training course was held in conjunction with the regional WIPPAC Congress in November 1996 and others are planned to prepare women for forthcoming elections in several Pacific countries in the next two years.

The Regional Conference on Women in Decision-Making in Cooperatives, organized in 1997 in the Philippines, outlined six strategies to enable women to have a greater say in decision-making in cooperatives:

- Instituting gender-sensitive cooperative laws, by-laws and policies to increase their membership of cooperatives and participation in decision-making.
- Promotion of transformation leadership to enhance gender equality in cooperative development.
- Building women's capacity for leadership and decision-making in cooperatives.
- Developing, promoting and implementing a gender-disaggregated data collection and utilization system for cooperatives.
- Creating an enabling environment for improving women's participation in leadership and decision-making in cooperatives.
- Establishing a Leadership Development Fund for Women in Cooperatives, to be used for carrying out the actions outlined in the Platform of Action drawn up by the Conference.

Summary

- Women's share of decision-making and leadership is small and, in most parts of the world, shows no clear trend toward improvement.
- By 1995, only 24 women had ever been elected as heads of State of Government in modern times. In this case the trend appears more encouraging: half had been elected to office since 1990. Between 1987 and 1995, the number of countries where women held no ministerial posts fell from 93 to 59. However, less than 6 per cent of cabinet ministers were women in 1994 and women held more than 15 per cent of ministerial positions in only 16 countries. Changes in women's participation in government show no clear trend.
- The pragmatic, efficiency-based argument for women's participation in decision-making and leadership also starts from recognition that women and men have different needs, interests and priorities arising from their specific roles and situations.

Self-Learning Activity

Try to answer the following questions on your own:

1. Why should women share decision-making and leadership?
2. What do you suggest to involve women in decision-making and leadership?

9 Women's Movement and Its Role in Development

This chapter focuses on the women's movement and its role in development. It describes the development activities of women at the international, regional, national, and local levels, outlining why the overall development scenario should include women's activism and organizing skills.

WOMEN'S MOVEMENT

The global formation of the women's movement is unlike the human rights and ecological movements. There are not single large organizations with a global membership base clearly associated with the goals of the movement in the public arena. The women's movement resembles, much more, the constantly growing and shifting cobweb characteristics of new politics in the global age. In many ways, the amorphous character of the movement may reflect an earlier stage in organizing, a more effective utilization of the institutions of the United Nations, or a unique characteristic of the type of organizing that is unique to women's issues. Whether more formal linkages would be useful is an open question.

The women's movement does indeed resemble a constantly growing and shifting cobweb, one made up of thousands of large and small local, national, regional, and international women's groups and organizations, connected and unconnected to each other and involved in traditional and non-traditional activities. What all of these women's groups and organizations have in common is that for the most part they have been left out of the history of development as currently written.

The reasons for this are many. Perhaps the biggest one is that the women themselves, especially women's groups in the South, have recorded very little about their activism and their efforts to organize for their rights within their communities.

International Women's Organizations and Networks

Women historians have made recent efforts to record the history of women's international non-governmental organizations (NGOs), and much of these efforts have focused on the work of affiliated groups in the South.

As part of its centennial celebrations in 1994-95, the World Young Women's Christian Association (YWCA) undertook to record the history of 100 years of women's organizing and activism on women's issues and concerns. I selected this organization as an example because it holds a unique position in the history of the women's movement. Very early in this organization's history, women set up autonomous national YWCA groups in Africa, Asia, Latin America and the Caribbean, and later in the Pacific. Then, with assistance and support from a world office, these groups planned and built permanent headquarters for their programmes. This has given women a kind of bastion or stronghold, which they themselves control, in more than 80 countries. Each national YWCA is engaged in activities — with, for, and by women — in training, health, non-formal education, human rights, public affairs, energy and the environment, and other community and social work.

The YWCA trains women for jobs in the community and positions of leadership in all facets of the organization. This creates a core of women leaders who often go on to become leaders in other parts of community life. Each national YWCA has complete control over management, programmes, and future directions. The world office provides a set of guiding principles and, when requested, support for fund-raising and leadership-training opportunities.

Having a central building and a staff of trained leaders gives the YWCA a head start in influencing the development of a community and providing a place for other forms of activism and organizing. Women are given the opportunity to be managers, trainers, decision-makers, and planners in an atmosphere that is women centred, non-threatening, and safe. And remarkable achievements have come out of this safe atmosphere:

- The beginnings of political movements for more democratic societies.
- The introduction of appropriate technologies for women in rural and semi-urban areas.
- New and innovative training methods for women with little or no educational background.
- Participatory forms of group organizing.
- A host of other activities that have moved women into the forefront of development, both within their countries and around the world.

For example, many women on national delegations to the United Nations gained their leadership training and experience as committee or board members of the YWCA in their respective countries.

Not much work has yet been done to record the history of international women's networks. Networks are a more recent phenomenon. More flexible than an organization and much more reliant on each individual or group to keep the web of contacts alive, a network arises to fill a need and then often disappears when the need is gone. A true network has no headquarters, main offices, or staff. However, variations on this theme are more common, usually with a group taking on the responsibility of keeping the contacts alive, using some full- or part-time staff.

During and since the United Nations International Women's Year (1975) and the subsequent Decade for Women (1976-85), international women's networks emerged to fill a need that women's groups had for better contact with others and for access to information and resources. Best known among these networks are Isis International (Manila and Santiago), Isis Women's International Cross Cultural Exchange, the Women's Features Service (India), and the International Women's Tribune Centre (IWTC). Neither the Isis groups nor IWTC have affiliated members such as belong to the World YWCA and other more established international NGOs (for example, the World Association of Girl Guides and Scouts, the International Federation of Business and Professional Women, and the Associated Country Women of the World [ACWW]). The Women's Features Service came out of the Inter Press Service and functions as a news wire service, providing news stories by and about women for the world's media.

The Isis groups and IWTC have "constituencies" of women's groups in every world region, most of which are not formally affiliated with any other group and have previously functioned in relative isolation. The main channel of communication is a journal or newsletter used to inform member groups of issues and available resources on women-or gender-and-development activities and plans and preparations for upcoming events and conferences, etc.

In the case of IWTC, the mailing list also includes government women's bureaus and ministries, United Nations departments and specialized agencies, donors, and other support groups for women- or gender-and-development activities worldwide. Both IWTC and the two Isis groups undertake training and technical-assistance activities on request, and both collaborate with national and regional groups to develop manuals, guidebooks, bibliographies, and other women- or gender-and-development resource materials. In recent years, their emphasis has been on training women to use computers for desktop publishing, for electronic networking, and for developing resource centres and databases for women involved in development activities.

Regional Women's Organizations and Networks

As in the case of the international women's organizations and networks, very little has been written about the history of their regional counterparts. Perhaps an exception is the Women and Development Unit (WAND) of the University of the West Indies in Barbados. Several booklets and articles have been written about WAND's history, and newspaper features on various aspects of WAND's development and work are disseminated regularly.

WAND grew out of a regional conference held in Jamaica in 1977, where women's groups from across the English-speaking Caribbean gathered to draw up a plan of action for women in their region. One of the needs expressed at this conference was for a central agency to provide resources, technical assistance, and training for the women's groups and projects. This would keep isolated women's groups a little more in touch with the women's movement.

WAND has forged a path that intersects with the development of women's bureaus in the Caribbean, the regionalization of resources, and the burgeoning of women's human rights as a major focus among women activists and groups in the Caribbean. WAND epitomizes the work and dedication of regional women's organizations by providing women- or gender-and-development information from a central resource centre and database, helping to develop project proposals and search for funds for projects, and leading the way in lobbying regional governments for legislation that moves ahead on women's human-rights issues and concerns.

Regional women's networks, especially those concerned with the flow of information within regions, have grown in importance during and since the United Nations Decade for Women. Women's regional media networks can now be found in every world region (Africa, Asia and the Pacific, Europe, Latin America and the Caribbean, the Middle East, and North America). They usually operate within the framework of alternative media, sending their information directly to women's groups. But increasingly these networks are crossing over into the world of mass media and mainstream media channels.

Fempress (a women's alternative media network for Latin America) began in 1981 as a clipping service. Working out of offices at the Institute for Studies of Transnationals in Latin America, two women began collecting clippings about women's activities in Latin American countries and pasting them together in a magazine format for distribution to every country in the region. Having expanded into a regular monthly magazine of original articles and clippings, Fempress is now acknowledged as one of the leading networks, linking women activists across Latin America and putting forward the cause of women's human rights and women's equality of opportunity in every country in the region.

Fempress operates on a simple but extremely effective logic — it has a correspondent in each country, who notes what is happening in that country, clips relevant articles, and writes an article on a major issue concerning women each month. These are published at the Fempress headquarters in Santiago, Chile, in its monthly magazine. Fempress also prepares and distributes radio broadcasts of interviews and talks by various women in each country of the region. Fempress puts out a quarterly compilation of clippings and writings on specific subjects; this quarterly is known as *Mujer Especiàl* (Women's Space).

National Women's Organizations and Networks

The National Councils of Women (NCWs) have been foremost among national women's organizations and networks. NCWs comprise national women's organizations (such as Maendeleo ya Wanawake of Kenya, a network of women's groups in Kenya that are affiliated with ACWW; national YWCAs, which are affiliated with the World YWCA; and national women's groups that have member groups within the country but are not affiliated with any international organization).

NCWs are usually set up to unite the efforts of national women's groups to lobby government or to improve facilities and programmes for women in their country. Over the years, NCWs have had mixed reviews. Combining the efforts of national women's groups that have sometimes had long histories in a country before the inception of an NCW is not easy. But most of the member groups of an NCW come together when there is a common cause, such as the need to develop a national plan of action for women or to promote legislation on issues related to women's human rights.

Maendeleo ya Wanawake is the major national women's organization of Kenya. Maendeleo has member groups in every town and village, an impressive headquarters in Nairobi, and a full-time staff of administrators and trainers. It undertakes projects in a wide variety of areas and has been responsible for village water-pump projects, schemes for craft production and marketing, workshops for leadership training, and a multitude of other rural and urban development activities — with, for, and by the women of Kenya. Increasingly, Maendeleo ya Wanawake has become involved in political and government activities, in addition to its programmes for training and project implementation, and this has provoked much discussion of the roles and responsibilities of women in Kenya. Maendeleo is a member group of the Kenyan NCW.

The Friends of Women (FOW) project was set up in Thailand by women concerned about the rising numbers of young girls and women lured from villages to work as prostitutes in Bangkok. The women of FOW set themselves up in a couple of rooms in the centre of Bangkok and began to make contacts with groups and individuals across the country and region and eventually with groups in other countries around the world. Their efforts and continuing concern for the welfare of young women in Bangkok have now become a national network of people fighting against violations of women's human rights and specifically against luring girls from poor families into a life of sexual slavery.

FOW is not just a lobbying group, however. It provides counseling to young girls and their families, both in the village and in town; workshops for young leaders and helpers; resource materials, including flash cards and posters for group sessions; and a newsletter, which is published in both Thai and English. It is a network, rather than an organization, because it does not require membership, and its activities focus on needs as they arise, rather than on any set programme. Anyone interested can take part in FOW activities.

Local Women's Organizations and Networks

Because women's groups function in so many different ways and the definitions of an organization and a network become blurred, it is better to discuss examples of women's local activities than to discuss specific women's groups.

In Santiago, Chile, during the long years of dictatorship (1972-89), women's groups organized for the right to democratic elections and women's equality in decision-making positions in government. Beginning with a few established women's groups, protest marches were organized each year on 8 March (International Women's Day). Momentum grew each year, with many thousands of women from every walk of life marching through the streets of Santiago or gathering in the sports stadium, demanding democratic rule and equality of opportunity for women. Individual women courageously approached soldiers and police in the streets and shouted "Give us back our country!"

When democratic rule returned in Chile, credit was given in large part to the relentless activism of women's groups, and the new government appointed women to positions of power and authority.

In Ahmedabad, India, women's work in the informal sector received little recognition and, therefore, little was done to make these women's livelihoods more economically sustainable. Within the trade-union movement, Ela Bhatt tried to push forward the cause of these women but had little success. She decided to form a breakaway union for self-employed women, those who work at home or within women's groups — rather than in factories or other businesses — and have a hard time making ends meet. The Self-Employed Women's Association (SEWA) was the result. It now has many thousands of members and maintains a type of revolving bank: all the members donate a small amount each month, and money is available when they need it to purchase equipment or set up a small business. Women around the world often cite, and try to emulate, SEWA's example.

From a small village at the foot of Mount Meru, Kenya, generations of women traveled each day down a large hill to collect water and carry it back up the hill for use in the village. Some days, a woman would make several trips to the river below, carrying heavy pots full of water on her head as she strained up the slippery path to the village. One day, at a meeting of the village women's group, the women decided that enough was enough. They did not want their daughters to suffer as they were, with bent backs and endless pain in their old age. Offering their savings from work in nearby tea plantations, they asked the men to buy water pipes when they went to town — one at a time over a period of years.

An expert from the Food and Agriculture Organization was approached to assist in setting up a simple pump at the foot of a waterfall in the river. Slowly, the women laid the pipes. Up the hill the pipes went, branching off at each woman's hut. Then large plugs were made of corklike materials and inserted into the pipes, and finally the pump was started. Now every woman in that village has her own water supply, which has, not only improved the health and well-being of the village but also ensures that future generations of girls and women will not have to damage their backs and live in pain from carrying heavy pots on their heads up the mountain each day.

In Suva, Fiji, the newly established YWCA decided to open multiracial kindergartens. At that time, all education in the country was segregated by language, with Fijian children attending Fijian-language schools, Indian children attending Hindi-language schools, and children of expatriates (from Australia, New Zealand, and the United Kingdom) attending English-language schools. The facilities and standard of education were vastly different in each type of school, with the English-language schools having the most advanced facilities and teaching. Although much could be said for maintaining the cultures and traditions of each linguistic group, in reality, children in the non-English schools were receiving a poorer education, diminishing their future career prospects.

In keeping with its long-time principle of ensuring equal opportunity, the YWCA began multiracial kindergartens, open to everyone. The effect was dramatic. Educationalists came from all over the country to observe the experiment. There was considerable doubt about the wisdom and propriety of the project. The time came when several Fijian and Indian parents wanted their children to attend the better equipped and better staffed "European" primary school. The YWCA asked the Education Department whether this was possible. A top-level meeting was called. Clearly, this had been a racial and not a linguistic matter before, but now the authorities were faced with making a precedent-setting decision. Amid much consternation, the decision came down that any child could attend the European school if they passed an English-language test. All of the children passed and were accepted. All schools in Fiji are now multiracial. It is the official policy of the country. English, Fijian, and Hindi are Fiji's official languages, and all official documents and materials are printed in each one of these languages.

WOMEN'S ACTIVISM AND ITS ROLE IN DEVELOPMENT

As discussed earlier, anthropologists have often identified the stages of modernization and "progress" as hunter-gatherer or foraging, horticultural, agricultural or agrarian, and so on Feminist anthropologists have argued for giving greater weight to the organization of social and production relations, patterns of social stratification, family structure (monogamous or other), patterns of property ownership, and forms of work and production.

Perhaps "organization of social and production relations," as suggested by feminist anthropologists, would encompass some of the activities outlined here. But the activities and efforts of women worldwide are much more likely to be totally left out of the development matrix. By adding "patterns of women's organizing and activism," we could write a whole new chapter in development theory.

It should be obvious by now that the activism and continuing efforts of women's groups have been responsible for a great deal of what has happened in the history of the world, and more specifically in the area of development and "modernization". Each women's organization and network discussed, whether international, regional, national, or local, illustrates the extent to which women have been actively involved in the major changes taking place in their country and in the world. And yet, it is impossible to conclude this chapter without giving the following examples of how the activism and organizing skills of women have changed the course of history.

Women Activists at the International Level — the early years

Seventeen women were among the delegates at the founding meetings of the United Nations in San Francisco in 1946. Initial discussions revolved around setting up a commission on human rights. The women met and decided that the rights of women were not being given the priority they deserved. So a sub-commission on the Status of Women was agreed on. Still, the women were dissatisfied. At an introductory meeting of the sub-commission, they decided a full commission on the Status of Women was required.

The United Nations Commission on Human Rights (UNCHR) had its first meeting in January 1947. The United Nations Commission on the Status of Women (UNCSW) had its first meeting in February 1947. Insufficiently funded and having no secretariat or centre of its own, the UNCSW nevertheless placed women's rights firmly on the agenda of the United Nations.

Women Activists at the International Level — the 1990s

In the two years before the historic United Nations World Conference on Human Rights in Vienna in 1993, women held worldwide hearings on violations of women's human rights and collected more than 500,000 signatures on a petition demanding that women's human-rights issues (particularly violence against women) be placed on the conference agenda of the UNCHR and not merely discussed by a small group during sessions of the UNCSW. UNCSW was hampered by a lack of resources and the lack of an official protocol to deal with violations of women's human rights. In addition, women requested the appointment of a Special Rapporteur on Violence Against Women and asked for a tribunal on crimes against women.

The final documents to come out of the World Conference on Human Rights are a testament to the organizing and activism of women worldwide. The Vienna declaration put violations of women's human rights on the world's agenda, and the Plan of Action called for a Special Rapporteur on Violence Against Women.

Women Activists at the Regional Level

Deciding that progress on women's rights issues was too slow in Latin America and the Caribbean and mindful of the fact that a large number of countries in the region were military dictatorships with little or no regard for the equal right of women to be decision-makers in their own countries, a small group of activists organized a feminist *Encuentro* (encounter) in Colombia in 1981. About 200 women participated over a 4-day period. Reveling in the freedom of the occasion, the women made plans of action for the region and decided to hold an *Encuentro* every two years in a different Latin American country.

By 1983, word had spread. Feminists from across the region made plans to travel to Lima, Peru. Seven thousand eventually turned up, to the consternation of organizers, who were unprepared to receive this many delegates. But creativity and goodwill prevailed, and the women crafted major plans and decisions to strengthen the feminist movement in the region. Two years later, emergency plans had to be made to cope with the crowds in Sao Paulo, Brazil. Almost 10,000 women participated, with more clamouring to get in from the *favelas* (urban slums) and urban areas of Sao Paulo.

And so the feminist movement in Latin America has continued to grow and develop from those small beginnings in Colombia. Feminist *Encuentrosin* Taxco, Mexico (1987), Mar del Plata, Argentina (1990), and El Salvador (1993) consolidated the feminist cause, with more and more women taking part in the political campaigns, assuming positions of responsibility in local and national councils, and becoming informed about women's human rights and equality under the law.

Perhaps it was no coincidence that in 1995 the region was rid of military dictatorships.

Women Activists at the National Level

In Tanzania, as in most countries worldwide, the issue of violence against women was becoming a national disgrace in the 1980s. A group of women met to discuss and map out plans to face this growing problem.

They decided they needed a multifaceted plan of action. Information had to be placed in front of the country at large to give everyone a clearer picture of the situation and just how it was violating the rights of women and damaging the very fabric of the nation. Men as well as women needed to be educated about the rights of women and to see more clearly that violence was never an answer to a problem within the home, or anywhere else. At the same time, the government had to be lobbied to pass legislation that would give women some protection against the violence they were experiencing. Women also needed safe houses and refuges where they could go, with or without children, to escape beatings.

From this meeting of women in Tanzania, the Tanzania Media Women's Association (TAMWA) was formed, with a special mission to face head-on the question of violence against women. TAMWA now has a regular newsletter, a resource centre, a crisis centre, and a refuge for women. Laws have been passed strengthening the rights of women, and women lawyers have joined the effort to put an end to violence against women.

Women Activists at the Local Level

Stories of women activists in their own small villages, towns, and settlements are numerous, and it seems almost impossible to choose one over another.

The Suva Crisis Centre in Fiji is the result of a group of local women activists who saw the need to set up a place for women to go when they have been violated in some way, whether by beating, rape, or any other form of violation.

Local women activists in Croatia, Bosnia-Herzegovina, and Serbia regularly held peace vigils and marched across front lines to face soldiers and take home sons and fathers involved in the battles. Women in Serbia ran rape-crisis centres for women of Bosnia-Herzogovina and organized protest marches against the leaders of their country who perpetuated war.

Local women activists protest against the custom of burning brides and widows in India and protect women who have been threatened or hurt by domestic violence.

Local women activists in refugee camps in Croatia, Guantanamo Bay, India, Liberia, Somalia, Thailand, and many more parts of the world are the ones who lobby for justice, run the soup kitchens, educate the children, and look after the health of the family.

Summary

- The women's movement does indeed resemble a constantly growing and shifting cobweb, one made up of thousands of large and small local, national, regional, and international women's groups and organizations, connected and unconnected to each other and involved in traditional and non-traditional activities.
- It should be obvious by now that women activism and continuing efforts of women's groups have been responsible for a great deal of what has happened in the history of the world, and more specifically in the area of development and "modernization.

Self-Learning Activity

Try to answer the following questions on your own:

1. Write about National Women's Organizations and Networks.
2. What is women's activism?

10 Gender Objectives and Good Practices

OBJECTIVES	EXAMPLES OF GOOD PRACTICES
Objective 1 To promote equality in rights for women and men through international and national policy reform.	• Development and implementation of equal opportunities policies in employment. • Gender aware approaches in all international and national agreements and regulatory frameworks for enterprise development, banking and trade. • Development of new tools for gender analysis of enterprise interventions and international and national enterprise policy-making, including better statistics on women's entrepreneurship and work.
Objective 2 To secure greater livelihood security, access to productive assets, and economic opportunities for women as well as men.	• Improved access to financial services for women. • Improved access for women to affordable energy, water and sanitation, and transport services. • Reforms to land and inheritance laws. • Improved information flows, particularly for women farmers and entrepreneurs. • Adherence to core labour standards • Development of 'family friendly' employment practices.

OBJECTIVES	EXAMPLES OF GOOD PRACTICES
Objective 3 To further close gender gaps in human development, particularly education and health.	• Micro-finance programmes which give loans for education and health of women and girls. • Enterprise training integrated with basic literacy, numeracy and/or other types of education. • Support for enterprises which provide health and education services for women, for example loans for equipment for midwives, family planning suppliers, women health practitioners and women home tutors.
Objective 4 To promote the more equal participation of women in decision-making and leader-ship roles at all levels.	• Micro-finance programmes which provide an organisational basis for women's political awareness campaigns and develop leader-ship skills. • Enterprise training which gives women entrepreneurs the organizational and advocacy skills to organise to defend their interests and influence economic policy at local, national and international levels. • Enterprise training for both women and men which promotes images of strong women entrepreneurs in non-traditional sectors.
Objective 5 To increase women's personal security and reduce gender-based violence.	• Micro-finance programmes which provide a forum for discussion and support network to enable women to expose and challenge gender-based violence. • Enterprise training for both women and men which raises issues of gender equality in the household and community. • Awareness-raising of women's economic rights among police and judiciary, including the rights and needs of women informal sector workers.
Objective 6 To strengthen institutional mechanisms and national machineries for the advan-cement of women in govern-ments and civil society.	• Micro-finance programmes which support women's mobili-sation as part of civil society. • Enterprise training integrated with civic education.

OBJECTIVES	EXAMPLES OF GOOD PRACTICES
Objective 7 To promote equality for women under the law and non-discrimination access to justice.	• Reform and strengthening of criminal and civil law relating to enterprise in ways which reinforced rather than undermine women's rights. • Micro-finance programmes which facilitate the access of women's groups to legal education. • Enterprise training integrated with legal education on women's rights.
Objective 8 To reduce gender stereo-typing and bring about changes in social attitudes in favour of women.	• Support to media projects and campaigns promoting positive images of women entrepreneurs, women's economic rights, family friendly working practices and other topics relevant to women's economic empowerment. • Support to women's business organisations and labour organi-sations. • Awareness-raising among policy-makers and political leaders about women's economic role.
Objective 9 To help develop gender aware approaches to the manage-ment of the environment and the safeguarding of natural resources.	• Gender aware planning and women's participation in the development of National Strategies for Sustainable Deve-lopment. • Strengthen tenure and common property rights in line with gender equity. • Ensure that local planning and access to natural resources is gender aware. • Improved data and research on gender and environmentally sustainable livelihoods.
Objective 10 To ensure that progress is made in upholding the rights of both girls and boys within the framework of Convention on the Rights of the Child.	• Improved data, research and statistics on child labour, particularly of girls. This should include investigation of the potentially positive impact of women's income levels in freeing their children on child labour and/or potentially negative impacts of both parents working in the absence of adequate childcare facilities. • Support to programmes to eliminate the worst forms of child labour particularly girls and including domestic service, sex tourism and other occupations where girls predominate

Summary

- There are gender objectives and good practices as rights for women, equality, access to assets, closing gender gaps, women in decision-making and leadership, etc.

Self-Learning Activity

Try to answer the following questions on your own:

1. Write about gender based violence and practices.
2. Give an account of gender equality objective and good practice.

11 Women Empowerment

Does women's increasing role as economic producers increase their decision-making power in the household and community? The evidence from the literature is not consistent. Early researchers focused on the poor and often abusive working conditions that working women encountered in *maquilas* and agricultural processing and packing firms. More recently, some scholars have mentioned a positive relationship between women's wage work and their status in the household. It appears that women who work off-farm as wage workers and directly receive their wages have more control over those wages, over how it is allocated, and therefore have more power in household decision making. With the exception of female-headed households, women who work as unremunerated family workers are less likely to increase their status and decision-making power.

Dolan and Sorby suggest that the point that needs exploring is that "gender equality is not simply a matter of equal numbers of men and women in employment but rather the degree to which their work contributes to women's well-being and empowerment".

We will examine the impact of employment on women's empowerment in two areas: the gender division of labour and control over income.

Reproductive Work and Responsibilities

As women increase their time in wage work and cash cropping, their traditional responsibilities within the home are not assumed by men. Studies in Ecuador, Colombia, South Africa, and Kenya cited by Dolan and Sorby demonstrate that women and their daughters continue to put in the overwhelming majority of hours needed for domestic tasks. When women are away at work, their daughters take over the household work. This may mean that daughters are pulled out of school in order to stay at home to take care of younger siblings. The major exception is single women without children: they are able to escape household work while at work since they have no children to care for.

Control Over Income

In Deere's analysis for Latin America, she concludes that the benefits of wage employment for women include economic independence, mobility, and increased ability to make their own decisions. In addition, women working in the non-traditional agricultural export industry earn more than women in other rural occupations, particularly if they work in a processing or packaging plant. Single women have almost complete control over their wages; nonetheless many of them do handover part of their income to their mothers, particularly if they are living at home. For married women, while it increases their decision-making power in the household, in some cases it also contributes to increased conflict and domestic violence in the home.

A study in the Dominican Republic in the fresh fruit industry analyzed time-series data to measure changes in well-being of agricultural household between 1991 and 1996. It was found that while both male and female-headed households in agriculture have lower well-being indicators than households in other economic sectors, women are not worse off than men. More importantly, it appears that employment opportunities in export industries are giving women more control over household financial resources.

Dolan and Sutherland also found that single women working in Kenya's vegetable industry manage and control their income, but that married women either decide jointly with their husband how to allocate their wages or turn over their entire wages to their husbands.

With regard to smallholder women's increasing participation in cash cropping, it has been suggested that these women status is not significantly improved. Katz (1995) found in Guatemala's smallholder export sector that although wives work in almost all agricultural tasks of vegetable cash cropping, the male household head is the manager, makes most of the decisions, markets the harvest, and controls the income from production. In addition, male-controlled income is allocated to male goods, not the household. Women who are able to control production and income are those few women who own land, particularly those in female-headed households. Several other studies in Guatemala concluded that peasant production for the export market increased women's workload, decreased their access to independent income, made them more dependent on men's allocation of household income, and resulted in women's lost bargaining power within the household.

Later studies in the same area of Guatemala cited by Deere found that women have acquired a higher level of decision-making power in the household over land-use and over income allocation. In part, this finding may be a result of a much higher percentage of women owning land in this study, particularly as independent owners. In sub-Saharan Africa where men control the overwhelming majority of land, women's work in high-value cash crops does not seem guarantee their control over the income generated by these crops. Kasente et.al. in Uganda found in the late 1990s that even though women put in as much labour as men, more than 90 per cent of income from vanilla production was controlled by men. And in Kenya, 90 per cent of French bean export contracts to smallholders were issued to male household members who received the payment and controlled family labour allocation, even though most of the production was done on women's usufruct parcels. Women supplied almost three-quarters of the needed labour but were given only 38 per cent of the income. Women's increased contribution to cash income in smallholder households does not seem to alter the gender division of labour. Women's work on cash crops increases their overall work burden since they are still responsible for domestic chores and reproductive work. In some regions, particularly sub-Saharan Africa, women are also responsible for producing the household food on parcels given to them by their husbands. As we already saw in the previous section, women's work on cash crops often competes with the time they need to put into their food crops. This may have effects on family welfare as studies have found that women's food production is reduced.

DIFFERENTIATED ACCESS TO PRODUCTIVE RESOURCES AND MARKETS

Some of the studies cited in the previous section suggest that the potential for women empowerment and improved status, within the context of new economic opportunities offered by wage employment and cash cropping is influenced by their access to productive factors.

Women's Land Rights

Because of the patriarchal nature of most rural societies, women generally do not have the same rights to land as men. Sons, not daughters, inherit the family's land and marital property practices in most of Latin American and sub-Saharan Africa results in wives not inheriting land from their husbands, nor receiving an equal share of marital property in case of divorce. State programmes that allocate land, such as land distribution, land resettlement, and negotiated land reform programmes, have targeted men as beneficiaries. In addition, women's secondary status constrains their ability to access land on the land market (rental or sale), as well as other productive factors, such as credit and labour. In Latin America, even though men own more land than women, the most common way for women to acquire land is through inheritance. Recent legal reforms (in inheritance, marital property, and land titling) have improved women's legal land rights.

As women become more educated and legally informed, they are better able to claim these rights.

There is some evidence that cash cropping by smallholders is resulting in women losing access to land provided to them by their husbands. In Guatemala, as smallholder land is dedicated to vegetable production, women are losing access to garden plots where they traditionally grew food crops for the household and for sale. Dolan also found that in Kenya one-third of women were obliged to use their usufruct plots to grow vegetables for export and that their husbands either controlled income from that production or retracted their wives' rights to the land. Vegetables in Kenya are traditionally grown by women on their usufruct plots and they control income from vegetable production. With the introduction of contract farming, these cultural norms and practices were modified or reinterpreted. Since contracts are made with landowners, women do not obtain contracts in their own name and the export firms pay men for the sale of vegetables. While women provide three quarters of the labour, they receive only one-third of the income. This has resulted in gendered struggles over land, labour, and income.

Whitehead observes that in Africa, cultural norms strongly support women's customary claims to land through their husbands and through other means (such as borrowing). The problem is that women's indirect rights to land prevent them from gaining access to productive resources such as capital and labour. In addition, their claim to land is for the production of food to feed her family, not for producing income for self use through cash cropping. Furthermore, land titling and privatization of land rights has weakened women's claims to land.

Women's claims also become weaker where land is becoming scarce. As we saw in the case in southern Niger, increasing land scarcity resulted in male household heads no longer allocating land for food production to wives and resorting to the Islamic seclusion of women in order to justify their withdrawal, from agricultural production. Since women in southern Niger are no longer receiving land from their husbands, they have been increasingly insisting on inheriting land from their birth families based on Islamic inheritance law. Customary inheritance norms that had only sons inheriting land, had previously trumped Muslim inheritance that permits daughters to inherit a fraction of what sons inherit.

Data Gaps in Coverage on Women's Labour

Women provide a large proportion of the labour that goes into agricultural production, even though official statistics based on census and survey instruments often underestimate women's work and contribution to national wealth. Problems persist in the collection of reliable and comprehensive data on rural women's work in agriculture and other productive sectors because of:

1. Invisibility of women's work
2. Seasonal and part-time nature of women's work.
3. Unremunerated family (mostly women and children) labour.

Deere and Katz, who scoured data sources and studies in Latin America, conclude that the data regarding women's work in agriculture is deficient, inadequate, and conflicting. They found little data on whether rural women who work in agriculture are non-remunerated family members, self-employed farmers, or wage workers. They were unable to determine how much total wage labour and total labour in agriculture (agricultural EAP) has increased. Both traditional export and peasant agriculture in Latin America have declined, but there is no adequate information on the size and distribution of the agricultural labour force across agricultural sectors: smallholder production, traditional exports, and non-traditional exports.

Deere (2005) for Latin America and Whitehead for sub-Saharan Africa mention several sources of under-counting and reporting of women's work. *First of all,* there is the practice for census takers to count only income-producing activities as work.

Secondly, there is also the tendency for women to report themselves as housewives. Whitehead mentions with regard to sub-Saharan Africa that women seem to be reluctant, except in the case of female-headed households, to reveal their decision-making power within the household and in agricultural production. *Thirdly,* with regard to agricultural data, agricultural production is limited to fieldwork, ignoring house gardens, small animal production, and post-harvest storage and processing work. *Fourthly,* national agricultural statistics do not break down the household holdings to collect household members' participation in agricultural production or disaggregate labour and managerial tasks by gender. One consequence is that data on women's own-account farming is deficient. *Finally,* census data on agricultural production is taken from previous week—since much of women's agricultural work tends to be seasonal (both in own-farm and wage agricultural wage work), their work may not be counted. Also, since the man is considered the main producer, other family members are considered part-time family labourers.

Deere compares household surveys in 19 Latin American countries implemented in the 1990s by the Banco Inter-Americano de Desarrollo (BID) and the Instituto Interamericano de Cooperacion para la Agricultura (IICA) with the agricultural censuses. The comparison showed that women are much more active in agricultural production, either as family members or as main producer, than the national censuses have shown. In fact, the under-reporting of women's work in agriculture ranged from 60 per cent to 500 per cent across the 19 countries.

Some surveys, such as the Living Standard Measurement Survey (LSMS), attempt to collect all productive activity of all family members, regardless of the time worked. FAO has also made recommendations since the early 1990s to improve gender-differentiated data, including women's work activities, in agricultural census and household surveys (see, for example, FAO 1993). These efforts are too recent, however, to be able to compare trends over time.

In summary, what is known is that in Latin America as well as in Africa women have been employed in increasing numbers for the production and processing of many non-traditional and high-value agricultural exports such as fruits, flowers, and vegetables. Women make up a significant proportion of field workers and a majority of process plant workers. And there is scattered evidence that women's work as independent producers and unremunerated family workers is also increasing. Yet, since women's participation in traditional cash cropping and in smallholder agriculture is not well known, it is difficult to determine whether women's work across all sectors of agriculture today represents a feminization of agriculture.

MICRO-FINANCE AND EMPOWERMENT OF WOMEN

Concept and Features of Micro-finance

The term micro-finance is of recent origin and is commonly used in addressing issues related to poverty alleviation, financial support to micro entrepreneurs, gender development etc. There is, however, no statutory definition of micro-finance. The task force on supportive policy and Regulatory Framework for Micro-finance has defined micro-finance as "Provision of thrift, credit and other financial services and products of very small amounts to the poor in rural, semi-urban or urban areas for enabling them to raise their income levels and improve living standards". The term "Micro" literally means "small". But the task force has not defined any amount. However, as per Micro Credit Special Cell of the Reserve Bank of India, the borrowal amounts upto the limit of Rs. 25000 could be considered as micro credit products and this amount could be gradually increased up to Rs. 40000 over a period of time which roughly equals to $500 – a standard for South Asia as per international perceptions.

The term micro-finance, sometimes is used interchangeably with the term micro-credit. However while micro-credit refers to purveyance of loans in small quantities, the term micro-finance has a broader meaning covering in its ambit other financial services like saving, insurance etc. as well.

The mantra "Micro-finance" is banking through groups. The essential features of the approach are to provide financial services through the groups of individuals, formed either in joint liability or co-obligation mode. The other dimensions of the micro-finance approach are:

- Savings/Thrift precedes credit
- Credit is linked with savings/thrift
- Absence of subsidies
- Group plays an important role in credit appraisal, monitoring and recovery.

Basically groups can be of two types:

1. *Self-help Groups (SHGs):* The group in this case does financial intermediation on behalf of the formal institution. This is the predominant model followed in India.
2. *Grameen Groups:* In this model, financial assistance is provided to the individual in a group by the formal institution on the strength of group's assurance. In other words, individual loans are provided on the strength of joint liability/co-obligation. This micro-finance model was initiated by Bangladesh Grameen Bank and is being used by some of the Micro-finance Institutions (MFIs) in our country

Promises and Ambiguities

Among financial institutions serving poor households around the world, micro-finance programmes have emerged as important players. These programmes typically make small loans—sometimes as small as $50 to $100, and sometimes as large as several thousand dollars—to households lacking access to formal sector banks. One important achievement of the micro-finance movement has been its relative success in deliberately reaching out to poor women living in diverse socio-economic environments.

Of the nearly 90 thousand village bank members worldwide that have received loans from the Foundation for International Community Assistance (FINCA), 95 per cent are women. The Association for Social Advancement (ASA), one of the most prominent micro-finance institutions in Bangladesh, has provided US $200 million exclusively to women borrowers.

In Malawi, 95 per cent of loans provided by the Malawi Muzdi Fund go to women borrowers. Since 1979, Women's World Banking has made more than 200,000 loans to low-income women around the world. Literally hundreds of similar examples can be found in Asia, Africa, and Latin America. The premises behind such targeting are two-fold: (1) that micro-finance is an effective tool in improving women's status; and (2) that overall household welfare is likely to be higher when micro-finance is provided to women rather than men. Women's status, household welfare, and micro-finance interact in the following ways:

- A woman's status in a household is linked to how well she can enforce command over available resources. Increased ability to tap financial resources independently enhances her control, and, therefore, her influence in household decision-making processes.

- Newly financed micro enterprises open up an important social platform for women to interact with markets and other social institutions outside the household, enabling them to gain useful knowledge and social capital. Many micro-finance programmes organize women into groups, not just to reduce transactions costs in credit delivery, but also to assist women in building and making effective use of these opportunities.
- Women's preferences regarding household business management and household consumption goals differ from men's, particularly in societies with severe gender bias. In such situations, placing additional resources in the hands of women is not a mere equalizer: it also materially affects both the quality of investments financed by the micro-finance programmes and how extra income is spent. IFPRI studies have underlined the importance of women's control of resources in achieving better welfare outcomes in food, nutrition, education, and other health statuses of children and their families.
- Women are thought to make better borrowers than men: timely repayment of loans is more likely to take place when women borrow. An IFPRI study in 1997, for example, shows that Bangladeshi groups with a higher proportion of women had significantly better repayment rates.
- Loans are not simple handouts. If micro-finance programmes are designed to cover all costs, a potential win-win situation emerges. Development goals related to women's empowerment and improved household welfare are self financing and no subsidies are required. Unfortunately, positive empowerment effects cannot be unconditionally guaranteed. In some male-dominated societies, men may use the agency of the woman to gain access to micro-finance funds, diminishing women's role to being mere conduits of cash. Even if women can maintain autonomy in how they access and use micro-finance services, their management of newly financed enterprises and shouldering of all attendant risks may alter inter-household dynamics. Since loans have to be repaid even if the project fails, new activities may increase exposure to financial risks and may impose additional pressures on the already overburdened woman. Finally, in societies following the practice of female seclusion, the new pressures to interact in the marketplace may initially involve a difficult learning period and trigger negative responses. Project failures may lead to serious reprimand and additional negative sanctions against the woman, especially if household resources have to be diverted to repay outstanding debt.

Emerging Evidence

If the arguments presented thus far about the impact of micro-finance on women's empowerment are ambiguous, then does empirical evidence resolve the ambiguities? While the record on outreach has been quite impressive, evidence on impact is not yet conclusive. Part of the problem is methodological.

First, "empowerment" is not readily observable, necessitating the use of proxy indicators. Empowerment is most strongly manifested in the decision-making process; but when outcome variables—such as changes in income and education levels—are used as proxies, not much light is shed on either the decision-making dynamics or the mechanism of impact. *Second,* "empowerment" is a cultural and personal concept; the informant and the researcher may frequently have differing notions of what empowerment means and how it is expressed. *Third,* there is the perennial problem of bias arising out of self-selection in programmes. If micro-finance programmes tend to attract already empowered women, ignoring this fact will overestimate the empowerment effect. Similarly, an underestimate of the empowerment effect will result if programmes attract or seek out relatively more oppressed women.

Despite these shortcomings, what does the empirical evidence on impact show? Much of the completed research on empowerment effects of micro-finance comes from Bangladesh, where the campaign to use micro-finance as a vehicle for women's empowerment has been most aggressively pursued.

However, policymakers must be careful not to generalize findings from Bangladesh to other socio-cultural settings. The most widely cited series of studies on gender-differentiated impacts of micro-finance, and one that takes special care to control for selection bias, was recently completed by the World Bank based on data collected during 1991-92 from 87 villages in Bangladesh. The study found that welfare impacts on the household were significantly better when borrowers were women. For every Bangladeshi taka lent to women, the increase in household consumption was 0.18 taka, compared to 0.11 taka when borrowers were men. Only when women borrowed was there a large and important effect on the nutritional status of both sons and daughters. Assets other than land also increased substantially when women borrowed—but not when men borrowed. Similarly, it was only when women borrowed that education of girls (rather than just boys) increased. Men, on the other hand, tended to take more leisure as a result of borrowing. Other studies have more directly attempted to assess impact on empowerment. One widely cited study that made special efforts to construct measures of empowerment incorporating client perspectives is based on a 1996 survey of 1,300 married Bangladeshi women members of the leading micro-finance institutions, Grameen Bank and the Bangladesh Rural Advancement

Committee (BRAC). The study found that married women participating in these credit programmes scored higher than non-participating women on a number of empowerment indicators such as involvement in major family decision-making, participation in public action, physical mobility, political and legal awareness, and the ability to make small and large purchases. An IFPRI study in Bangladesh similarly indicated significant positive impacts on physical mobility of women and increased social interactions in the community.

However, empirical studies point out that positive gender effects cannot always be taken for granted. Many women, lacking skills and confidence, lean on their husbands to make use of their loans. A 1995 study in Bangladesh indicated that while 94 per cent of Grameen Bank's borrowers are female, only 37 per cent of them are able to exercise control over loan use.

Another survey in Bangladesh in 1998 indicated that only 3 per cent of the 150 women borrowers surveyed used the money on their own. The others gave it to their husbands or other male relatives. In fact, some conclude that women's lack of empowerment is what makes it easier for programme managers to enforce loan conditions, therefore making women preferred borrowers. Micro-finance institutions tend to downplay this plausible but not yet widely accepted conclusion.

WOMEN'S EMPOWERMENT AND MICRO-FINANCE: DIFFERENT PARADIGMS

Concern with women's access to credit and assumptions about contributions to women's empowerment are not new. From the early 1970s women's movements in a number of countries became increasingly interested in the degree to which women were able to access poverty-focused credit programmes and credit cooperatives. In India organizations like Self-Employed Women's Association (SEWA) among others with origins and affiliations in the Indian labour and women's movements identified credit as a major constraint in their work with informal sector women workers.

The problem of women's access to credit was given particular emphasis at the first International Women's Conference in Mexico in 1975 as part of the emerging awareness of the importance of women's productive role both for national economies, and for women's rights. This led to the setting up of the Women's World Banking network and production of manuals for women's credit provision. Other women's organizations worldwide set up credit and savings components both as a way of increasing women's incomes and bringing women together to address wider gender issues. From the mid-1980s there was a mushrooming of donor, government and NGO-sponsored credit programmes in the wake of the 1985 Nairobi women's conference (Mayoux, 1995a).

The 1980s and 1990s also saw development and rapid expansion of large minimalist poverty-targeted micro-finance institutions and networks like Grameen Bank, ACCION and Finca among others. In these organizations and others evidence of significantly higher female repayment rates led to increasing emphasis on targeting women as an efficiency strategy to increase credit recovery. A number of donors also saw female-targeted financially-sustainable micro-finance as a means of marrying internal demands for increased efficiency because of declining budgets with demands of the increasingly vocal gender lobbies.

The trend was further reinforced by the Micro Credit Summit Campaign starting in 1997 which had 'reaching and empowering women' as it's second key goal after poverty reduction (RESULTS 1997). Micro-finance for women has recently been seen as a key strategy in meeting not only Millennium Goal 3 on gender equality, but also poverty Reduction, Health, HIV/AIDS and other goals.

Feminist Empowerment Paradigm

The feminist empowerment paradigm did not originate as a Northern imposition, but is firmly rooted in the development of some of the earliest micro-finance programmes in the South, including SEWA in India. It currently underlies the gender policies of many NGOs and the perspectives of some of the consultants and researchers looking at gender impact of micro-finance programmes (e.g. Chen, 1996; Johnson, 1997).

Here the underlying concerns are gender equality and women's human rights. Women's empowerment is seen as an integral and inseparable part of a wider process of social transformation. The main target group is poor women and women capable of providing alternative female role models for change. Increasing attention has also been paid to men's role in challenging gender inequality.

Micro-finance is promoted as an entry point in the context of a wider strategy for women's economic and socio-political empowerment which focuses on gender awareness and feminist organization. As developed by Chen in her proposals for a sub-sector approach to micro-credit, based partly on SEWA's strategy and promoted by UNIFEM, micro-finance must be:

- Part of a sectoral strategy for change which identifies opportunities, constraints and bottlenecks within industries which if addressed can raise returns and prospects for large numbers of women. Possible strategies include linking women to existing services and infrastructure, developing new technology such as labour-saving, food processing, building information networks, shifting to new markets, policy level changes to overcome legislative barriers and unionization.

Based on participatory principles to build up incremental knowledge of industries and enable women to develop their strategies for change (Chen, 1996). Economic empowerment is however defined in more than individualist terms to include issues such as property rights, changes intra-household relations and transformation of the macro-economic context. Many organisations go further than interventions at the industry level to include gender-specific strategies for social and political empowerment. Some programmes have developed very effective means for integrating gender awareness into programmes and for organizing women and men to challenge and change gender discrimination. Some also have legal rights support for women and engage in gender advocacy. These interventions to increase social and political empowerment are seen as essential prerequisites for economic empowerment.

Poverty Reduction Paradigm

The poverty alleviation paradigm underlies many NGO integrated poverty-targeted community development programmes. Poverty alleviation here is defined in broader terms than market incomes to encompass increasing capacities and choices and decreasing the vulnerability of poor people.

The main focus of programmes as a whole is on developing sustainable livelihoods, community development and social service provision like literacy, health care and infrastructure development. There is not only a concern with reaching the poor, but also the poorest.

Policy debates have focused particularly on the importance of small savings and loan provision for consumption as well as production, group formation and the possible justification for some level of subsidy for programmes working with particular client groups or in particular contexts. Some programmes have developed effective methodologies for poverty targeting and/or operating in remote areas. Such strategies have recently become a focus of interest from some donors and also the Microcredit Summit Campaign.

Here gender lobbies have argued for targeting women because of higher levels of female poverty and women's responsibility for household well-being. However although gender inequality is recognised as an issue, the focus is on assistance to households and there is a tendency to see gender issues as cultural and hence not subject to outside intervention.

Although term 'empowerment' is frequently used in general terms, often synonymous with a multi-dimensional definition of poverty alleviation, the term 'women's empowerment' is often considered best avoided as being too controversial and political. The assumption is that increasing women's access to micro-finance will enable women to make a greater contribution to household income and this, together with other interventions to increase household well-being, will translate into improved well-being for women and enable women to bring about wider changes in gender inequality.

Financial Sustainability Paradigm

The financial self-sustainability paradigm (also referred to as the financial systems approach or sustainability approach) underlies the models of micro-finance promoted since the mid-1990s by most donor agencies and the Best Practice guidelines promoted in publications by USAID, World Bank, UNDP and CGAP.

The ultimate aim is large programmes which are profitable and fully self-supporting in competition with other private sector banking institutions and able to raise funds from international financial markets rather than relying on funds from development agencies. The main target group, despite claims to reach the poorest, is the 'bankable poor': small entrepreneurs and farmers. This emphasis on financial sustainability is seen as necessary to create institutions which reach significant numbers of poor people in the context of declining aid budgets and opposition to welfare and redistribution in macro-economic policy.

Policy discussions have focused particularly on setting of interest rates to cover costs, separation of micro-finance from other interventions to enable separate accounting and programme expansion to increase outreach and economies of scale, reduction of transaction costs and ways of using groups to decrease costs of delivery. Recent guidelines for CGAP funding and best practice focus on production of a 'financial sustainability index' which charts progress of programmes in covering costs from incomes.

Within this paradigm gender lobbies have been able to argue for targeting women on the grounds of high female repayment rates and the need to stimulate women's economic activity as a hitherto underutilized resource for economic growth. They have had some success in ensuring that considerations of female targeting are integrated into conditions of micro-finance delivery and programme evaluation.

Alongside this focus on female targeting, the term 'empowerment' is frequently used in promotional literature. Definitions of empowerment are in individualist terms with the ultimate aim being the expansion of individual choice or capacity for Self-reliance. It is assumed that increasing women's access to micro-finance services will in itself lead to individual economic empowerment through enabling women's decisions about savings and credit use, enabling women to set up micro-enterprise, increasing incomes under their control. It is then assumed that this increased economic empowerment will lead to increased well-being of women and also to social and political empowerment.

These paradigms do not correspond systematically to any one organisational model of micro-finance. Micro-finance providers with the same organisational form, e.g. village bank, Grameen model or cooperative model may have very different gender policies and/or emphases and strategies for poverty alleviation. The three paradigms represent different 'discourses' each with its own relatively consistent internal logic in relating aims to policies, based on different underlying understandings of development. They are not only different, but often seen as 'incompatible discourses' in uneasy tension and with continually contested degrees of dominance. In many programmes and donor agencies there is considerable disagreement, lack of communication and/or personal animosity and promoted by different stakeholders within organisations between staff involved in micro-finance (generally firm followers of financial self-sustainability), staff concerned with human development (generally with more sympathy for the poverty alleviation paradigm and emphasising participation and integrated development) gender lobbies (generally incorporating at least some elements of the feminist empowerment paradigm). What is of concern in current debates is the way in which the use of apparently similar terminology of empowerment, participation and sustainability conceals radical differences in policy priorities. Although women's empowerment may be a stated aim in the rhetoric of official gender policy and programme promotion, in practice it becomes subsumed in and marginalised by concerns of financial sustainability and/or poverty alleviation.

MICRO-FINANCE INSTRUMENT FOR WOMEN'S EMPOWERMENT

Micro-finance is emerging as a powerful instrument for poverty alleviation in the new economy. In India, micro-finance scene is dominated by Self Help Groups (SHGs) — Bank Linkage Programme, aimed at providing a cost-effective mechanism for providing financial services to the "unreached poor". Based on the philosophy of peer pressure and group savings as collateral substitute, the SHG programme has been successful in not only in meeting peculiar needs of the rural poor, but also in strengthening collective self-help capacities of the poor at the local level, leading to their empowerment.

Micro-finance for the poor and women has received extensive recognition as a strategy for poverty reduction and for economic empowerment. Increasingly in the last five years, there is questioning of whether micro-credit is most effective approach to economic empowerment of poorest and, among them, women in particular. Development practitioners in India and developing countries often argue that the exaggerated focus on micro-finance as a solution for the poor has led to neglect by the state and public institutions in addressing employment and livelihood needs of the poor.

Credit for empowerment is about organizing people, particularly around credit and building capacities to manage money. The focus is on getting the poor to mobilize their own funds, building their capacities and empowering them to leverage external credit. Perception of women is that learning to manage money and rotate funds builds women's capacities and confidence to intervene in local governance beyond the limited goals of ensuring access to credit. Further, it combines the goals of financial sustainability with that of creating community owned institutions.

Before 1990's, credit schemes for rural women were almost negligible. The concept of women's credit was born on the insistence by women-oriented studies that highlighted the discrimination and struggle of women in having the access to credit. However, there is a perceptible gap in financing genuine credit needs of the poor, especially women, in the rural sector.

There are certain misconceptions about the poor people that they need loan at subsidized rate of interest on soft terms, they lack education, skill, capacity to save, credit worthiness and therefore are not bankable. Nevertheless, the experience of several SHGs reveal that rural poor are actually efficient managers of credit and finance. Availability of timely and adequate credit is essential for them to undertake any economic activity rather than credit subsidy.

The government measures have attempted to help the poor by implementing different poverty alleviation programmes but with little success. Since most of them are target-based involving lengthy procedures for loan disbursement, high transaction costs, and lack of supervision and monitoring. Since the credit requirements of the rural poor cannot be adopted on project lending approach as it is in the case of organized sector, there emerged the need for an informal credit supply through SHGs. The rural poor with the assistance from NGOs have demonstrated their potential for self help to secure economic and financial strength. Various case studies show that there is a positive correlation between credit availability and women's empowerment.

Summary

- We can examine the impact of employment on women's empowerment in two areas: the gender division of labour and control over income.
- The term micro-finance is of recent origin and is commonly used in addressing issues related to poverty alleviation, financial support to micro entrepreneurs, gender development etc.
- "Empowerment" is not readily observable, necessitating the use of proxy indicators. Empowerment is most strongly manifested in the decision-making process; but when outcome variables— such as changes in income

and education levels—are used as proxies, not much light is shed on either the decision-making dynamics or the mechanism of impact.

- "Empowerment" is a cultural and personal concept; the informant and the researcher may frequently have differing notions of what empowerment means and how it is expressed.
- There is the perennial problem of bias arising out of self-selection in programmes.

Self-Learning Activity

Try to answer the following questions on your own:

1. Define women empowerment.
2. Discuss micro-finance as an instrument for women empowerment.
3. Write short note on: Feminist Empowerment Paradigm?

12 Legal Reform and Women

> As long as women do not have the same rights in law as men, as long as the birth of a girl does not receive the same welcome as that of a boy, so long we should know that India is suffering from partial paralysis. Suppression of women is inconsistent with principles of *ahimsa* (non-violence).
>
> Mahatma Gandhi, *Harijan*, August 18, 1940

The legal system is an important tool for social change and reform. It is capable of establishing an equitable and transparent framework for the functioning of a civilized society and for protecting the rights of vulnerable groups including women. Many constitutions of the world recognize equality before the law and prohibit discrimination on the basis of sex. Statutory laws aim to reform discriminatory customary practices, and an active judiciary can further protect women's social, economic, and political rights. India and Ethiopia provide two examples where the legal framework has sought to protect the interests of women. In both countries, the constitutions prohibit discrimination on the basis of sex, although they uphold the application of customary laws to personal matters. Women have obtained equal access to property and are able to participate freely in economic activities. These laws also give women inheritance rights equal to those of men and in Ethiopia even give women equal rights to matrimonial or common household property. Such a potentially powerful instrument of change still only weakly protects the rights of the most vulnerable groups. Equal protection laws have not yet benefited the majority of women who remain unaware of their rights or unable to seek protection of the law. Working mostly in the unregulated informal labour markets, these poor women experience the law as harassment, not assistance. This brief asks why legal systems in these two countries are unable to protect poor women, identifies reasons why previous legal reforms may not have worked, and highlights some principles that may be useful for undertaking future legal reform.

Laws Protect the Interests of the Powerful

In many countries, laws protect the interests of the state. In India, laws inherited from the British created a system of centralized control and sanctions to protect the state's access to rich forests and communal lands, limiting the rights of those who had for centuries lived near them. The colonial forest laws effectively destroyed communal systems of forest management that gave no one entity or individual proprietary rights over these resources, but expected both men and women to share and protect them through community-approved rules. Modern laws continue to vest ownership in the state and issue licenses for commercial use without enforcing accountability to protect the resources effectively.

The system of landownership imposed by the colonial regime and continued by postcolonial East African rulers provides another example. Prior to the introduction of English land law, women often had customary rights to parcels of land for cultivation. Any produce or revenue generated through their labour belonged to them. However, the colonial regime introduced individual titling to facilitate the free transfer of land.

Following the patriarchal practices of nineteenth century English law that colonial powers imported into East Africa, communal landholdings legally became the property of male household heads while customary rules remained unchanged. Women continued to work the land as part of the family labour, but no longer controlled its products. Legal reform had reduced the legitimacy of women's control over economic resources.

In both Ethiopia and India, women work mostly in the informal labour markets and in agriculture. These women bear great economic risks and shocks, and yet, with few exceptions, have no protection from the state or the legal framework. Where they work for wages, they have no work security, little or no access to social security or assistance, and no access to care services. Their contact with the law is frequently negative. They are harassed by officials for bribes when hawking petty goods without licenses or collecting raw products from protected forests.

Laws are Based on Different Values

Laws are often more difficult and costly to implement when based on values alien to those they are supposed to help. In India, the reform of personal laws for the Hindu majority imposed values different from those based on principles of *dharma* or obligations. New laws adopted an individual-rights approach and assumed a community of nuclear families. In Ethiopia, imposing a rights-based Judeo-Christian value system on people applying different customary rules to govern personal relationships and property meant that the more egalitarian principles of the new Civil Code never took root.

Egalitarian laws and norms work best when both men and women have economic opportunities. When poor, uneducated, and often illiterate women have little chance of attaining economic independence, they cannot take advantage of egalitarian laws to assert their individual rights. Exiting out of inequitable contexts has high social and economic costs. They may instead choose options offering less individual freedom but lower social costs, lessening the impact of egalitarian legislation.

Despite good intentions, legal reforms may have unintended effects on women's property rights. The dowry system in India, for example, shifted from a familial obligation to provide a share of family property to daughters at marriage to a *de facto* right of the bridegroom's family to demand compensation. In response, the Dowry Prohibition Act (1961), while not banning dowries, prohibited gifts given or taken in consideration for marriage. Unfortunately, it also reduced the willingness of families to provide property to their daughters at marriage, while maintaining preferential rights of male members of joint families over inherited properties. In the end, daughters' claims to family property were weakened.

Legal Reform Needs to be Holistic

For effective legal reform, both substantive and procedural issues must be addressed; piecemeal legal reform is ineffective. Emperor Haile Selassie changed the substance of the law when he abolished Ethiopian customary laws with one sweep of his royal pen. The 1960 Civil Code gave women more rights than their contemporaries in the United States or United Kingdom.

However, the civil code maintained the age-old tradition of dispute settlement by personal arbitrators, normally older men within the family or community selected by the disputants. The arbitrators, unfamiliar with or unsympathetic to the new laws, continued to apply old customary laws. The *de jure* system had nothing to do with the *de facto* reality that existed for the next 30 years.

Legal institutions are also important. Women had been familiar with and comfortable in their community-based legal institutions. Judges were community members and personally accountable for ensuring the peace. New legal systems transferred dispute settlement authority to institutions outside the immediate community. Judges were impersonal officers of the court and their concern was not the peace of the community but upholding of laws prescribed by the state. With increasing importance given to inflexible written laws and judicial precedents, the illiterate and the poor became more disempowered. Court and advocate fees and complex procedural rules ensured that the process of seeking justice became expensive and difficult for the poor, let alone for women.

Some Potentially Promising Reforms

Gender-based legal reform that is sensitive to tradition is necessary. Values are not static, but successful legal reform must build on positive traditional values rather than impose different values. New and creative solutions must be found. The Ethiopian constitution found a striking way of addressing the conflict between conservative customary laws and the progressive egalitarian provisions of the Civil Code. First, after prolonged debate, the constitution revoked the abolition of personal laws (customary and religious). It then allowed the disputant to participate in the determination of the laws applicable to the personal dispute. If any party to a dispute does not wish to apply personal laws, she or he may opt for the application of the Civil Code provisions. Anecdotal evidence indicates that this has had unanticipated results. Personal-law arbitrators and courts are rethinking the application of outdated customary law provisions out of fear that women disputants may prefer to transfer the decision to the civil courts, thereby weakening the customary bodies.

Experience in other countries also suggests that strong gender-aware local institutions make a difference. Affirmative action programmes are increasing the participation of women in political and social activities. In India and Uganda, for example, an affirmative action programme requires 33 per cent of seats in the local government councils be reserved for women. In India a percentage of these seats is reserved for lower-caste women, recognizing that women are not a homogeneous group.

Observers report that in both countries women are gradually gaining greater social recognition and increasing their involvement in development decision-making. A seat at the table is helping to catalyze the process of social change at the village levels. Examples from Uganda illustrate that women's increased access to the newer institutions have resulted in speedier and less costly legal decisions. But the process remains constrained by issues of governance, an inadequate number of gender-aware judges, and general lack of training of counselors.

Uganda has therefore initiated a gender-sensitive capacity building programme for both men and women councilors. If one message comes out of these promising reforms, it is the importance of participation of both women and men in legal reform. Legal reform has always been top-down, starting with the assumption that the state knows best. The state should realize that those who are to be governed know best about what works and what does not. Legal reform needs to move away from a focus on norms to a focus on ensuring a transparent process to establish the norms—a process involving the informed participation of both women and men. Although there are attendant risks to such a process-based approach, the present norm-based legal system has failed to protect the majority. It is time to test another method, and the new approaches in Ethiopia and India are examples of the first stumbling steps in the right direction.

Summary

- The legal system is an important tool for social change and reform. It is capable of establishing an equitable and transparent framework for the functioning of a civilized society and for protecting the rights of vulnerable groups including women.
- Laws are often more difficult and costly to implement when based on values alien to those they are supposed to help.
- Gender-based legal reform that is sensitive to tradition is necessary. Values are not static, but successful legal reform must build on positive traditional values rather than impose different values. New and creative solutions must be found.

Self-Learning Activity

Try to answer the following questions on your own:

1. Laws are based on different values. Comment.
2. Discuss the gender-based legal reforms.

Part II — Gender Issues in Cooperatives

13 Gender and Cooperatives

Gender and Cooperatives

Women in many parts of the world have a very low status and are often treated as second-class citizens. Some progress has, however, been made in the last ten years since the UN Decade for Women (1975-85). Nevertheless, the disparities that exist between North and South, rural and urban, rich and poor, still give rise to particular concern. Cooperatives as instruments of growth and development and the shield of the poor have to play a prominent role in improving the economic conditions of women. Cooperatives all over the world are expected to give importance to the problems and issues of women.

Attaining equality of opportunity between men and women is a long process and cooperatives in all parts of the world still have a long way to go before they are able to claim that they are truly gender-responsive. However, the very fact that cooperatives, as opposed to other types of enterprise, have to pay attention to the needs and interests of their members, gives them a special role to play. Members, clients and customers very often perceive cooperatives as having a high regard for business ethics, therein included equality issues, so in order to attract new members and loyal clients and customers, cooperatives should take advantage of this. The Cooperative Commission of the UK states in its Report (2001):

> "Active equal opportunities management can open up new opportunities and improve market share by broadening the customer base, particularly where the customers can identify with the specific policies and practices, e.g. gender, disability, race and age. Conversely, bad practice can lead to a loss of reputation and customers..."

Many cooperative businesses today have clearly formulated policies on equal opportunities but practice may, of course, differ. Very few cooperatives, for example, actually have a percentage of women in decision-making positions that corresponds to the percentage of women in the membership. A key starting point is therefore to ensure that cooperative leaders and management are sensitized to gender issues. It is only with a understanding of the issues and a commitment to systematically address them that proactive measures will be taken by the leaders and managers. Ensuring that gender concerns are mainstreamed in all cooperative policies, legislation, mission statements, visions, by-laws, strategies, plans and programmes is also essential. Gender analysis can be used as a tool to help reveal areas needing change. Examining the rights, resource allocations and decision-making processes within cooperatives can give an indication of the constraints and challenges facing women and provide a key to designing policies and strategies to enable them to take better advantage of the opportunities that exist.

Empowerment has always been fundamental to the cooperative idea where people get together to achieve goals that they would not be able to achieve on their own. The goals are decided by the members themselves and, since cooperatives are organized on the principle of one person - one vote, the cooperative form of enterprise provides women with the opportunity of participating on equal terms with men. Cooperative enterprises can take on different forms: They can be set up by a group of enterprises or by individual entrepreneurs wishing to benefit from shared services, cheaper goods, easier access to markets or higher prices for their products. But what they all have in common is that, as a group, members are able to create economies of scale and increase their influence and bargaining power.

In many developing countries women work individually, often isolated, in the informal economy, operating at a low level of activity and reaping marginal income. Joining forces in small-scale cooperatives can provide them with the economic, social and political leverage they need. A good example of this can be seen in the achievements of SEWA in India. For the member entrepreneurs, cooperatives provide the setting for collective problem-solving and the articulation of strategic and basic needs. The support and mutual encouragement that a group of entrepreneurs can give each other can also be crucial in helping to maintain or boost their self-confidence. Solidarity, social responsibility, equality and caring for others are among the core values on which genuine cooperatives are based. But are women able to fully utilize the potential that the cooperative method of doing business represents? And do the traditional cooperatives recognize and make full use of the potential that women members and employees represent?

Women form half of the population in all societies. They must be given equal rights and responsibilities. Neglect of women by any society will lead to the very neglect of such society. The main objective of all development programmes in countries must be focused on women. The main objective of the development programmes is to raise the socio-economic status of women in order to bring them into the mainstream of national development. The approach was to inculcate confidence in the minds of women and create awareness about their potential for development as also their rights and privileges through agencies like cooperatives.

Considering the aspects regarding the status of women, it is necessary to take a fresh look at the existing gender relations in cooperatives and redefine the role and status of women members in relation to their contribution made to the society and cooperatives in particular. This is to ensure that women get equal opportunities in cooperatives with due weightage to her additional burden of domestic responsibility.

In cooperative sector, women need to be empowered in membership, employment, management, administration and decision making, because women are the prime consumers and the prime producers. The cooperative values of honesty, selfhelp, openness, social responsibility, solidarity and caring for others are the basic women's values. As cooperatives are trying to identify with these values, women are identified with such values to promote cooperative activities.

Women and Cooperatives in Africa

The following discussion will give a picture about the role of women in the Cooperative Movement of certain countries in Africa. Because the concern for women is significant in Africa than in other continents. Success stories as well as failures have been pointed out here. At a conference in 1988 of African Women in Cooperatives, however, it became clear that there was almost universal discrimination against women in African cooperatives. It was reported:

> In most countries, the majority of women were excluded from membership of agricultural production and marketing cooperatives in the state sponsored sector, because of membership regulations, which only recognize one member, the 'household head', per family ... this excludes married women.

Women in cooperatives, where they are admitted, have generally been treated as less than full members and their labor has often been exploited. This is said to be the reality of Harambee, the widespread cooperative movement in Kenya. In some places, such treatment has led to the collapse of the cooperative, since the women simply reduced their work input in response to their poor reward.

For women to form their own cooperatives, nonetheless, requires experience and resources. There are reports of successful women's cooperatives in Mozambique, Botswana and Angola, where women play a major role in agriculture because of the migration of men to the towns or to South Africa and because of government encouragement of women's political involvement.

Successful cooperative projects have also been reported from Cameroon and as elements of integrated projects in Tanzania, Kenya, Senegal and Cameroon (MIDENO), 'which are known to have provided women with resources and input, extension services and training and income'.

Cooperatives of small-scale farmers in Zimbabwe include a growing number of women's cooperatives. They are reported to be producing 50 per cent of the nation's marketed maize, the national staple food.

Most of these example are of rural agricultural cooperatives, but in Tanzania women cooperatives in Dar es Salaam have been established in tailoring and soap making with government assistance, and in Uganda the new government is said to have 'contributed much to the development of women's cooperatives by, e.g. funding their purchases of new inputs, especially machinery and spares'.

Women were still, not being treated as equal in the cooperatives. It is reported that the women took less part than men in decision-making in the clubs not only because of their domestic workloads, but also because of male prejudice. This inequality was very strongly expressed in an earlier inquiry by the Zimbabwe Women's Bureau into the working of Master Farmers Clubs. The women interviewed said that they still had to do most of the work, not only in the home, including the fetching of the water and fuel, but also in the fields and in the transporting produce to the market. Husbands kept the earnings and some would not pay the fee for the women to join the clubs.

The experience in Zimbabwe is of particular importance both because it emphasizes the value of grassroots democracy in rural development and because it shows how women's projects can be integrated into large-scale agricultural development. In other countries, where women's projects have been components of larger integrated development schemes, money failures have been recorded. The chief reasons for failure, according to Joyce Endely of the University Center of Dschang, Cameroon, appear to be the following:

(*a*) Refusal to identify women as equal participants with legal rights.

(*b*) Stereotyping of women's work, e.g. vegetable gardening, child care, sewing and Backing, with no access to machinery.

(*c*) Lack of women advisors, extension workers and manager.

(*d*) No consideration in project design of the whole life of a woman as mother, housekeeper as well as worker outside the household.

(*e*) Neglect of the potential of women for training in new skills.

(*f*) Dependence of projects on outside government or NGO management and intiative.

As a result of all the limitations on women's contribution to rural cooperatives, many projects focusing especially on women, far from narrowing the existing gender gap in rural life, have served only to widen the gap still further. This often appears to be the deliberate intention of government aid for women's cooperatives. One example comes from Sudan, where the Productive Family Programme encourages women to engage in a handicrafts and backyard gardens, explicitly 'to keep them working within the home sphere'.

The major handicap for African women farmers developing their full potential remains their neglect by government agencies in the provision of extension education and technological support. Women farmers have been shown in several country surveys to be most desirous of extension contact and to have established contact as much as men. Improvement in results does not always follow. The reasons are several. The educational level of women is generally lower than that of men. If improvements involve the use of animals or machinery, that is men's work and not women's. Most agricultural research is done by men and many of the technical recommendations concerning crops that are regarded as men's responsibility – maize and other cash crops – and not the vegetables and food crops like cassava, sweet potatoes, millet and sorghum, which are in the care of the women. Most extension agents also are men and, although in the inquiries made both in Nigeria and Kenya women said that they preferred male agents, this could be because the male agents talked mainly about farming and the women agents about home economics.

A new perspective for women's organizations in Africa has been opened up by the egalitarian ethos of the liberation movement both in Ethiopia and Eritrea, particularly in the later. Even under the Mengistu regime in Ethiopia, there was some rhetorical encouragement of cooperatives, but women formed only about 7 per cent of the membership of the producer and service cooperatives in the 1980s. Yet groups of mainly Christian immigrants in Addis Ababa with much larger women's representation were able to take advantage of government encouragement to make a success of food-growing cooperatives as a 'coping strategy' in the city itself.

Summary

- Cooperatives as instruments of growth and development and the shield of the poor have to play a prominent role in improving the economic conditions of women. Cooperatives all over the world are expected to give importance to the problems and issues of women.

- Women were still, not being treated as equal in the cooperatives. It is reported that the women took less part than men in decision-making in the clubs not only because of their domestic workloads, but because of male prejudice.
- Women cooperatives are emerging in all fields to encourage women involvement in cooperatives.

Self-Learning Activity

Try to answer the following questions on your own:

1. Describe gender and cooperatives.
2. Give an account of gender involvement in cooperatives.

Gender Issues in Cooperatives

What is Gender Issue?

Gender issue is problem and concern brought up in the distinction and roles of women and men. When we put line to divide males and females based on activities they do, resource they have and so on, problems happen, which can be best explained as problem of inequality and gender issue is nothing but this problem that concern every body as member of society. Women are always part and parcel of male as *Plato* describe them, they are our Mother, Wife or Sister. Institutional factors reinforce this problem of inequality since gender issue is related to political, economic and social issues. Gender issue can be developmental issue; but *why is Gender a development issue*? As we all know human potential is a huge resource that is underused everywhere, partly for reasons linked to gender, so considering gender issue is integrating this half part of the society in to development activity. Gender Issue is also Justice and human right issue, the Ethiopian constitutions say, "All persons are equal before the law" which is to mean everybody should be treated equally without any discrimination on grounds of race, colour, sex, gender, language, political opinion, national origin, wealth etc. If half of the Ethiopian population receives fewer resources than the other half, it shows that there is a problem and it is violation of human right.

What are gender issues in cooperatives?

Below are some specific gender issues of concern to cooperatives, and questions that cooperative leaders can ask themselves:

- Low level of participation in cooperative development and particularly that of women. Are efforts being made to increase the membership?
- Quality of women's participation in cooperatives. Are women involved in decision-making processes?

- Constraints to participation in cooperatives such as social, cultural, economic and political restrictions on women, their heavy workload, level of education, or the selection criteria for members etc. If any of these constraints exist, what is being done to address the situation?
- Access to and control over resources such as credit, education, training, production inputs and marketing outlets. Do men and women have equal access and control over resources?
- Cooperative training and education programmes. Do these programmes address women's needs? Are efforts being made to involve women, e.g. are meetings conveniently timed and are childcare facilities available?
- Financial and social benefits. Is it advantageous for women to form cooperatives? Do cooperatives support income- generating activities for women?
- Possible existence of gender bias. Do gender-blind policies, practices and services exist within the cooperative?
- Lack of strong cooperative support and commitment to gender issues. How are they addressed? Are gender sensitization programmes carried out?

Need for Gender Issues in Cooperatives

Gender issues in cooperatives are important as cooperatives are user organisations and women are the main users of the services of cooperatives. In spite of this, women's participation in cooperatives is low because men are involved in cash crops while women concentrate on food crops in societies like Ethiopia. Thus women are marginalised in economic sector and have not become active members of cooperatives. Gender integration is a strategy in cooperatives for the development of women.

Gender is an issue in the society, it is an issue in Cooperative societies as well due to a number of factors among which the following are the major ones:

- *There is inequality between women and men in society:* In all societies including the advanced societies, we can find inequality among men and women. Such inequality is wider in developing countries like Ethiopia due to various socio-economic factors like lack of education, lack of employment opportunities, lack of recognition for female children etc.
- *There is gender oppression in every aspect of life:* In traditional societies deliberate subordination of women and their rights is common in any society. It is more so in developing societies. The causes for such operation are treating women as inferior to man, a thinking that women are not intelligent enough to manage problems and bias towards women.

- *Gender relation is not based on equality:* The power relation is that of male dominance and women's subordination, best for the patriarchal system of the society. The bias towards women by men dominated society treats women as unequal and is not giving the basic rights of human beings, equally for men and women.
- *Differences between women's and men's need, responsibilities and constraints are not realized, among development planners and workers:* Women form half of the human population and they have all rights to share the benefits equally with men. But in the planning schemes and developmental activities proper place in employment, income generation, education etc is not given to women.
- *There is gender bias in formulating policies, in planning, implementing programs, and making decisions in society due to biased traditional beliefs:* In economic and social development process gender bias used to occur due to the bias towards women. In many societies the planning policies are prepared by men administrators and the implementation process is also left mainly to the men folk. This natural process makes the planning and implementation activities partial towards men. In traditional societies such differences are wider that developed societies.
- *Indifference in Cooperatives:* Like the imbalance in economic development process, in the case of cooperatives also the gender issues dominate. Women are neglected in the cooperatives in the areas of admission, sharing benefits, representation in the management bodies and decision making. In many cases women themselves are not coming forward to exploit the benefits of cooperatives due to their inferior complex, work burden in the family and self imposed laziness.

Gender issues as such in cooperatives

Below are some specific gender issues of concern to cooperatives:

- *Low level of participation in cooperative development and particularly that of women:* This is one of the major gender issues in cooperatives. The poor participation of women in the business activities and management of the cooperatives is a great concern to the cooperative movement of developing countries including that of Ethiopia.
- *Quality of women's participation in cooperatives:* Quality denotes the deepness of participation by women in the affairs of the cooperatives. They must save money with their cooperatives, while attending meetings they must ask questions about the working of the cooperatives and they must watch the working of the cooperative keenly by not allowing any corruption or mismanagement.

- ***Constraints to participation in cooperatives:*** Constraints such as social, cultural, economic and political restrictions on women may prevent them in joining the cooperative and enjoy the benefits of cooperatives. Their heavy workload in the house may prevent them in the participation of the cooperatives. The low level of education may inhibit them to take interest in the cooperatives. Some times the selection criteria fixed may prevent them to become members. In several countries, including in Ethiopia land ownership vests with men, which prevents women without land to become members of cooperatives.
- ***Access to and control over resources such as credit, education, training, production inputs and marketing outlets:*** Denial of access to such services is also a concern to women and becomes a major gender issue in cooperatives.
- ***Cooperative training and education programmes:*** Do these programmes address women's needs? Are efforts being made to involve women, e.g. are meetings conveniently timed and are childcare facilities available?
- ***Financial and social benefits:*** Is it advantageous for women to form cooperatives? Do cooperatives support income-generating activities for women? Such are the questions to be answered in the context of gender issues in cooperatives.
- ***Possible existence of gender bias:*** Do gender-blind policies, practices and services exist within the cooperative? Discussion on such areas are found in detail in later parts of this module.
- ***Lack of strong cooperative support and commitment to gender issues:*** The way in which such supportive measures are addressed and their commitment to gender issues also hold good in the context of gender issues in cooperatives. Gender sensitization programmes must be carried out to give importance to gender issues in cooperatives.

Summary

- Gender issues in cooperatives are important as cooperatives are user organisations and women are the main users of the services of cooperatives. In spite of this, women's participation in cooperatives is low because men are involved in cash crops while women concentrate on food crops in societies.
- The poor participation of women in the business activities of the cooperatives and in the management of the cooperatives is a great concern to the cooperative movement of developing countries.
- There are gender issues such as financial, cultural, participation, access to land, credit, legal constraints, etc.

Self-Learning Activity

Try to answer the following questions on your own:

1. Why gender issues in cooperatives?
2. Discuss about quality of women participation in cooperatives.

15 Place of Women in Cooperatives and the Role of Women in the Development of Cooperatives

One of the agencies suitable for the empowerment of women in cooperatives. The 4th World Conference on Women held in September 1995 at Beijing stressed on the economic empowerment of women. The economic empowerment of women aims at bringing the women in the mainstream. In cooperative sector, women need to be empowered in membership, employment, management, administration and decision making because they are prime consumers and prime producers. The cooperative values of self-help, honesty, mutual help, openness, social responsibility and caring for others are the basic women's values. The Beijing Conference was determined to ensure the full enjoyment by the women and the females of all human rights and fundamental freedom and take effective action against violence of rights and freedom.

Involvement of women in cooperative movement as members and as active participants is both a means and an end to their development in totality. This grants women opportunities of decision-making, planning and accessibility to cooperative services. On the other hand, women get a self-managed institutional forum for expressing their views and measures on important legislative and administrative policies concerning women. With the principle of open membership and democratic management, cooperation is the most appropriate form for the overall development of women, especially the women belonging to socially handicapped and economically weaker segments of the country's population.

PLACE OF WOMEN IN COOPERATIVES

The place of women in cooperatives can be discussed in four ways viz.,

1. As a member of a cooperative society;
2. As a leader of a cooperative society;

3. As an employee of a cooperative society;
4. As a user of a cooperative society.

The purpose behind these four roles of women may be different but specific importance is given during these days to strengthen their position in the cooperatives. Because, too often women are considered to be the users of cooperative services or passive observers of programmes, which may radically change their living conditions.

As a Member of Cooperative Society

As a member of a cooperative society, women have every right to enjoy the rights and benefits of a cooperative society. As a member of a cooperative society, they can participate in the democratic functioning and they can become office-bearers of such cooperative societies. At the same time, a women member must be aware of the following:

(*a*) *Member should be loyal and committed to the society's objectives:* After becoming the member of cooperatives, the women members should express their loyalty by means of participating in the business, attending the meetings, closely watching the activities and pointing out the mistakes of their cooperatives to the committee members and the manager of the Cooperatives

(*b*) *Member should exercise overall supervision through the general assembly over the adminis-tration of the society:* The women members of the cooperative must attend the general assembly meetings regularly without fail. They must raise questions relating to the activities of the cooperative and must compel the board to take actions on the wrong doings and mismanagement. They must also take the responsibility to elect the competent, honest, and efficient committee members.

(*c*) *Member should have the responsibility to feed the necessary capital to the society:* To run a cooperative efficiently, a cooperative must have strong financial basis. The capital structure of a cooperative is formed by owned and borrowed funds. Owned funds consist of share capital and reserve funds. Borrowed funds consist of deposits and loans. Women can contribute their capital towards share capital and deposits. They can play a greater role in contributing more deposits to their cooperatives. By nature women have mentality to save and they are good financial administrators. They must convert these abilities towards their cooperatives.

(*d*) *Member should patronize the society as much as possible by doing business with the society:* Cooperatives like consumer cooperatives, cooperative banks and handicraft cooperatives are patronized mainly by women. The success of such cooperatives depends on the active business participation of women members. Only through their effort the volume of business can increase and the profitability of the cooperatives will increase.

(e) *Member should keep herself regularly informed about the activities, problems, and prospects of her society:* The women members must compel the cooperative to provide them all the informations needed for their cooperatives. Any problems faced by the society must be seized by women members and they must clarify such problems in the forums like general assembly, management committee and sub-committees. The audit report must be prepared every year and the mistakes pointed out in the audit report must be rectified with the effort of the women members.

Woman As a Leader of a Cooperative Society

Innovation and entrepreneurship are the two guiding principles of leadership. In cooperatives, limited opportunities are given to women to develop as a leader. But with hard work and motivation from other women members, they can become leaders of various cooperatives and they can represent their cooperative society in various forums and at the higher-level cooperative structure. The leadership role of women in cooperatives can be performed as follows:

(a) Whenever elections come, eligible women members must stand for election and get elected.

(b) During the times of election unity among women must be created to elect the efficient committee members.

(c) When they become committee members, they must be active in attending the committee meetings and by means of participating regularly in the meetings.

(d) Wherever committee meetings are held, they must raise questions, clarify issues, and suggest solutions for the efficient working of the cooperative.

As Employees of a Cooperatives

Women can become employees of various types of cooperatives at par with men. Exclusive women cooperatives can also be established in the fields of cooperative banking, cooperative dairying and consumer cooperatives to expand their employment opportunities. Women as employees of a cooperative society can enlist customer attraction and loyalty from the users.

Enormous scope awaits for women to organize cooperatives in new fields like handicrafts, finance, etc., to promote their employment opportunities. The following activities are needed to promote more employment opportunities for women in cooperatives.

(*a*) In cooperatives, a percentage of jobs must be reserved for women.

(*b*) Cooperative promoters must encourage the formation of women cooperatives.

(*c*) Special types of training must be arranged for women employees in cooperatives to improve their working efficiency.

(*d*) Financial institutions must come forward to lend money liberally to the cooperatives organized by women.

As users of a Cooperative Society

The success of many cooperatives like thrift and credit societies, dairy cooperatives, consumer cooperatives and handicrafts cooperatives depends on the patronage provided by women. The success of consumer cooperatives in Japan and Sweden highlight the role of women as users of cooperatives.

The following measures are suggested to increase women's participation in the business of cooperatives:

(*a*) Women must purchase their household needs only through the cooperatives and they must encourage their friends and neighbors to purchase through cooperatives.

(*b*) They must watch the price of commodities in the open market and inform about them to their cooperatives.

(*c*) In cooperatives like consumer cooperatives, they must guide the management in purchasing quality goods and must insist for bulk purchase.

(*d*) Any mismanagement in their cooperatives must be pointed out by women members and such problems must be solved immediately.

(*e*) To keep the image of the cooperative high among the public the women members must be helpful to the cooperatives. Then only more members and non-members will patronize the cooperative.

(*f*) To improve the efficiency of the cooperative, they must work for the transparency and honesty of the management.

RURAL WOMEN IN AGRICULTURAL COOPERATIVES

Women are represented in various forms and in various types of cooperatives in the Region. In most of the South-Asian countries women membership in mixed membership cooperatives is generally lower as compared with those from other countries in the Region. In societies where culture restricts women's membership in cooperatives, women-only cooperatives proliferate. It is in women-only cooperatives that women feel freer and less restricted in their participation in cooperatives. In countries like India, Nepal, Bangladesh, Sri Lanka and Pakistan, women comprise just 7.5 per cent as compared to men 92.5 per cent of the total membership. In Malaysia it is around 30.6 per cent. In many of the Asian countries women's membership is low (ranging from 2 to 10.5%) in agricultural cooperatives. This reflects the age-old stereotype that men are the farmers and not the women, and the title of the farm property should be in the name of the man. This situation automatically prohibits women to be the members. Out of a total of 450,000 cooperatives with a total membership of 204.5 million in India, there were 8,171 women-only cooperatives with a total membership of 693,000. It is also known that the women-only cooperatives, e.g., cooperative banks, consumer stores, fruits and vegetable vendors, have done exceedingly well and provided a whole range of services to their members. In India, with a view to involve women in the process of decision-making in local self-government bodies including cooperatives, a 33 per cent representation has been instituted and in a number of states all boards of directors have women serving on them. There has also been a discussion to have a similar representation in state and national legislatures as well.

The highest number of women in cooperatives in the Region comes from the credit and consumer sectors. In Japan the membership of women in agricultural cooperatives and in decision-making organs is low. No discriminatory provisions preventing women's participation in agricultural cooperatives are contained in the agricultural cooperative law nor in the bylaws of the agricultural cooperatives. In the majority of the bylaws, membership is based either on land-ownership or work on the farm for more than 90 days a year. Despite this, women membership has not increased mainly due to the fact that most cooperatives have a membership policy that allows only one member per household, based on the idea that a household is the minimum unit for production. In addition, it is customary that women follow their husbands in the village life and decision-making. Women themselves do not want to cause troubles by challenging such a tradition. Therefore, men became the majority of directors and delegates and women quietly accepted the situation. However, the concept of plural membership from households is being encouraged. There are still some prevailing laws which place barriers for women's participation in agricultural cooperatives and/or farmers' associations, like landownership and head of the household. In many societies the very women who need to organise to cooperate and prosper, lack the time for participation due to multiple work demands.

Cooperatives being people-centered movement had recognised these limitations placed on women by the society and economic institutions. Experiments made in different parts of the world clearly indicate that women's participation in cooperatives and other local government bodies not only provides them an opportunity to articulate their problems but it also helps them to be an active partner in decision-making process.

Relationship between Women and Cooperatives

The relationship between women and their cooperatives in the context of gender integration can be summarised as under:

- A cooperative being a social development agency should play an active role in advocating for gender equality.
- Since women have been active in development work, they should play central role in development.
- The cooperative can be a venue to improve women's social status and economic conditions,
- Thus, cooperatives should promote women's empowerment by integrating gender concerns and formulating a strategy that would address gender issues.

In terms of the ratio of membership of women in agricultural cooperatives, the percentage is rather low, but they have a strong influence on them through the heads of the household. Certain obvious barriers restrict their direct and formal entry in agricultural cooperatives. Agricultural cooperatives, in present times, everywhere have come under dark clouds due to heavy competitions and pressures of open market economy systems. They are now expected to meet the challenges which they had never anticipated before. Their business methods remain traditional and they expect government support in the form of protection and subsidies. These are no longer available and will not be available in the near future. In several countries, agricultural cooperatives have either folded up or are under massive reorganisation.

Challenges faced by Agricultural Cooperatives

The challenges faced by agricultural cooperatives can be enumerated as under:

- Need to improve professional management skills of those who provide advisory or guidance services to cooperatives and of the managers and some key members of primary level cooperatives.
- Establishment of a marketing intelligence system within the Cooperative Movement to enable the farmer-producers follow market trends and plan their production and marketing strategies.

- Assured supply of farm inputs (quality seeds, chemical fertiliser, farm chemicals, credit and extension services).
- Establishment of business federations through cooperative clusters to undertake primary agro-processing marketing of local products and to cover financial requirements.
- Be aware of quality controls and standardisation of farm products to be able to compete effectively in the open market.
- Participate in efforts to conserve natural resources which directly and indirectly, influence farm production and rural employment.
- Need for providing information to the farmers and farmers' organisations on the implications of restructuring, globalisation and WTO agreements.

Constraints faced by Rural Farm Women

Based on the experiences of farm extension workers, field advisors and rural farm women in the Asia-Pacific Region, the following are the general constraints faced by them:

- High illiteracy rates and poor living conditions among rural women.
- Lack of leadership and inadequate participation in the organisational and economic affairs of their agricultural cooperatives.
- Absence of property inheritance rights, restriction on acquiring membership of agricultural cooperatives consequently being deprived of farm credit etc.
- Inadequate health care services in rural areas.
- Inadequate water supply for household and farm operations.
- Lack of appropriate agricultural technology aimed at reducing the physical burden of farm women.
- Inadequate access to credit and agricultural inputs and other services.
- Lack of female farm extension workers.
- Lack of marketing facilities and opportunities.
- Traditional, religious, social and cultural obstacles.
- Less participation in decision-making – even within the household.
- Male migration/urban drift which increases pressure on women.
- Lack of opportunities to improve socio-economic status of farm women.
- Lack of skills and attitudes in leadership and management development.
- Lack of secretariat supporting functions for women's organisations and allocation of funds for them in cooperative organisations.

ROLE OF WOMEN IN THE DEVELOPMENT OF COOPERATIVES

The role of women in the development of cooperatives can be discussed as under:

Membership drive

The women can look for the growth of membership of fellow women who have not so far become members of various cooperatives. They alone can explain the advantages of cooperatives to other women. They can relieve the families from the exploitation of moneylenders, traders and middlemen.

Bodies like ICA insist that, in the long run, a cooperative must enroll all the individuals including women within its area of operation as members. Member mobilization is necessary for the following purposes:

1. To show gender equality, all eligible women must be made as members.
2. To increase the capital base of a cooperative, member mobilization is necessary.
3. To increase the volume of transactions new members must be enrolled every year.
4. To run the cooperative on profitable basis, there is a need for growth of membership and increased volume of business.
5. To improve the bargaining power of the farmers, works, etc they must be brought under the fold of cooperatives.
6. To make a primary cooperative to undertake multipurpose functions, sound membership is necessary.

Savings and deposits

Women can work for augmenting the financial resources of cooperatives in the form of share capital and deposits. Cooperatives give attractive interest to the deposits of members and public. Cooperatives can become good avenues for the savings of women. Such savings will be useful for the family for education, marriage and ceremonial purposes.

Micro-credit

Through cooperatives, women can get micro-credit of small amounts to promote small trade and business. History has shown the sufferings of women at the hands of moneylenders. Micro credit can abolish moneylenders.

Productive use of credit

Women can help the cooperatives by way of directing other members to use the credit given by the cooperatives for productive purposes.

Productive utilization of credit alone can ensure the repayment of loan in time to the cooperatives. Today's credit cooperatives in developing countries are facing the problem of non-repayment of loans by the borrowers. Women can influence the men folk to repay the loans in time to the cooperatives.

Leadership

Ethiopian women can take the leadership in their cooperatives by means of taking leadership positions like directors. They can inculcate ethics and non-corrupt practices to their men folk. In India, large number of dairy cooperatives are run by women.

Employment generation

Through cooperatives, Ethiopian women can promote employment opportunities for themselves. Exclusive women cooperatives can provide employment opportunities to educated women. Self-employment can also be created for women by the cooperatives by providing loans to do small business.

Price control measures

Women can help to control the price of consumer goods by means of promoting consumer cooperatives and cooperative super-markets. Consumer cooperatives in several countries have brought down the market price.

IMPROVING THE MEMBER BUSINESS PARTICIPATION

Women members of cooperatives must extend their role in improving the business of their cooperatives. To improve the member business participation, the women members must insist the following steps:

1. *Giving high price for produces:* Cooperatives must provide higher prices for their produce, than the market price. As cooperatives keep low operating costs, they can provide higher prices to the members.
2. *Charge low price for inputs:* Through bulk purchases, cooperatives can charge lower prices for agricultural inputs like seeds, fertilizer and pesticides. In practice, cooperative unions in many parts of Ethiopia are supplying inputs for lower price.
3. *Providing better infrastructural facilities:* By producing better services like transport, storage, processing etc. cooperatives can bring more business from members.
4. *Value addition:* By providing value addition to the produces of the farmers, business volume can be increased. To have value addition, cooperatives must undertake processing activities like sugar production, powdering coffee, engaging wheat flour manufacturing, etc.

5. ***Exclusive women cooperatives:*** In many countries exclusive women's cooperatives are organized and run successfully.

Summary

- Involvement of women in cooperative movement as members and as active participants is both a means and an end to their development in totality. This grants women opportunities of decision-making, planning and accessibility to cooperative services.
- The place of women in cooperatives can be as members, as leaders, as employees and as users.

Self-Learning Activity

Try to answer the following questions on your own:

1. Women as leaders of cooperatives — comment.
2. How to improve women role in business participation of cooperatives?

16 Gender Integration in Cooperatives

Why gender imbalance in cooperatives?

The gender imbalance in cooperatives takes place due to the following factors:

- *General imbalance in the particular society:* If gender imbalance exists in a particular society, it may reflect in the cooperatives also. Such gender imbalance in societies exist due to low level of women education, culture with hierarchy, tradition and disrespect to women. In cooperatives it is reflected in the form of non-admission of women, denying opportunity for women members to contest elections and denying due share in the services and benefits of the cooperative.

- *Imbalance in the men's and women's income:* This is a general factor which affects the imbalance in cooperatives also. Men and women doing the same job are not given the same salary. In spite of so many legislative and legal measures this imbalance persists in all societies, including advanced societies. This is due to wrong impressions people have on female labour productivity and the hard working nature of female workers.

- *Refusal to give active participation:* Even when women are admitted as members of various cooperatives they are not allowed to take active participation in the affairs of cooperatives. In very many cooperatives in the remote areas in Ethiopia men used to attend meetings on behalf of their wives. If women members want to take loan or get services of their cooperatives, the cooperative asks the guarantee of their husbands as the guarantors.

- *Poor educational level:* Due to the lower educational level of women than men, in many cooperatives, the active role of women is not recognized or other men leaders never like their participation due to sheer dislike for women or wrong notions about women. The problem in this respect can be tackled only by getting good education by women members of cooperatives.

- *Lack of participation in meetings:* Women push themselves to be neglected by men due to their inactive participation in committee meetings and general assembly meetings. This automatically lead to gender imbalance in cooperatives.
- *Lack of training opportunities:* Compared to men, training opportunities for women is low. In common training programmes men are preferred over women. Women get benefited only in specialised training programmes meant for women. As has been mentioned earlier, the planners of various training programmes are most likely men, which naturally do not allow women's participation.
- *Lack of bylaw provisions:* In the bylaws of various cooperatives no provision has been made for the special privileges for women in the form of reserving seats in the management committee or in the resources of cooperatives. In countries like India in several regions, the bylaws of cooperatives insist to reserve one-third of the seats in the board of directors for women. Such aspects should come to Ethiopian cooperatives also.
- *Lack of empowerment of women members:* Women members in cooperatives must assert their rights and responsibilities in the forums like the general assembly. But in many instances they never bother to be neglected or sidelined by the men members or men leaders. They also never use the forum like the general assembly to raise their voices.
- *Absence of women cooperatives:* Absence of the organisation of women cooperatives has also become one of the causes for the gender imbalance in the cooperative movement in a country. Women cooperatives are good outlet for women to express their views and to do things what they like. The inhibitions like shyness, reservations and fear complex could be overcome by women cooperatives.
- *Inactive role by the initial women members:* While starting a new cooperative, initially some women members might have been admitted and they might have shown poor performance, which might have led to the general neglect of future women members also.

How cooperatives can help women's integration?

Training, education, and information, have an important role to play in increasing women's involvement in cooperatives. But they would be more effective if:

- programmes were better adapted to women's broad concerns (health, electrification, housing...).

- more female trainers were available, making it easier for women to join in the courses.
- less stress were placed on written training materials, of little use to illiterate women.
- radio cooperative programmes were provided more in local languages (all too often they are in the "colonial" language).
- timing took account of the women's daily schedules.

Women can also be groomed to play their role in mixed societies by first learning group leadership roles in exclusively women's cooperatives. Such cooperatives, and other rural groups, can also serve as training grounds in participatory development, teach methods of group decision-taking, and develop trust and self-assurance. They also provide a valuable apprenticeship in the conduct of business: successful women's groups demonstrate to skeptical men (and women) that women are capable of developing their own business and can thus be valuable participants in mixed societies.

As breeding grounds for democracy and participation, cooperatives could be used to empower women by enhancing and upgrading their specific knowledge and capacities. For instance, indigenous knowledge in areas such as traditional healing, frequently transferred through the female members of the family, is under severe threat from modern medicine. Cooperatives could institute programmes whereby such knowledge would be systematically called on and preserved, and proposed as a service where modern health services are being cut back.

With greater freedom to decide on the types of business to conduct through a cooperative, the way is open for the development of activities of specific interest to women such as small cooperative mills, food storage and preservation, production of household necessities like soap and clothing, small animal raising and handicrafts. More stress should also be laid on cooperatives' social function by organising services which would relieve women from certain of their tasks: child-care services or drudgery-reducing activities, or assist with organising marriages and other ceremonies.

Such activities are already taking place through so-called informal groups. In Benin, while only 8 per cent of rural women are members of cooperatives, 90 per cent belong to traditional groups. An important reason for this apparent imbalance is that they keep control over their own money and can use it flexibly when it is channeled (invisibly) through women's groups. Experience has shown that women prefer to stay independent both of cooperative laws and more especially of interference and domination by men.

Finally, more active female participation in rural cooperatives will have an additional bonus. A debate on gender division of labour for agricultural and domestic tasks, especially in the light of evolving technologies, would almost certainly develop through the regular cooperative meetings. The male members may then become convinced that there are more efficient ways of allocating tasks and resources than the current ones, to the greater good of the whole village and household social and economic set-up.

Why is gender integration important?

When we come to cooperative organizations, you can see a number of areas where the need of gender issue is unquestionable, first for reasons related to cooperative principles. While emphasizing one of the Principles of Cooperation, the Third Principles Commission has pointed out that:

> "Cooperatives are open to all persons able to use their services and willing to accept the responsibilities of membership without gender, social, racial, political or religious discrimination".

Secondly, women have got a number of useful contributions in the development and advancement of cooperatives.

- Active, equitable participation of members, both men and women, is a necessity for sustainable cooperative development. Active participation in the cooperative context means that members are involved in all the functions of a cooperative including planning, decision- making, implementation and financial and management control.
- Cooperatives are based on the values of self-help, mutual responsibility, equality and equity. They practice honesty, openness and social responsibility in all their activities. In order to enhance the credibility of cooperatives as democratic people-based movements in the eyes of the public and cooperative members, cooperative values must be respected and adhered to.
- Cooperative principles state that cooperatives are democratic organizations without gender discrimination. But can they be regarded as truly democratic if women members do not have equal access to decision-making levels? If women are under-represented or not represented at all in decision-making, they may find it difficult to accept the legitimacy of decisions taken which do not take their interests into consideration.
- Experience has shown that women in leadership positions are more likely to address gender issues and safeguard the interests of women. As the cooperative movement worldwide incorporates so many women (yet few in management positions), it is important that more women are integrated into the system.

Importance of Gender Integration in Cooperatives

Gender integration in cooperatives is important due to the following reasons:

- *Gender as an analytical tool:* The concept 'Gender' is an important analytical tool in the planning, management, monitoring and evaluation of development programmes or cooperative projects require that women be considered in relation to men in a socio- cultural setting and not as 'isolated' group. Because in almost all societies women form half of the population and they undertake heavy domestic, social and economic participation.
- *To understand the equitable role of women:* Understanding of the roles and positions of men and women in cooperative in their socio-economic environment is important to identify and address their different needs, to be able to develop their strengths and potentials and to ensure an equitable distribution of resources and benefits of cooperative development. Women, in addition to their equitable role have added responsibilities to perform, which needs to be addressed by all cooperatives.
- *For the sustainable growth of cooperatives:* Gender integration in cooperative development is also essential because active and equitable participation of members, both men and women, is a necessary condition for sustainable cooperative development. Active participation from cooperative context means that members are involved in all the functions of cooperative, including planning, decision-making, implementation and financial and management control. Any cooperative to grow from strength to strength needs to increase their volume of business and operational efficiency. This calls for the due role to be given to women members.
- *Social capital and cooperatives:* Cooperatives are based on the values of self-help, mutual responsibility, equality and equity, which are all the result of strong social capital; the ability of people to work together, they practice honesty, openness and social responsibility in all their activities. Women members of cooperatives play notable role in enhancing the social capital towards their cooperatives.
- *To respect cooperative democracy:* In order to enhance the credibility of cooperative as democratic people-based movements in the eyes of the public and cooperative members, the cooperative values must be respected and adhered to. One of the basic components of cooperative democracy is equality, which insists the importance of gender equality also.

- *Legitimacy of decision making:* Cooperative principles state that cooperatives are democratic organizations. It is to mean that cooperatives are the place where people exercise their right without gender discrimination. But can they be regarded as truly democratic if women members do not have equal access to decision-making, under-represented and not at all represented some times. Women may find it difficult to accept the legitimacy of decisions taken without their participations, which do not take their interests in to consideration. Having women in leadership positions is of great importance to women in cooperatives.
- *Underutilised human capacities:* Women represent 50 per cent of the world's human resources, cooperatives will benefit from this under-utilized human resources by enhancing women's productive capabilities. Many women have special skills in, for instance, marketing and trading, while others have special knowledge and capabilities, which have been at all unacknowledged. The active involvement of women (the invisible workforce) will make cooperatives economically and politically strong.
- *Involving creative ideas:* In today's fast changing socio–economic and political climate the need for innovative thinking and creative ideas is becoming exceedingly important, also for the cooperative sector. By involving more women in decision–shaping and decision–making within the cooperative movement, one will enhance the prospects of cooperatives, diversify activities and fortify the cooperative movement.
- *To diversify the cooperative activities:* In order to grow vertically and horizontally, cooperatives need to diversify their operations by means of adding additional functions for the benefits of the members. It is also significant that the involvement of more women in cooperatives will broaden the scope of cooperatives and improves their social role by empowering them to decision-making level.

A number of experiences have shown that initiatives taken by women in cooperatives have accelerated the progress and change of socio-economic situations both for women and the society at large.

The Indian self-employed women's association and the Bangladesh Garment Bank are examples. In case of Agricultural Cooperatives, the involvement of more women in economic activities would result in a more integrated production of food crop and cash crops. This would enhance food security and have a positive effect for the entire society.

Benefits of Gender Integration

- Women represent fifty per cent of the world's human resources. By enhancing women's productive capabilities and developing their capacities, cooperatives will benefit from this hitherto under-utilized human resource. Many women have special skills in, for instance, marketing and trading, while others have special knowledge and capabilities which have been unacknowledged.

- Cooperatives will become a stronger economic and more influential political force if more women (the invisible workforce) are actively involved.
- Men and women often tackle and solve problems differently. In today's fast changing socio-economic and political climate the need for innovative thinking and creative ideas is becoming exceedingly important also for the cooperative sector. By involving more women in decision-shaping and decision-making within the cooperative movement, one will enhance the prospects of cooperatives, diversify activities and fortify the cooperative movement.
- In the case of agricultural cooperatives, the involvement of more women in economic activities would result in a more integrated production of food crop and cash crops. This would enhance food security and have a positive effect on the environment as monoculture causes soil erosion and degradation.
- Involving more women in cooperatives will broaden the scope of cooperatives and improve their social role. Women's and men's priority areas often differ. Women are, for example, often more concerned with social development issues such as employment, health, the environment and children than men.
- Experiences have shown that initiatives taken by women in cooperatives have accelerated the progress and change of their socio-economic situation. The trainer/moderator can give examples here. Women's involvement in thrift and credit cooperatives in Africa have, for example, been particularly successful. In India the Self-Employed Women's Association (SEWA) is immensely successful and likewise the Grameen Banks in Bangladesh.
- By involving women in the affairs of the cooperatives, better and justifiable decision-making process will take in the cooperatives. The decisions taken in any organisation must involve the key stakeholders and major beneficiaries, women happened to such decision makers.
- The cooperatives can cover entire population in its area of operation. The International Cooperative Alliance insists cooperatives of member countries to bring the entire population under their fold, including eligible women members.
- Gender integration improves image of the cooperatives as the best social and economic organisations suitable to improve the living conditions of the poor and deprived population.

- By involving women members in decision making, cooperatives can introduce thrift and cost-saving operations in their working, as women exercise such habits in their household operations.
- The competitive power of the cooperatives increases through gender integration. The private trade is keenly watching the activities of the cooperatives and they are ready to demoralize the activities of the cooperatives .This can be stopped by the cooperatives by giving active role to women.

How to integrate more women into cooperatives?

- The first thing is to include gender on their agendas. The formulation of gender-sensitive policies, strategies and plans is essential. These should be drawn up in a joint effort between women and men.
- Cooperatives should address equality issues and make a firm commitment in their mandate to correct imbalances where they exist. For example, cooperatives can state their intention to address the problems of women's access to credit, land, equipment, extension services etc., and/or to take positive measures to include more women in their training programmes, in decision-making and leadership positions.

Some Suggestions

- Through awareness creation, gender sensitization, education and lobbying cooperatives can help remove the obstacles to women's equal participation (e.g., membership criteria or legal, traditional, financial, attitudinal constraints).
- Through training and education programmes which are sensitive to women needs, cooperatives can help strengthen women's capacities and capabilities, resulting in their increased self-confidence and enabling them to participate more fully in decision-making and assume leadership positions.
- Cooperatives can consult and involve women when decision are being taken, particularly those regarding women or which are in women's interests.
- Cooperatives can review their policies and plans periodically to ensure that they are gender-sensitive? Cooperatives can focus on gender in their action plans.
- Cooperatives can establish "gender committees" or units whose tasks can, for example, be to identify gender-related problems; to ensure that gender awareness training programmes are carried out; to be responsible for gender analysis in programme planning etc. It should be noted here that by establishing a special unit or office for gender issues or programmes, one risks that the gender issue becomes a side-issue that

has been "taken care of" and that women continue to be marginalized in mainstream activities. A gender unit must therefore be part of mainstream activities or have direct access to policy and decision-making levels.

- Cooperatives can use their national organizations and networks to collect gender disaggregated data and help identify different types of projects focused to women's needs which can help them increase their income-earning capacities and alleviate their workloads. For example, they can investigate how much time men and women spend on various chores and activities and how this fits in with potential and economically viable and sustainable cooperative activities.

Strategies for Integration of Women in Cooperatives Development

Regarding strategies for the integration of women in cooperatives development and decision-making levels, the following points can be mentioned:

- The cooperative organization or sector must first include gender on the agenda. The formulation of gender-sensitive policies, strategies and plans is essential and these should be drawn up in a joint effort between women and men and not solely on men's terms.
- Cooperatives should address equality issues and make a firm commitment in their mandate to correct imbalances where they exist. For example, cooperatives can state their intention to address the problems of women's access to credit, land, equipment, extension services etc., and/or to take positive measures to include more women in their training programmes, in decision-making and leadership positions.

The trainer/moderator can also ask participants to suggest other areas where action can be taken by cooperatives to enhance women's participation and access to decision-making levels. Based on the information given earlier regarding women's constraints and areas of concern, the participants should be able to suggest some of the following solutions with some guidance from the trainer/moderator (when necessary):

1. Through awareness creation, gender sensitization, education and lobbying cooperatives can help remove the obstacles to women's equal participation (e.g., membership criteria or legal, traditional, financial, attitudinal constraints).
2. Through training and education programmes which are sensitive to women needs, cooperatives can help strengthen women's capacities and capabilities, resulting in their increased self-confidence and enabling them to participate more fully in decision-making and assume leadership positions.

3. Cooperatives can consult and involve women when decisions are being taken, particularly those regarding women or which are in women's interests.
4. Cooperatives can review their policies and plans periodically to ensure that they are gender-sensitive? Cooperatives can focus on gender in their action plans.
5. Cooperatives can establish "gender committees" or units whose tasks can, for example, be to identify gender-related problems; to ensure that gender awareness training programmes are carried out; to be responsible for gender analysis in programme planning etc. It should be noted here that by establishing a special unit or office for gender issues or programmes, one risks that the gender issue becomes a side-issue that has been taken care of and that women continue to be marginalized in mainstream activities. A gender unit must therefore be part of mainstream activities or have direct access to policy and decision-making levels.
6. Cooperatives can use their national organizations and networks to collect gender disaggregated data and help identify different types of projects focused to women's needs which can help them increase their income-earning capacities and alleviate their work burden. For example, they can investigate how much time men and women spend on various chores and activities and how this fits in with potential and economically viable and sustainable cooperative activities.

Areas for Gender Integration in Cooperatives

The following are the important areas for gender integration in cooperatives.

- *Membership drive:* One of the important areas of gender integration in cooperatives is increasing the membership, especially increasing women membership. Efforts should be made to increase women membership so as to enhance women participation in cooperative development.
- *Organising women cooperatives:* Identification of practical and strategic needs of women and organization of women cooperatives on the basis of the need identification.will help women to get the fuller benefits of cooperatives. To organise exclusive women cooperatives, initial difficulties may be there, but it could be overcome later by careful handling of the administration.
- *Special programmes for women:* Each cooperative can create on-going mechanism within the cooperatives to facilitate implementation of the programmes for women development. Such special programmes may be related to employment generation, poverty reduction, income generation, awareness creation, experience sharing, etc.

- *Gender awareness programmes:* Sensitization of members, elected management and the employees of the cooperatives about the significance of the gender integration through gender awareness programmes. Such gender awareness programmes can be undertaken by associating various development departments, women bureaus, HIV counselling centres and health departments.
- *Bylaw provisions:* A model bylaw must be prepared by the Cooperative Authorities, which can be implemented at all levels. Creation of necessary legislative framework, which would ensure women's involvement and participation in cooperatives. Such model bylaw must contain regulating and corrective provisions and should encourage gender integration, gender priority and must sort out gender imbalance.
- *Linkages with other development agencies:* Establishment of linkages with sister cooperative organizations, government, development agencies and NGOs to materialize the objectives of the gender integration, must also be considered to give overall attention to gender integration in cooperatives.

Methods of Integrating Women in Cooperatives

Now we have come to the method, how to integrate women in cooperative and its development, we can have few points.

- *Inclusion of gender in the agenda:* Cooperative sectors or organization must include Gender on the Agenda. The formulation of Gender-sensitive policies and plans is essential and these should be drawn up in a joint effort between women and men and not solely on men's terms. Cooperatives should address equality issues and make a firm commitment in their mandate to correct imbalances wherever they exist. *For example,* cooperatives can state their intention to address the problems of women's access to credit, land, equipment, extension services etc. and/or to take positive measures to include more women in their training programmers if there, in decision making and leadership positions.
- *Training and education:* Through training and education programmes, cooperatives can help strengthen women's capacities and capabilities, resulting in their increased self-confidence and enabling them to participate more fully in decision-making and assume leadership positions.
- *Involvement of women in decision making:* Cooperatives can consult and involve women when decisions are being taken; particularly those regarding women or which are in women's interests. During election times the management committee, the male members can consult the women members, and even try to put up women nomination unanimously.

- *Action plans:* Action plans are the formulation of schemes to be implemented for the welfare of the members. Cooperatives can review their policies and plans periodically to ensure that they are gender-sensitive. They can focus on gender in their action plans.
- *Forming gender committees:* Cooperative can also establish "gender committees" or units whose tasks can, for example, be to:
  - Identify gender-related problems
  - Ensure that gender awareness training programmes are carried out
  - Be responsible for gender analysis in programme planning etc.

It should be noted here that by establishing a special unit or office for gender issues or programmes, one risk that the gender issue becomes a side issue that has been taken care of and that women continue to be marginalized in mainstream activities. A gender unit must therefore be part of mainstream activities or have direct access to policy and decision-making levels.

Ways and means for achieving equality

Following are some of the ways and means of helping women to achieve equality with men in cooperatives:

- *Provision of employment and service:* To overcome poverty, the cooperatives should help women members and employees by providing employment in acceptable conditions; provide credit at non-exploitative terms and lobby for women's economic rights. Savings and credit cooperatives should introduce gender sensitive services.
- *Access to education and training:* To ensure women's access to education and training, cooperatives should give special attention to improve the educational status of women members and employees. Cooperatives should facilitate greater involvement of female child and women in education by helping to reduce the burden of household work and by making available income, which they can control independently of men. Cooperation as a subject giving due importance to gender issues should be included in the curriculum of schools and colleges.
- *Access to information:* In order to provide adequate healthcare for women, cooperatives should create community health services at low cost. By means of cooperative literacy and education programmes, women should be given access to information on nutrition, health, family planning, childcare and intra-family relations.
- *Reducing violence against women:* By providing secured employment in conditions of dignity and equality, the cooperatives play an important role in empowering women and reducing the financial stress, which

contributes to violence against women. Housing cooperatives can initiate programmes to tackle domestic violence and health cooperatives can provide for counseling and rehabilitation of women victims.

- *Providing economic security:* Cooperatives are significant means whereby groups of women are able to pool their resources in order to protect the assets and enhance opportunities for viable economic activity. Association with cooperatives provide women with opportunities, empowerment and economic security.
- *Ground to gain experience:* Cooperatives are schools of democracy and member participation involves gaining experience in decision-making. Cooperatives offer a channel for gaining experience and for upward mobility in the power structure of the movement itself.
- *Awareness creation:* Cooperative media provides substantial amount of information on the experience of women members/ employees in all areas of life and keeps women informed on political issues. Cooperative meetings and training programmes provide immense opportunities for awareness creation.
- *Promotion of business activities to ensure equality:* Non-discrimination on the basis of gender is a part of basic cooperative principles. Efforts should be intensified to increase women participation and membership to ensure that the business activities promote women's equality.

Summary

- Training, education, and information, have an important role to play in increasing women's involvement in cooperatives.
- Cooperatives should address equality issues and make a firm commitment in their mandate to correct imbalances where they exist.
- Cooperatives can establish "gender committees" or units whose tasks can, for example, be to identify gender-related problems; to ensure that gender awareness training programmes are carried out; to be responsible for gender analysis in programme planning etc.

Self-Learning Activity

Try to answer the following questions on your own:

1. How do cooperatives help women's integration?
2. What are the benefits of gender integration?

17 Causes for Poor Participation of Women

Why is female participation so low?

The world over, statistics show that women's participation in cooperatives is low, especially in rural cooperatives. This is perhaps more difficult to explain in the developed countries where gender discrimination has, in principle, been overcome. In the developing world, cultural and religious factors are often evoked: women's "inside" role, discretion, not speaking in front of men, traditions of men negotiating and handling money matters, illiteracy, supposed inferior abilities, and social pressures make it difficult for women to play an active and visible public role. The types of business cooperatives deal in, particularly cash crops which tend to be male precincts, is another factor, and male resistance to women's participation also go a long way to keep them out. Absolute lack of time to join up with other women seems to be a major factor everywhere.

The position of women in many rural cooperatives is illustrated by the Anand pattern dairy cooperative, which has come to symbolise female agricultural enterprise. Unfortunately, this positive image does not correspond to reality in the villages. According to one study, despite efforts by the National Dairy Development Board, the government and NGOs, female membership is still only around 16 per cent nationally, even though "in virtually every part of India women are the primary dairy producers responsible for most of the activities involved in dairying" (Radhika Philips. *Member Participation and Cooperative Performance*, FAO, December 1994).

There is no need here to develop the negative effects. This has in societies where the family unit is no longer so solid and especially where the male head of family is often absent for long periods in search of work and income. Cooperative law often condones such discrimination by providing that the head of family attends meetings. The fact that the wife is often *de facto* or even *de jure* head of family is not always seen as enough reason for her to participate.

This is compounded by provisions to the effect that only owners or tenants of land may be members of agricultural cooperatives. This is most often the male who, however, frequently shares much of the labour with his wife. Use of land should be substituted for tenure or ownership as a criterion to overcome this obstacle.

Being virtually absent from most meetings, women stand little chance of influencing decisions, and even less of being elected to Boards or other posts. There would appear, however, to be one exception, both in Africa and Asia: the post of treasurer. Women have a reputation for greater honesty and dedication than men and therefore have some chance of election to this key, if not very influential, post. Of course, on the other hand, when women treasurers lack self-assertion and experience, they are open to abuse by unscrupulous men such as the secretary or president.

"Mixed" cooperatives have tended to be synonymous with "men's" cooperatives. But the importance of certain agricultural cooperatives in village life, and their repercussions on agricultural production, processing and marketing, as well as on family life and on women's chores, is too great for the exclusion of women from the decision-making process to be accepted as inevitable. When cooperative laws are revised, all provisions which make for gender discrimination should therefore be weeded out to avoid aggravating the problems faced by women in their attempts to be integrated into the participatory cooperative structures.

General Factors for Women's Low Participation

In the developing world, cultural and religious factors are often evoked: women's "inside" role, discretion, not speaking in front of men, traditions of men negotiating and handling money matters, illiteracy, supposed inferior abilities, and social pressures make it difficult for women to play an active and visible public role. The types of business cooperatives deal in, particularly cash crops, which tend to be male precincts, is another factor, and male resistance to women's participation also go a long way to keeping them out. Absolute lack of time to join up with other women seems to be a major factor everywhere.

The position of women in many rural cooperatives is illustrated by the Anand pattern dairy cooperative, which has come to symbolize female agricultural enterprise. Unfortunately, this positive image does not correspond to reality in the villages. According to one study, despite efforts by the National Dairy Development Board, the government and NGOS, female membership is still only around 16 per cent nationally, even though "in virtually every part of India women are the primary dairy producers responsible for most of the activities involved in dairying".

There is no need here to develop the negative effects this has in societies where the family unit is no longer so solid and especially where the male head of family is often absent for long periods in Search of work and income. Cooperative law often condones such discrimination by providing that the head of family attends meetings. The fact that the wife is often *de facto* or even *de jure* head of family is not always seen as enough reason for her to participate. This is compounded by provisions to the effect that only owners or tenants of land may be members of agricultural cooperatives. This is most often the male who, however, frequently shares much of the labour with his wife. Use of land should be substituted for tenure or ownership as a criterion to overcome this obstacle.

Inherent Difficulties of Women

Women face number of difficulties in their cooperatives. This is due to their inherent difficulties like lack of formal education, lack of awareness, suppression by male dominated society, lack of time to devote to the cooperatives, poor decision-making capacity in their cooperatives, lack of training, lack of provisions in the cooperative proclamation and bylaws, and their own apathy about the potentialities of cooperatives in solving economic problems of the members. Apart from the above reasons the following structural reasons are quoted here below:

Other Constraints

Legal Constraints

The Cooperative Proclamation/Laws and the bylaws of cooperative societies are apparently gender neutral but in real terms they are gender blind. There are no major women specific provisions in the statues which can be clearly stated to be framed for the benefit of women. There is a provision of "one family one member", in the cooperative legal terms. It is quite apparent that if only one member from a household is to become the member of a cooperative, it will be the husband or the male member of the family, as assets and the properties are in the name of the head of the household. Women, therefore are deprived of the membership as well as decision-making power in the cooperatives. Because the access to assets and resources are vested with the male members of the family. There is no joint membership in agricultural cooperatives or other cooperatives, which again can not put any check over the male domination. The Cooperative Proclamation or the bylaws of any cooperatives do not provide for reservation of seats in membership or in the elected management committee of the cooperatives, where women may participate in the decision making.

Social Constraints

The main reasons for socio-economic inequalities can be attributed to the structural obstacles arising from the fundamental conflict between the feudal culture and the cooperative culture. While the feudal culture is based on hierarchy an unequal relations, among people, at every basis of cooperative culture is equality amongst members. The four key social institutions namely the family, community, the market and the state (government) not only govern human existence but form the very basis of social construction for both men and women within them.

Family

Women are discriminated from the cradle to the grave and even before birth. Within the family, the members are governed by a set of norms and practices made by the head of the family, who exercise control, power and authority over other members of the family. Since men have access and control to the resources, their role is clearly defined as the "bread winner" and women are supposed to confine themselves to the role of "home makers" and thus they are unable to take an initiative to become the member of the cooperatives. Division of functions of men and women must be redefined as their roles are changing. The rural women have a low self-image and do not consider themselves to be making a substantial contribution even though they are engaged in production and constructive process.

Community

Community in developing countries reinforces men's dominant position, women's restricted mobility within the family leads to further restricting her mobility in the community and traditional values reinforce women's home-maker role. Such community rigidities play a negative role and forbid women to mobilise on common platform and work in the cooperatives.

Market

Market is characterized by rigid timings often not suitable for women due to their reproductive chores. Mostly men have access to village markets. The market awareness of men is higher than women.

State (Government)

Men dominate as the policy makers of cooperatives and cooperative legal system is shaped by men folk at the national and regional levels, which primarily exclude women's interests.

Financial Constraints

Financial and professional assistance to women in cooperatives is also negligible. There is no special financial benefits given to women members of cooperatives. Resources tickle down slowly to women members. This will change the very complexion of the society. The future of Ethiopia lies with the women. When the women move, the family moves, the community moves, the village moves and the whole country moves.

Administrative Constraints

In many countries there is no national policy defining the role of cooperatives in the socio-economic development of women. There are no specific programmes either relating to cooperative credit, marketing or training for bringing self-employed women or women in unorganised sectors into the cooperative fold. The impact of this indifference is well reflected in the profile of participation and membership of cooperatives.

Educational

The facilities of cooperative education and training is very much limited in developing countries. The meager opportunities available are grabbed by male members of the cooperatives. Without special training programmes for women members, no training can be given to the women members.

The above constraints must be removed through legal and administrative efforts.

Situation of Women in Cooperatives in Asia-Pacific Region

The scarcity of official sex-disaggregated statistics on entrepreneurship in the region, in particular in women's entrepreneurship, makes it difficult to assess the situation of women's entrepreneurship. Stronger government initiatives in data collection on women's entrepreneurship are an important step for greater analysis of women's entrepreneurship and its impact in the region and economic development. According to the 2006 Economic and Social Survey of Asia and the Pacific, small and medium-sized enterprises (SMEs) account for more than 60 per cent of formal sector employment in most developing countries in the region. More than 86 per cent of the labour force in Thailand is employed by SMEs. More than 70 per cent of the labour force is employed by these firms in the Republic of Korea and in Vietnam. Although the scarcity of data makes mapping and regional assessment of women's entrepreneurship among Asian and Pacific countries difficult, micro, small and medium-sized enterprises appears to be one area where large numbers of the region's working poor, including large numbers of women, are concentrated. In the formal sector, women appear to head about 35 per cent of registered small and medium-sized enterprises. The full numbers of women in the economic production sphere are likely to be even larger than official records due to the large numbers of women working in the informal sector and subsistence businesses where the fine line between subsistence activities for the household and formal entrepreneurship becomes blurred and difficult to measure or quantify.

- A number of small-scale surveys enable some idea of women's entrepreneurship within the region.
- According to Chinese official statistics, the majority of Chinese women work in collective enterprises, most of them small and medium-sized enterprises. It has also been reported that women initiate about 25 per cent of new business start-ups.
- In the Philippines, women constituted more than half of the self-employed working in manufacturing and trade and up to 70 per cent in social/community and personal services.
- In Japan four out of five small business owners are women.
- In Vietnam in 1997, four out of five restaurants, cafes, hotels and wholesale retail shops and garment and leather manufacturing enterprises were owned and run by women. Supporting local level self-help women's groups to develop their own collective capacities and pursue policy advocacy for women's entrepreneurship is a crucial component for ensuring the sustainability of initiatives for the promotion of women's entrepreneurship.

By forming cooperatives and self-help women's groups, women entrepreneurs can through a cooperative effort undertake initiatives which individually would not be feasible and channel their collective strength. These include undertaking collective marketing, the creation of shared facilities, bulk purchasing, group lending, etc. Although formally pledging gender equality, cooperatives in the region are still characterized by strong gender inequities, in particular with regard to women's participation. Data shows that the percentage of women who are members of cooperatives is low (Table 17.1). Information presented in table 17.1, collected from seven countries (India, Islamic Republic of Iran, Japan, Malaysia, Singapore, Sri Lanka and Thailand) in the Asian and Pacific region shows that, while the percentage of women in decision-making and leadership positions is improving at the state apex-level, it is still low in particular at the primary level. Overall the percentage of women in decision-making and leadership positions is low in comparison with the percentage of women who are cooperative members.

Table 17.1: Women's participation at decision-making level in cooperatives

	National apex	State apex	Primary co-op
Leader	11.49%	4.0%	14.16%
Manager	23%	50%	7%
Staff	37%	51.62%	46.53%

Source: ICA, 2005.

The data clearly reflect an overall trend toward strong gender prejudice in the traditional cooperative system and the difficulties involved in introducing structural change to balance the gender inequity. They also suggest that gender inequity is more strongly prevalent in certain types of cooperatives than others.

Effects on Gender Relations in Cooperatives

- Stereotyping of women's role in cooperatives and lack of gender awareness.
- Women are assigned to positions that are an extension of their traditional roles (such as secretaries, treasurers), whilst men are groomed for managerial and leadership positions. The potential that women represent is not fully utilized and developed. Traditional gender roles are reinforced.
- Lack of sex disaggregated data and information. Lack of awareness and understanding of gender issues.
- Cooperative leaders and policy-makers are gender insensitive. Lack of gender-responsive cooperative policies. Absence of support services such as day-care facilities, which could restrain women's active participation. Family friendly policies, such as paternity leave, not given priority. Leaders not sensitive to the needs of women members and employees, which in turn leads to their disaffection.
- Unequal access of women and men to cooperative education and training.
- Women's self-development and career opportunities are restricted, whilst men's are increased.
- Imbalanced development. Few women in decision-making. Unequal opportunities and treatment in personal and career development.
- Limited number of women in management and leadership.
- Policy, planning and decision-making dominated by men.
- Potential of women not utilized, faster turn-over of female employees. Decision-making gender insensitive. Unequal access of men and women to credit and other services.
- Limits women's productive activities and economic independence. Increases men's economic opportunities and reinforces the gender stereotypical role of men as the main breadwinners.

Summary

- The world over, statistics show that women's participation in cooperatives is low, especially in rural cooperatives. This is perhaps more difficult to explain in the developed countries where gender discrimination has, in principle, been overcome.

- There are constraints for low participation of women in cooperatives; they are to be overcome to increase their participation.

Self-Learning Activity

Try to answer the following questions on your own:

1. Why is there low participation of women in cooperatives?
2. What are the effects of gender relations in cooperatives?
3. Write short note on Social constraints of women.

18 Legal Constraints

Women's Economic Participation

Overview of Legal Constraints

It is essential to take account of a country's whole legal framework, and particularly timely in the current context of amending existing or adopting new cooperative legislation, in order to meet the emerging needs posed by the changing international economic and political environment. During the last decade, at least 15 sub-Saharan African States have adopted new cooperative laws as well as India, the Philippines and Thailand. In addition, other countries are also considering to update their cooperative legislation, hence the importance of drawing the attention of the legislator to the existing shortcomings and to the possible solutions in order to increase women participation. However, despite the fairly recent adoption of cooperative laws in several countries in order to palliate shortcomings with regard to equal opportunities for women, the results in practice remain unsatisfactory, as women's participation has not increased accordingly.

Within the framework of the national policy of Burkina Faso, for example, the Government views cooperatives as important for income generation and job creation for women and men alike. However, despite the consecutive adoption of four new cooperative laws since 1973, the latest being in 1999, the situation of women has not been noticeably improved. In effect, statistical research undertaken in the country during 1997-1998 in the framework of an agricultural popularization campaign, indicates that women represent less than a third of the members of the identified cooperatives and an even lesser number in various cooperative type associations (4,694 women of a total of 25,516 members), even though they constitute more than half of the population. Similarly, in Cameroon, the percentage of women members in cooperatives is estimated at 25 per cent only. This rate a'so fluctuates according to the respective cooperative sectors, such as in Ecuador, as women's representation is low in the transport and agricultural sectors but higher in credit and savings cooperatives, where it is assessed to approximately 55 per cent. Other figures likewise display an overall low women proportion, as women-only cooperatives in Morocco represent hardly more than 3 per cent of the country's cooperative undertakings, mainly in the sectors of handicraft, agriculture and services. These figures illustrate the need to investigate further and deeper into the legislative framework in order to identify the legal shortcomings at all levels and address them accordingly.

In order to have a more comprehensive understanding of the legal constraints that women face in their full and equal participation in cooperative enterprises, a brief overview of the general legal framework in which these enterprises operate is necessary as cooperative legislation takes various forms worldwide, and as other related legislation may also seriously impair women participation. By way of example, provisions contained in civil or commercial legislation that restrict women's access to property rights have a direct bearing on their capacity to form cooperatives and enter into cooperative business relations as these require financial assets.

Cooperative legislation in its broad acceptation varies considerably from country to country, and accordingly with respect to its consequences on women's participation as several laws may be of application and contain discriminatory provisions that hamper women's legal freedom of action. In a number of countries, such as India and Thailand, one single cooperative law of a general scope encompasses all types of cooperative enterprises. In other countries, such as Uruguay, different cooperative laws govern specific cooperative sectors, for example, agricultural, services, housing or credit cooperatives. In addition to cooperative specific acts and regulations, particular provisions or chapters contained in other legislation such as the civil, commercial or rural code have a direct bearing on cooperatives as they supplement cooperative law through rules governing contracts, enterprise activities, winding up of enterprises and so on. In the few countries that have not passed a specific cooperative act, such as China, Denmark and Norway, the applicable legal texts to cooperative enterprises are laws, customs and rules adopted for individual enterprises in different areas, including labour standards. Third, in Federal States, cooperative legislation that is applicable to the whole country may co-exist, or not, with individual State laws. This is, for example, the case in India where a federal law is of application in parallel to the state laws.

Above described legislation, together with judicial decisions, regulate cooperative matters ranging from membership, participation in ongoing activities, formation of cooperative enterprises, access to services and to property, as well as to leadership. However, in the specific case of women's participation, an investigation into other laws proves necessary as, even in the case of gender sensitive cooperative legislation, women's involvement remains very low compared to men's. Whereas in certain cases, the legislation does not outwardly discriminate against women, its application may nonetheless lead to discriminatory treatment of women as succession rules in a number of countries exclude women from the right to inherit property from their deceased husbands, and thus deprive them from the necessary means to adhere to a cooperative or to participate more actively in its activities. An analysis of the overall legislation that may have a direct bearing on the situation of women in society in general comprises:

- the Constitution;
- Cooperative Acts, regulations and by-laws
- in addition, rules contained in the following legislation limit women's legal autonomy;
- affect theirs access to property;
- matrimonial law;
- succession law;
- civil and commercial legislation; and
- land legislation.

Moreover, it has to be noted that the barriers that women face are not only of a legal nature but also to a large extent cultural. Even in a gender equitable legal framework, women will often neither attempt to exercise their rights nor have them legally enforced by the court system due to consequences they risk facing, such as exclusion from the social groups they belong to. In many cases, they do not express themselves publicly in cooperative meetings due to lack of confidence or due to social norms that restrict them. In such cases women are less likely to be considered competent to take up leadership positions in mixed gender cooperatives. Women's participation in cooperatives depends in general on their status and hence, gender awareness at all levels of society is essential.

Language Used in Legislation

Gender biased language in legislation can be either directly or indirectly discriminating, depending of the legal constructions that prevail in a given country. Expressions such as *Alos socios, el Gerente, el Presidente, los funcionarios@* as stated in Ecuadorian legislation are outwardly discriminating, as they are written in the masculine form and can hence be interpreted as referring to men only. Similarly, reference to the family head in laws is also directly discriminating since this expression usually refers to men.

Moreover, even though the language used in legislation may not be outwardly discriminating, the legal system may be construed as discriminating against women in concrete terms. By way of illustration, even though the Constitution in certain cases includes gender in the list of prohibited grounds for discrimination, it may however refer explicitly to other written legislation which in effect contains discriminatory provisions against women. Or, in other cases, the Constitution upon listing prohibited grounds for discrimination such as race, age, ethnic origin, etc., omits any reference to gender and thus paves the way for legitimising women discrimination in the countrys laws. This is the case of Zimbabwe, whose Constitution states in section 23 that:

> Subject to the provisions of this section, (a) no laws shall make any provision that is discriminatory either in itself or in its effect; and (b) no person shall be treated in a discriminatory manner by any written law or in performance of the functions of any public office or any public authority ...

Whereby, it follows that a law action is considered discriminatory only if it contravenes one of the listed discrimination grounds. As gender is not included among the prohibited discrimination grounds quoted in subsection (2):

> For the purposes of subsection (1), a law shall be regarded as ... discriminatory ... if, as a result of that law or treatment, persons of a particular description by race, tribe, place of origin, political opinions, colour or creed are prejudiced.

Discrimination against women is thus not illegal. The Constitution may also refer expressly to the parallel applicability of custom, which leads to gender discrimination as customary rules contain a number of unequal conditions for women in general. These pertain in particular to inheritance and matrimonial rules restricting women's access to property, such as land and credit, which have direct repercussions on their participation in cooperative enterprises. In the case of Zimbabwe, the Constitution states further in its section 23(3):

> Nothing contained in any law shall be held to be in contravention (of the above provision) to the extent that the law in question relates to any of the following matters: (a) adoption, marriage, divorce, burial, devolution of property on the death or other matters of customary law...

This means that customary law is constitutionally acknowledged as regulating above matters all of which are directly related to women's life, a legal construction that expressly sanctions a policy of gender discrimination.

Similarly, statutory provisions referring to the culture of the country, for instance, in the Philippines, have a comparable effect since, according to cultural values, women do not participate in society on an equal footing with men. In this particular case, section 4 of the Cooperative Code of the Philippines (1990), provides. Every cooperative shall conduct its affairs in accordance with Filipino culture, which is reported to imply particular risks in very traditional communities where men dominate. In addition, inconsistencies between different applicable laws in the Philippines contribute to an unclear situation which leaves the door open to gender discrimination. This is, for example, to be found in the contradictions between the Family Code, which was recently revised to redress women's situation and put them at par with men, and the Civil Code, which contains provisions that impair women's full contracting rights, which in turn paves the way for gender discriminatory treatment.

In addition to the above-described explicit legal discrimination against women, the very technical formulation of cooperative legislation can render it inaccessible to people with poor legal literacy. This is often the case of cooperative members, especially in the rural areas where many may be illiterate or have only basic education. Even though the difficulty to understand the legal language affects both men and women, it affects women in particular in that they will have benefited from less school years than men and thus attain a lower education level. By way of example, in the urban areas of Burkina Faso, 67 per cent of women are reported to be illiterate compared to 46 per cent of men whereas the respective numbers in the rural areas are of 91 per cent as opposed to 76 per cent. Due to poor legal literacy, women are moreover unaware of their rights and accordingly are not in the position of having these rights enforced through legal enforcement mechanisms.

Obstacles at the Implementation Level of Legislation

Women also face legal obstacles at the implementation level of legislation. The causes behind these barriers are several and can be found even in gender-perfect legislation, where problems of applying the law remain. The absence of political commitment to enforce the laws once adopted and the tendency of the judiciary authorities to apply a restrictive and gender insensitive interpretation of the law, constitute a first explanatory cause to discriminatory enforcement of the law. Inconsistencies between existing and pending legislation, national laws and international conventions, written law and religious or customary laws, are also reported to contribute to a deficient application of the valid legislation. Such a situation results from a lack of coordination between the competent authorities, of resources and of will to enforce the laws. By way of example, and as already mentioned in above section, while family legislation in the Philippines has been updated to take account of gender issues, rules contained in other legislation, such as in the Commercial Code, impair women's legal capacity to enter into business transactions and lead to arbitrary legal situations.

Moreover, the judiciary is generally male dominated and judges have tended in a number of cases to pronounce unfavourable sentences towards women. Increasing the percentage of women in the judiciary, as suggested in the Philippines case study, where women represent only 10 to 15 per cent, would contribute to rendering court decisions more gender equal, a measure that needs, however, to be coupled by awareness raising activities. Another obstacle to applying a gender sensitive law may consist in its lack of practical applicability as the Philippine example of revised Family Code reveals. In this case, women in a poor rural area highlighted that even though separated women are legally entitled to obtain family support from their husbands, such a right is hardly enforceable since the men can hardly provide for their own subsistence.

In addition, as stated earlier, the complexity and technical character of the language used in cooperative legislation, including the by-laws, renders the text difficult to understand, particularly for disadvantaged women and men who lack access to legal aid or affordable legal services. As a result of lack of awareness of their rights or how to access the legal system, including the courts, they will not be in a position to exercise their rights and have them enforced. Accordingly, the judiciary court system is not only male dominated and gender biased but, in addition, women do not make use of the courts as often as they could since they are either unaware of their rights or mistrust the applicable legislation and judiciary enforcement system. In addition to purely legal barriers, cultural considerations play a role as women will often not attempt to have their rights enforced due to the many social sanctions that can result thereof. Furthermore, in cases where husbands, for example, do not grant their consent to transactions entered into by their wives, the latter, notwithstanding their legal rights, are not likely to jeopardise their relationship with their husbands by taking legal action against them. On a socio-cultural level, women are moreover reported to simply accept this situation as men's prerogative. Finally, the special case of duality or plurality of applicable norms, e.g. customary or Islamic law, in parallel to written law, also raises the question of legal enforcement mechanisms, which strongly undermine the position of women. In effect, notwithstanding a favourable legal environment created by the adoption of a new Cooperative Act in 1999 in Burkina Faso, women remain at a disadvantage as customary rules continue to be applicable especially in the rural areas, which is partly due to the fact that the legal enforcement mechanisms fail to set aside customary law. Along these lines, despite the rights provided for widows in written inheritance rules, as in the Ivory Coast, for example, customary law will prevail to the detriment of women, due to lack of political will to enforce the statutory law. Thus, in the absence of efficient legal enforcement mechanisms, customary law with its discriminatory norms towards women, will continue to be applied, despite the gender equal provisions contained in newly adopted statutory law. The section below will briefly describe some main substantive customary rules that discriminate against women.

Duality/Plurality of Norms

Women are exposed to dispossession through a number of legal provisions which, in addition to constitutional and statutory rules in certain countries, are mainly of a customary nature and pertain to matrimonial and inheritance regimes. In effect, these rules are detrimental to women's status in society in general and hamper their access to property such as land and credit, which has a direct impact on their participation in cooperative enterprises. Hence, a brief overview of how these rules restrict women's access to property as well as how certain statutory commercial law provisions put women at a disadvantage, will provide a framework against which women's low level of participation in cooperatives can be better grasped, bearing in mind that customs vary between countries and between regions within the same country. To the extent relevant Muslim legal provisions will also be looked into as in certain regions of Morocco and the Philippines, Islamic rules are applied.

In several sub-Saharan African countries, a married woman is under the custody of her husband. In Swaziland, for example, the husband is entitled to control his wife's person and property, and to represent her in court proceedings as she is unable to do so independently. Accordingly, a woman benefits from less legal protection for her business than a man, as she will need her husband's consent in order to be represented at court proceedings in case of commercial litigation. In such circumstances, business enterprises are reluctant to enter into commercial transactions with women as they risk, at a later stage, to have to deal legally with their husbands, who may decide not to continue cautioning their wive's commercial activities.

In Lesotho, women who attain majority at the age of 18 years, become minor again upon entering marriage and need thus their husband's prior consent to any commercial transaction they may wish to enter for the purpose of their business. For example, a woman cannot borrow money independently from a financial institution as she is under her husband's guardianship. This legal status remains after the death of her husband. She is placed under the guardianship of her husband's brothers, uncles or one of her sons if he is major. In Cameroon, not only customary norms but also statutory law contains provisions that severely limit women's legal autonomy as their property is confided to the husband who may dispose thereof without their wive's consent. However, in Morocco, statutory law affords a married woman freedom, whereas Muslim law, when abided by, provides for separation of goods between man and wife, which allows women to conduct their business independently, provided, however, that they dispose of property.

Secondly, in addition to matrimonial rules, a woman is barred from property through succession rules under which she is excluded from inheritance, both from her father and her husband. Once married, a woman very seldom inherits from her father's cattle or land, for example, and when she does, the inherited property generally comes under her husband's custody. In Lesotho, for instance, women, whether married or not, are not entitled to succession, and a widow is not only barred from inheriting from her deceased husband, but is to administer the property in consultation with her husband's male relatives if the deceased leaves no male heir or if the heir is minor. Even though statutory law in Cameroon expressly grants equal succession rights to female and male children alike, customary rules provide that women only benefit from a "right of use" to the property. Under Muslim law, women are entitled to inherit up to the share of one to two compared to male heirs. However, in a certain number of cases, the law is set aside for the exclusive benefit of men, as the Ouarzazate and Figuig regions of Morocco where women who claim their right to succession are culturally frowned upon in their community.

In Kenya, the Succession Act of 1972 excluded from its scope of application agricultural land and crops thereon and livestock, to be governed by law or customs applicable to the deceased's community, tribe, religion or sect as the case may be, which triggers the applicability of the following four systems of law:

- Customary law, under which women have only maintenance rights, but no inheritance rights.
- Muslim law, whereby widows inherit one eighth of the property if she has children or one fourth if she does not.
- Hindu law, granting women only a maintenance right.
- Statutory law, according to which a woman has security of tenure in the matrimonial home, right to benefit from her husband's assets under certain conditions. It thus appears that all above legal regimes discriminate women compared to men, as women at best are entitled to inherit under Muslim law, provided though that the rules are implemented in practice and not overruled by local traditions. Moreover, the parallel applicability of four legal systems in one given country leads to discrimination among the different groups of women, with consequent repercussions on women participation in cooperative enterprises.

The validity and applicability of custom may moreover be acknowledged through court decisions. In Togo, women can acquire assets of their own, through, for example their labour. However, similar to customary rules in Kenya or Lesotho, they cannot do so through succession since customary law, which denies women the right to inherit from their husband, has been recognized as applicable law by court decisions, notwithstanding the Constitution that explicitly prohibits gender discrimination. Thus, the duality of these legal systems in place leads to conflicting rights for women. They also lead to a lack of integrity in the hierarchy of laws as lower level laws (or custom) override higher level laws, including the Constitution which has direct consequences on the access to property, as the laws that afford women with property rights are being disregarded. However, some judges have pronounced decisions based on natural justice principles to set aside customary law, and to pose principles in contradiction with previous legal sentences. This was the case in Tanzania where in 1990, a court decision, while assessing whether statutory or customary law was applicable, upheld in favour of the former and hence that inheritance for women was lawful.

Above restrictions towards women can be partly explained by the concept underlying property in sub-Saharan Africa, particularly agricultural land, and partly by the influence that the introduction of the colonial rule had on customary law with regard to women's rights. In effect, before the colonial period, land was communally owned and women had an important agricultural role to play with ensuing rights of use. Such a conception contrasted with Western European law whereby property rights were individual and under which women had no independent economic role or no property rights, as their function were of a reproductive nature and consisted in the charge of the household. Consequently, the introduction of the colonial western law had important repercussions on landownership as men became afforded with individual land rights, a reform that led to a redefinition of customary land rights. Custom was invoked to justify the exclusion of women from both economic activities as well as decision-making where deliberations were male dominated, which consequently led to a reduction of women's rights compared to customary law prior to colonisation.

Thus, due to the economic interests of the colonising powers, men were given a formal title to land and as women's rights became increasingly identified through their husbands, they lost the guarantees of the traditional system. Initially introduced by the colonial powers, cooperatives were aimed at increasing cash crop production for export purposes, which implied a profound change in the prevailing community production structures. Accordingly, the traditional division of labour shifted towards men being involved in commercializing the crops, with an ensuing accrued commercial role in society, whereas women became confined to household production for subsistence purposes, losing thereby a recognition of their role in the national economy. Currently, agricultural property, i.e., mainly land, cattle and equipment, rely on family ownership which explains above succession rules as women, upon marriage, leave their family.

Accordingly, if they inherit assets from their parents, they will bring the acquired property to their new family, property which will thus be lost to their brothers and jeopardise the land equilibrium at community level. In conclusion, acquisition of property by women — whether in the form of land, work tools or credit — is severely hampered by above described matrimonial and succession rules, not to mention the case of women whose legal status is that of minor, such as in Lesotho.

Other provisions of applicability hamper even further women's right and use of property and are to be found in tax laws, business regulations, or other customary rules. Such discriminations can be illustrated by the following examples: women's right to income earnings may be reduced by discriminatory tax laws setting a higher rate for married women than for married men.Married women cannot apply independently for credits as banks require consent by the husband in a number of instances, e.g., in Lesotho and the Philippines, banks will require collateral for loans, in general less available to women. In addition, even though women are entitled to conduct business without the consent of their husband in certain countries such as Morocco, their independence may be hampered by social practices, whereas women in Lesotho cannot hire the necessary labour force and equipment for their farming operations, even if they are household heads and legally major.

Women's Participation in Cooperatives

Specific Legal Constraints

It is against this background that the specific legal constraints that women face in cooperative enterprises will be examined, as statutory cooperative legislation does not operate in isolation from other applicable laws, customary norms or cultural values. The identified legal constraints are articulated around the following four main and closely interrelated areas, namely cooperative membership, formation and access to services and decision-making, all of which will be analysed in the light of the recently adopted international instrument, Recommendation 193 on the promotion of cooperatives.

Access to Membership

In Section 1, (paragraph 2) of ILO Recommendation No. 193, a definition of cooperatives is given which corresponds to the definition formulated by the ICA in the Statement on the Cooperative Identity, "an autonomous association of persons united voluntarily to meet their common economic, social and cultural needs and aspirations through jointly owned and democratically controlled enterprise". The values, ethics and principles on which true cooperatives are based also incorporated in the text (paragraph 3). These emphasize the voluntary and open character of cooperatives, signifying that membership in cooperatives cannot be made compulsory, on one hand, and purporting to an open-door principle, on the other, according to which all persons applying for membership should be admitted, without any form of discrimination, and specifying among others "gender".

> Cooperatives are voluntary organizations, open to all persons able to use their services and willing to accept the responsibilities of membership, without gender, social, racial, political or religious discrimination.

The new standard furthermore explicitly refers to the promotion of gender equality in cooperatives and in their work in paragraph 8(c) and proposes giving special consideration to increasing women's participation in the cooperative movement at all levels, particularly at management and leadership levels in paragraph 7(3).

The case studies in this chapter present several factors that impede women's access to membership in cooperatives despite the recent adoption of cooperative legislation aimed at removing gender discriminatory conditions. One of these impediments is the cooperative rule whereby only one member per household may be admitted, who is usually defined as the family head, i.e. the man. Such a requirement is particularly common in agricultural cooperatives. The rule is motivated by two main concerns. Firstly, not to concentrate voting rights in the same family, which would thereby grant them unjustly high decision-making power compared to individual members, and secondly, not to jeopardize the family assets guaranteed for membership purposes. For example, in Tanzania, the new Cooperative Act, adopted in 1997, takes into consideration gender issues by stipulating, Cooperatives are voluntary organizations open to all persons able to use their services...without gender, social, racial, political or religious discrimination, but contains further the membership requirement of only one person per household, barring accordingly women's access to membership as their husbands will be considered the family head.

The one member per household rule may be statutory or contained in the by-laws of the cooperative, such as in India under the Andhra Pradesh Cooperative Societies Act, 1964, (APCS). However, under the more recent Andhra Pradesh Mutually Aided Cooperative Societies Act, 1995 (APMACS) this condition has been removed and thousands of women have consequently joined cooperatives. Such an impediment may be cultural, where for instance, in Thailand, under the prevailing traditions, agricultural cooperatives accept in practice the man as representing the family, despite the absence of any express provision in this direction.

A second legal constraint that severely hampers married women from acceding to membership, resides in their legal status, as they are considered to be minors under the law in certain countries. In the previously mentioned example of Lesotho, both statutory and customary law provide that men acquire guardianship of their wives upon their marriage, women being hence barred from joining a cooperative on their own initiative as they lack legal autonomy.

Similarly, laws that expressly discriminate against women are those that prohibit them from exercising certain activities without the consent of their husbands, and consequently bar them from membership in a cooperative enterprise, which is the case in Ecuador. Attention should in this regard be drawn to the relevant ratified international conventions, and in particular the ILO Discrimination (Employment and Occupation) Convention, 1958, (No. 111), as well as other international conventions which purport to gender equality such as the Convention on the Elimination of All Forms of Discrimination Against Women (CEDAW).

ILO Convention No. 111 defines discrimination as any distinction, exclusion or preference made on the basis of race, colour, sex, religion, political opinion, national extraction or social origin which has the effect of nullifying or impairing equality of opportunity or treatment in employment or occupation. The Convention's scope of coverage encompasses both employment relations and access to non-wage work. Regarding the latter category, "There should be no discrimination in access to the material goods and services (land, investment credit, etc.) required to carry on the occupation in question (in some countries, single women with no dependents cannot own land, ...). The Special Survey further enunciates, "Discrimination, especially on the basis of sex, arising from rules concerning marital or personal status must be countered, as in the cases where the inheritance system excludes certain categories of persons or where the right to enter into contracts is restricted by a requirement for the authorization of a third party (for example, family law in some countries requires a married woman to have her husband's consent in order to carry out a professional activity and perform the related transactions). Thus, restrictive membership provisions can hinder women from access to income generating activities, including the establishment of businesses, in direct infringement with the Convention, and the case of Ecuador was examined by the ILO Committee of Experts in 1993 who clearly referred to a provision requiring a married woman to obtaining authorization from her husband in order to become member of a cooperative. This rule is furthermore contrary to the spirit of the revision of the Civil Code in 1989 to abolish gender discriminatory provisions, which leads to inconsistencies between the two Acts, and jeopardizes accordingly legal clarity and predictability.

Along these lines, other legal provisions applicable in a country may also considerably restrict women's access to cooperative membership despite gender equitable cooperative legislation. For example, in section 2(2) of Act (No. 06 of 1992) relating to Cooperative Societies and Common Initiative Groups in Cameroon recognizes the principle of freedom to adhere to cooperatives without any form of discrimination.

Although gender is omitted as a discriminatory ground, the guidelines to the Act palliate this shortcoming by expressly referring to gender as a prohibited ground for discrimination. It can thus be assumed that women have free and equal access to membership under the Cooperative Act, however, Ordinance No. 81/02 is reported to severely limit this right. In effect, whereas its first section grants married women the right to exercise a separate profession from that of their husband, the latter is nonetheless entitled to oppose this autonomy, even if he needs to justify his refusal. As traditional cooperatives are considered as commercial enterprises, this Ordinance is applicable to them and women thus risk not having the right to join. This example reveals once more how inconsistencies between different applicable laws have repercussions on women's rights, even though cooperative legislation does not *per se* discriminate against them.

Third, the many legal obstacles to women benefiting from property rights and financial resources as described in the preceding section, have important repercussions on their admission to cooperatives. According to cooperative entry requirements, each member must pay a minimum number of shares fixed determined by the by-laws and is often liable for the debts of the cooperative up to at least the amount of subscribed shares. In addition, certain cooperative laws or by-laws may impose member's financial liability in the event that the cooperative cannot meet its debts, whereby the members are required to contribute with further payments. In a number of countries where customary law is applicable, succession rules exclude women from inheriting from their deceased husband's cooperative assets.

The lack of equal inheritance rights between men and women can constitute an added obstacle to women's access to membership. For example, the Hindu Succession Act (1956) in India, which governs the rights of Hindus, provides for the devolution of ancestral (not acquired) property. The Act applies to the whole country with such amendments as may have been made by the legislature of each state. In 1985, Andhra Pradesh introduced a few provisions providing for equal rights to daughters in co-parcenary property. Therefore, women can and do get a share of agricultural land. However, when they get married, they tend to live away from their parental families in the villages of their husbands, where they do not have a share in agricultural property. In primary agricultural societies where landownership is a requirement for membership, they are hence restricted.

Formation of Cooperatives

The case studies in this volume reveal that women face two main obstacles with regard to the creation of cooperative enterprises. Firstly, those resulting directly from the constraints related to membership and secondly, those linked to their lack of assets or access to financial resources. Additional obstacles include the legal formalism that characterizes cooperative legislation and traditional cultural and practices.

The membership-related constraints that impact on women's ability to set up cooperatives, reside in their legal status, on the one hand, and the consequences of the "one member per household" rule, on the other. Even though the recently adopted Cooperative Act in Cameroon (1992), for example, expressly excludes discrimination in the creation of cooperatives, stating in its Section 2(1).

> Persons shall be free to set up a cooperative society or a common initiative group. This shall be a right enjoyed by citizens who have attained legal majority or ... reality nonetheless shows that women's participation remains very low. As stated above under the preceding section, a married woman in the rural areas of sub-Saharan Africa, is often under the guardianship of her husband, and thus not entitled to enter freely into contractual liabilities. In other words, she needs her husband's consent to start a business or to engage the family's assets. As a consequence of the one member per household rule found in many cooperative by-laws, many women have opted to form women-only cooperatives. In the State of Andhra Pradesh in India, for example, women have, to a limited extent, been successful in creating consumer cooperatives under the APCS Act of 1964. However, they could meet further obstacles, as the Registrar can deny them the right to register their cooperative if he feels that their business might lead to excessive competition for the existing cooperatives in the area. This requirement has, however, been removed under the newly adopted APMACS Act, 1995, under which the Registrar no longer has this power. Consequent to this amendment, women have been able to create several cooperatives in the rural areas, particularly in the field of savings and credit, as well as milk marketing.

Moreover, as seen above, the considerable obstacles to women's access to financial resources reduce even further their possibilities to form new cooperative enterprises as their creation calls for initial capital requirements or for other assets such as land. Another example can be found in the Thai legislation, which does not *per se* discriminate against women owning land but, in the case of married women, it is the husband (or head of household) who acquires landownership and can thus use it to guarantee a loan for cooperative activities. Women are largely excluded from this possibility. Similarly, in the Philippines, where the Comprehensive Agrarian Reform Act (1988) grants women agricultural workers equal rights to ownership of land, practice has resulted in the registration of joint or conjugal land in the husband's name only. This puts women at a disadvantage in the event they wish to establish a cooperative. Women are also often excluded from agricultural cooperatives where landownership is usually a requirement for membership.

Limited access to credit constitutes a major barrier for women in many countries, who wish to set up cooperatives, even though formal legal restrictions in accessing credit generally do not exist. For example, despite equal access and control over resources expressly recognized by the Constitution of Ecuador, and despite the absence of any particular impediment in the cooperative legislation, statistical figures indicate that men and women have a credit stake amounting to 69.7 per cent and 30.3 per cent respectively. Hence, according to the case study, women face more difficulties in meeting the financial requirements of cooperative membership than men. Several other factors underlie women's and men's unequal access to credit, such as the inconsistencies between different legal texts, and notably provisions that favour married men with regard to conjugal property, irrespective of the Family Code revised from an equal rights perspective, which is reported to be the case in the Philippines.

Moreover, even though the Republic Act on Credit grants women equal rights and opportunities regarding contractual autonomy and entering into loan agreements, two limitations restrict their access to credit. The first is in the bank practice which requires the husband's consent for large loans involving property as collateral. The second restriction is found in the Civil Code rules, which provide that in the case of insolvency, the husband is the sole administrator of the communal property. This hampers women's capacity and autonomy to dispose of conjugal assets as well as their possibility to enter business ventures independently.

In sub-Saharan African countries where customary law plays a significant role, credit facilities will not be more readily available to women than other property rights. In Lesotho, as married women are under the custody of their husbands, they may be unable to provide the necessary collateral required by the financial institutions in order to start up a cooperative, unless their husbands consent thereto. In Morocco, statutory law is reported not to discriminate against women in their access to credit.

Muslim succession rules grant women one share as opposed to two for men. Married women are moreover allowed to carry out business transactions without marital consent as well as to dispose freely of their revenues and can hence invest in the establishment of a cooperative. However, in spite of this more favourable legal framework, traditional norms and practice prevailing in certain regions of the country do not look positively on this autonomy.

In addition to the obstacles related to land or credit, women face constraints of a more general nature, such as the legal complexity of the cooperative legislation or by-laws. Even if the very technical formulation of these texts affects both men and women, the latter are generally more disadvantaged, especially in developing countries, as they have often not benefited from the same educational opportunities as men. Handicapped by illiteracy and poor knowledge of their legal rights, many women may also not trust the efficiency of the available legal enforcement mechanisms. Cooperative legislation contains relatively complex legal procedures and requirements both in the establishment and running of cooperatives. Thus, instead of providing a facilitative tool for the formation of cooperatives, cooperative legislation and complex by-laws can in many cases act as a deterrent.

Finally, cultural traditions and practices vis-à-vis women's role and status in society add to the legal obstacles faced by women. However, with the currently changing economic context, where women play an increasing economic role even in the most traditional societies, their status is called to change accordingly. Thus in Lesotho where a significant number of men migrate for employment purposes, women become *de facto* family heads and have to adopt important economic decisions in the absence of their husbands. It is therefore important that women are afforded equal opportunities and treatment for example, in applying for credit to start their own businesses, as this would clearly benefits the country socio-economically as a whole. Likewise, in Cameroon, the economic crisis that has prevailed since the mid-1980s, characterized by drastic drops in incomes and declining standards of living, has resulted in deep mutations in the society. In this context, women have initiated economic activities in order to survive and their newfound "productive" role has had repercussions on the cooperative sector where women are today more active and numerous in number than ever before.

Access to Cooperative Services

Membership in cooperative enterprises entails obligations but also rights, among which are the use of the services provided by the cooperatives as stipulated in their bylaws. Cooperative legislation may also explicitly refer to members' equitable access to cooperative services without any form of discrimination. For example, in the 1992 Cooperative Act of Cameroon, it is stated —

> any member shall have the right to ... use the services and facilities of the cooperative society under the conditions ... (section 13(1)).

However, in the 1997 Cooperative Act of Tanzania, "gender" is expressly stated as a prohibited ground for discrimination upon providing cooperative services. Cooperatives provide a whole range of social and/or economic services to their members according to the type of cooperative and the economic sector in which they operate, be it agriculture, banking, consumer, housing, health, insurance and so on. However, a first limitation to women accessing cooperative services follows from the restrictions described above regarding the constraints women face in joining or forming cooperatives. As cooperative services are usually restricted to members only, which is the case for instance under the 1964 ACPS Act (India), women who are impeded from joining or forming cooperatives, are hence also barred from obtaining cooperative services.

Moreover, in Thailand, for instance, where the agricultural cooperatives apply the "one member per household" rule, women, even though they contribute to the work of the cooperative, do not benefit directly from its services as the male members do. In Burkina Faso, social prejudices appear to hamper women's access to cooperative services, and male members are consequently given priority. Accordingly, restricted access to membership and to creation of cooperatives, constitutes *per se* a first severely restricting constraint to women's access to cooperative services.

Other barriers pertain to the necessity of acquiring the husband's consent prior to benefiting from cooperative services as, in many cases, married women not only depend on their husband's approval upon joining or setting up a cooperative, but also at all subsequent stages. Such a situation is reported to prevail in the Philippines, where women under the Civil Code are limited from the enjoyment of full contractual rights, and cannot thus freely enter contracts for the purpose of benefiting from cooperative services without marital consent. Moreover, the applicable family property laws (with obvious consequences on access to cooperative services as family assets may be needed for the purpose of benefiting from certain of these services), grant the husband the final say in case of disagreement. A second example can be found in Thailand where the legislation requires marital consent equally from either the husband or wife before carrying out transactions that pledge common family assets, except for financial services. However, the legal enforcement of this prerequisite remains imbalanced. In practice, married women are always required to produce documents proving their legal status, whereas married men are seldom asked to do so due to traditional practices. Finally, despite existing legal court remedies available for women in order to contest their husband's decision, such remedies are rarely used as women lack resources, legal literacy as well as legal aid.

Education and training constitute an essential part of the services provided by cooperatives. One of the principles of the international cooperative movement states:

> Cooperatives provide training and education for their members, elected representatives, managers, and employees so they can contribute effectively to the development of their cooperatives...

ILO Recommendation No. 193 further recommends that measures should be adopted to promote the potential of cooperatives to develop the capacities and knowledge of the values, advantages and benefits of the cooperative movement through education and training (paragraph 4). Moreover, national policies should develop technical and vocational skills, entrepreneurial and managerial abilities, knowledge of business potential and general economic and social policy skills of cooperative members, workers and managers improve their access to information and communication technologies. The promotion of education and training in cooperative principles and practices at all appropriate levels of national education and training systems is also encouraged.

However, it appears that women are often excluded from cooperative training and education programmes. According to the case studies, this regularly occurs when the training courses require a certain level of prior education, knowledge or experience, which many women do not have, as they have not had the same opportunities as men due to cultural or other barriers. In addition, according to the Philippines case study, male rather than female members are more often selected to attend cooperative meetings and workshops. This is seen particularly in the case where traveling is involved, such as to regional workshops.

In this context, it is worth reiterating that if "Special consideration should to be given to increasing women's participation in the cooperative movement at all levels, particularly at management and leadership levels", as proposed in paragraph 7(3) of ILO Recommendation No. 193, more women members and employees of cooperatives should identified, encouraged and selected by cooperatives to participate in human resource development initiatives.

Other constraints, of a socio-economic or of a purely cultural nature, also hamper women from accessing cooperative services, such as in Ecuador where the concentration of cooperatives in large or medium sized urban centres impedes women from benefiting who live far away from the available cooperative services. A heavy workload of productive and reproductive tasks also renders it more difficult for women to profit from services as they have little time available for this purpose, let alone time to travel great distances. Finally lack of access to information, as reported to be the case in Ecuador, also hamper women in their access to services, as they are often not aware of the services available to them.

Access to Decision-Making

Decision-Making in cooperatives takes place on the membership-level through voting in general assemblies and on the executive-level through decisions taken by elected officials in management committees or boards of directors. The voting rights of members constitutes an essential characteristic of cooperatives as defined in the universally adopted cooperative principles: In primary cooperatives members have equal voting rights (one member, one vote) and cooperatives at other levels are also organized in a democratic manner. With regard to women exercising this right, their restricted access to membership in cooperatives is a hindrance as only members are entitled to vote. A second constraint reported in several countries, is of a cultural nature and relates to women members being afraid to or lacking the confidence to express their opinions publicly in meetings where men are present.

Decision-making in cooperatives also entails active involvement in designing policies and adopting decisions on behalf of the members in the different cooperative decision making bodies (e.g. management committee, supervisory committee etc.). According to the cooperative principles, men and women serving as elected representatives are accountable to the membership, acknowledging thereby explicitly gender equality and equity.

ILO Recommendation No. 193 refers specifically to women's participation in cooperative decision-making by recommending:

> "Special consideration be given to increasing women's participation in the cooperative movement at all levels, particularly at management and leadership levels."(paragraph 7(3)).

In this regard, cooperative legislation in a number of countries, such as in India or Lesotho, is reported not to discriminate against women, but a closer scrutiny of reality however reveals constraints to women involvement at the decision-making level. In effect, in addition to women's restricted access to membership, their similarly restricted access to educational and training facilities, hampers them in taking up leadership roles as they consequently lack the necessary experience, knowledge and skills required.

Thus, according to the Ecuador study, the limited extent to which women are involved in cooperative decision-making is a direct consequence of their limited participation in training activities. Figures reveal that, despite women representing an estimated overall 40 per cent of cooperative membership, their presence at management level does not exceed more than 8 per cent, a figure that moreover reflects women's participation at political level in general in the country. Additional reasons given in the case studies for the low proportion of women in high-level positions include the lack of institutional incentives to promote women and cultural values, particularly the belief that men possess natural leadership skills as opposed to women. In Fiji, women are also reported to have less access to cooperative specific training activities with direct negative repercussions on their representation at higher decision-making level. In Cameroon, women members can apparently benefit from cooperative services, including educational and training facilities. However, due to their heavy workload, their participation in training activities is low compared to that of men.

The educational level of women is generally not the only barrier to women being elected to decision-making positions in cooperatives, as the case study of Lesotho reveals. It is here reported that despite women's access to higher education in the country, they still remain largely under-represented in decision-making processes. Cultural factors and the traditional gender division of labour, whereby women are responsible for household tasks and the cultivation of family land, effectively bar them from acceding to decision-making positions in cooperatives.

The relationship between the educational level of women and their representation in decision-making organs becomes apparent when comparing the situation in rural and urban areas. Rural women generally have much poorer access to schools and training facilities, and thus frequently lack the necessary skills for active involvement in cooperative management, as reported in Tanzania. In urban centres educational facilities are more easily accessible. Likewise, in Morocco, it is reported that there are approximately 32 per cent women in leadership positions in enterprises in the formal economy, as opposed to 3.5 per cent in rural areas in the agricultural sector, a number that suggests a direct link between education level, leadership and traditions, as the latter are particularly prevalent in rural areas.

A further distinction should be drawn between primary, secondary and tertiary level cooperatives, as, under the 1964 APCS Act in India, even though women are involved in decision-making at the primary level, they are seldom elected into leadership positions in secondary level cooperatives or federations. Under this Act, certain types of cooperatives reserve two seats for women in the Management Committee, which has increased the number of women but has not brought them to key executive positions in the sub-committees. This provision is, however, only applicable to certain types of primary cooperatives and not to secondary or tertiary level cooperatives, with the consequence that women seldom reach leadership positions in the latter levels.

Even though subsequently withdrawn from the Act, another provision is worth mentioning, namely the prohibition of being elected to a leadership level position for a third consecutive term. This rule led certain men to promote their wives to be elected in their place, which allowed them to continue exercising their former functions *de facto* and thus to circumvent the rule. It also distorted the figures regarding the number of women in leadership positions.

In addition to constraints of a legal character, other barriers, of a cultural nature hamper women participating in the formulation and implementation of decisions in cooperatives. These, already partly depicted above, pertain to the position of women in society in general where, for example in Cameroon, men are considered to be the family head and thus assume the responsibilities incumbent to the household, as provided for in section 214 of the Civil Code. Although women in Cameroon generally tend to keep silent in meetings when there are men present, there are nevertheless, a number of cases where women's participation in decision-making is relatively high, such as in the common initiative groups. In certain Muslim areas, however, where traditional norms and practices are strongly adhered to, women cannot even sit on the same board or committee as men.

The case studies from the Philippines and Thailand report that even though legislation does not outwardly favour men for leadership functions, women are traditionally perceived as incapable of assuming leadership roles, which effectively bars them. Forming women only cooperatives may offer an appropriate means to enable women to exercise their activities without cultural constraints. Women would be free to organize themselves according to their specific needs, and to gain organizational experience, confidence and leadership skills. In the Philippines, for example, women-only cooperatives have succeeded in combining the strengths of women to stand against exploitative tendencies in society. Respect for women is often related to economic independence and experience has shown that women who participate in cooperative groups are often much less likely to be victims of violence since they are income earners but also because cooperatives offer them security and protection. Moreover, women's cooperatives and self-help groups have often been favoured by policy-makers and donor agencies and have consequently managed to build up women's organizational structures, which can function as an economical and political force to be reckoned with.

It must be added, however, that women-only cooperatives have not been particularly effective in changing the subordinate status of women in society. Women cooperatives have, in general, led to the separation of women from mainstream cooperative activities. It is therefore important that women cooperatives work together through local, national, regional and international structures and that these structures in turn promote, encourage and facilitate the advancement of women in cooperative decision-making.

Finally, it can be mentioned that women be benefited from increased and active participation in cooperatives. But equally important is the fact that cooperatives will also be benefited from gender integration. Women represent 50 per cent of the world's human resource but this human resource is under-utilized. By enhancing women's productive capabilities and developing their capacities, cooperatives can be benefited from this untapped resource. Many women have, for example, special indigenous knowledge, or particular skills in marketing and trading. In the case of agricultural cooperatives, the involvement of more women in economic activities would result in a more integrated production of food crops and cash crops. This would subsequently enhance food security and have a positive effect on the environment as intensive monoculture causes soil erosion and degradation. Involving more women in cooperatives and especially in decision-making, would also broaden the scope of cooperatives and make them a stronger and more influential political force. Men and women often tackle and solve problems differently. In today's rapidly changing socio-economic and political climate, the need for innovative thinking and creative ideas is becoming more and more important, especially for the cooperative sector.

CASE STUDIES

INDIA

Legal Constraints to Women's Participation in Cooperatives

In India, each state has enacted its own cooperative law. A state law applies to cooperatives whose membership is confined to persons from that state. Although state laws have dissimilarities, they have, overall, several common provisions, especially in relation to formation, registration, membership requirements, management, winding up of cooperatives, and the roles of the Registrar and the government vis-à-vis cooperatives.

Where a cooperative has members from more than one state, it is registered under the central law, that is, the Multi-State Cooperative Societies Act, 1984. Since 1995, states have begun the process of enacting an additional cooperative law for such cooperatives as do not have Government share capital, and are fully owned by their members. That is, since 1995, the states of Andhra Pradesh, Bihar, Jammu & Kashmir, and Madhya Pradesh have two cooperative laws - the older law with all its regulations, and a newer liberal law for existing and new cooperatives which do not seek/have Government share capital, and wish to be fully responsible for their own actions. A few other states are engaged in the process of introducing parallel laws. The co-existence of two cooperative laws is seen as a temporary feature, to enable cooperatives heavily dependent on Governmental financial and non-financial resources to make the shift to greater self-reliance and full autonomy. The interim period is also seen as a measure to enable over-sized departments of cooperation to become more compact, and not to expect to be deputed to cooperatives at their expense. In this review of cooperative legislation in India in relation to women's participation in the cooperative movement, three cooperative laws and their application have been reviewed:

- The Andhra Pradesh Cooperative Societies Act, 1964 (APCS Act).
- The Multi-State Cooperative Societies Act, 1984 (MSCS Act).
- The Andhra Pradesh Mutually Aided Cooperative Societies Act, 1995 (APMACS Act).

The three reviews together will present a wholesome, even though a far from complete picture, of legal restraints across India to women's participation in cooperatives. It needs to be remembered that in India the first cooperative law was enacted at the start of the twentieth century, primarily for the formation of farmers' thrift and credit cooperatives, in order to provide them with an alternative to usurious moneylenders. Since then, even though other forms of cooperatives have emerged, and even though thrift has been neglected, much of cooperative legislation across India is framed keeping in view cooperatives engaged in rural credit disbursement.

This report contains the findings of the study of the two cooperative laws currently operational in the state of Andhra Pradesh and of the cooperative law applicable to cooperatives with membership from more than one state. The findings are being presented under the following headings:

- Formation of cooperatives by women
- Membership of women in existing cooperatives
- Use of cooperative services by women
- Women's leadership in cooperatives

A summary of the reviews of the three cooperative laws is provided in the final section. Under each section, related legal provisions, if any, in each of the three laws studied, have been identified, and their impact on women's presence in cooperatives examined. Where there are no directly related legal provisions, the effect of related provisions in other laws, or of the absence of any legal provision in cooperative law has been examined.

Formation of Cooperatives by Women

APCS Act and Formation of Cooperatives by Women

Section 4 of the APCS Act provides that a society which has as its main object the promotion of the economic interests of its members, in accordance with cooperative principles, may be registered under this Act. Section 6(2)(b), however, requires that individuals applying for the registration of a cooperative must necessarily be from different families. Men and women belonging to the same family may well want to set up housing cooperatives or weavers cooperatives, or other cooperatives in which men and women have an equal stake. Because of this section, however, most such cooperatives are formed by men and, more often than not, women relatives do not become members even subsequently. Section 7(c) of the APCS Act requires the Registrar to be satisfied before registering a new cooperative, that its registration will not have an adverse effect on the development of the cooperative movement. The Indian countryside is dotted with primary agricultural credit cooperatives (PACs), which are used by governments and public funding agencies to channel subsidized credit to rural areas. The PAC is perceived by most Registrars as able to meet all the economic needs of all rural families. Any other cooperative for thrift and credit is, therefore, perceived as competition and likely to affect the viability of the existing PAC. Consequently, Sec 7(c) has often been used to deny registration to rural women who have wished to form their own thrift and credit cooperatives. Sections 6 and 7 have resulted in women being projected as consumers in the cooperative sector, as women's consumer cooperatives alone are easily registered. This is not to say that other cooperatives have not been formed by women under this Act, but they are insignificant in number. Rural women have been permitted to establish all women's dairy cooperatives but that is perhaps because the Registrar for credit cooperatives is different from the Registrar for dairy cooperatives.

Rule 52(5)(a) of the APCS Rules 1964, framed under the APCS Act 1964, when laying down the procedure to be followed in the seizure and sale of movable property of defaulting members specifies: "If the defaulter is absent, the sale officer shall serve the demand notice on some adult male member of his family". There is a clear assumption that membership is for men, and that women are not even competent to receive notices. In 1984, the Cooperative Development Foundation had commissioned an independent study on the APCS Act 1964. When the Study Group on APCS Act held public hearings in 1994 at several places in Andhra Pradesh, many women met the group and expressed their need to register formally their unregistered cooperatives. They expressed their unwillingness to register under the existing APCS Act, saying that even if the Registrar did agree to their registration, they did not want to lose their autonomy, and were very uncomfortable with several provisions in the Act. The Study Group observed in its report: "It is indeed ironic that individuals sincerely wedded to the principles are unable to get their association registered under cooperative law in the ordinary course, while some others are unwilling to be so registered for fear of undue interference and unreasonable restrictions. Some instances which struck us poignantly during the hearings are narrated below.

The President of the Rudramma Devi Mahila Podupu Sangham of Makdumpuram area of Warangal district met us and gave us the following details. The work of mobilizing women around thrift and credit began in 1990. These groups explained that they wanted to be registered as cooperatives, but were afraid of losing their right to control their own affairs; that they had been advised by their well-wishers to register as societies under Societies Registration Act rather than as cooperatives, since Government interfered too much in the latter. All had the same story to tell — that they began as small scattered groups, then merged voluntarily, that some are in the process of voluntary division, since in their view the membership had become unwieldy; that they appointed their own staff, locally, on terms set by them; that they elected their own leaders and replaced them when they did not perform; that they changed their by-laws when needed; that they had appointed their own auditor, and presented their printed annual report and audited accounts each year at their respective general body meetings which had more than 75 per cent member attendance; that they declared a bonus each year on thrift and on loans taken. This amount was not immediately disbursed, but set up as a separate fund in each member's account, to be withdrawn only in the event of resignation from membership, the interest accruing there from being used in the meantime to cover outstanding loans of deceased members. We were pleasantly surprised to hear that they have also taken up computerization of their accounts, and are in the process of setting up a common association for the purpose of providing important support services such as insurance. When asked what help they got from external agencies, they said that all they got was good advice and training. They were clear that they needed no other kind of help.

MSCS Act and Formation of Cooperatives by Women

Section 5 of the MSCS Act provides that a society which aims at economic and social betterment of its members, drawn from more than one state, through mutual aid and in accordance with cooperative principles, may be registered under this Act. Section 6 requires a minimum of 50 individuals to set up a cooperative, and unlike the APCS Act, this Act does not require that the applicants be from different families. It should be possible, therefore, for women to set up cooperatives, either by themselves, or with men, related or unrelated. It may be noted that the total number of cooperatives registered under the MSCS Act is less than 400, and of these, the majority are those which existed at the time when the Act came into force, and were "deemed" to be registered under this Act because of membership from more than one state.

Section 7 requires the Registrar to be satisfied that the proposed cooperative has a good chance of becoming viable, and that it does not have an area of operation similar to, and objects identical to that of another existing cooperative. As in the case of the APCS Act, this can be used to deny women the right to set up their own cooperative where men have already established a similar one. Registration under the MSCS Act is done in Delhi, and even if women did get together across states (and languages) to set up cooperatives, they would need to liaise with the Central Registrar in Delhi for registering their cooperative.

APMACS Act and Formation of Cooperatives by Women

Section 3 requires that those intending to form a cooperative under this Act frame bylaws in accordance with the cooperative principles. Section 4(1) requires that individuals wishing to form a cooperative must come from different families. As in the case of the APCS Act, this can come in the way of women/men joining men/women relatives in forming a cooperative with equal stakes. Section 4(4) dealing with the actual registration of a cooperative, does not provide for the Registrar to prevent the formation of a cooperative by women if another "similar" cooperative already exists in the same area. On the field, this has translated to several women's cooperatives being formed in rural areas especially around savings and credit, and around milk marketing.

Membership of Women in Cooperatives

APCS Act and Membership of Women in Cooperatives

There is nothing in the APCS Act which prevents membership of women in cooperatives, apart from the spirit of Section 6(2) already discussed. A special provision had been introduced permitting men and women from the same weaver families to have membership in weavers' cooperatives. This provision has since been deleted. Model by-laws of many cooperatives require that only one person from a family may be a member, and in practice, it is usually a man. Where women own agricultural land in their own names, they are permitted to be members of PACs. While male agricultural workers are given membership in PACs, women without land are very rarely taken in as members. Agricultural labourers rarely get good service from a PAC and, therefore, women's lack of access to membership in PACs may not be such a loss.

The Hindu Succession Act, 1956 governs the rights of Hindus, who form a majority of the population of India, and provides for devolution of ancestral (not acquired) property, and of interstate property. This Act applies to the whole of India with such amendments as may have been made by the legislature of each state. In 1985, Andhra Pradesh introduced a few provisions providing for equal rights to daughters in co-parcenary property. Therefore, women can and do get a share of agricultural land. However, as they tend to live away from their parental families, in the villages of their husbands, they are not residents of the villages in which they might have a share in agricultural property. This, too, is a reason for their not being members of PACs.

On the other hand, women are members in dairy cooperatives which permit only women to become members, as well as in dairy cooperatives with mixed membership. Women are members in consumer cooperatives, usually with all women membership, and in urban cooperative banks, exclusively of women. In some urban cooperative banks with primarily male membership, some women, too, have become members.

MSCS Act and Membership of Women in Cooperatives

There is nothing in the APCS Act which prevents membership of women in cooperatives, as there was nothing in it which came in the way of women forming their own cooperatives, or forming cooperatives along with men. However, perhaps because of the levels of mobilising and organizing skills needed to establish and manage cooperatives with membership from across various states, women's membership appears to be insignificant in cooperatives registered under the MSCS Act. As has already been mentioned, very few men, too, have established cooperatives under the MSCS Act. Many of the cooperatives registered under this Act are centred around savings and credit for the urban male workforce, in the organized sector, where the employer has branches in more than one state.

APMACS Act and Membership of Women in Cooperatives

There is nothing in the APMACS Act to prevent women from obtaining membership in cooperatives. As there is no provision for the framing of model bylaws by the Registrar, cooperatives are free to frame their own bylaws to accept women and men as members. As has already been mentioned, thousands of women have voluntarily joined as members of cooperatives under this Act. There are some instances of mixed membership, too, but not in any way comparable with membership in all women's cooperatives. The requirement under Section 4(1) that applicants for registration of a cooperative come from different families, is applied only for the time of registration. Subsequently more than one woman from a family, and women alongside male relatives become members of cooperatives, if they so wish to, and if the by-laws so permit. Each woman is treated as an individual, and not as a member of a family, except at the time of registration.

Use of Cooperative Services by Women

APCS Act and Use of Cooperative Services by Women

Under Section 22, every member is entitled to the services that a cooperative offers its members, subject to its availability. If a member is refused a service, s/he may approach the Registrar, who may direct the cooperative to render the service. This section is applicable to women and men. Even though very few women are members of cooperatives registered under this Act, there were no instances which came to light of women having approached the Registrar on grounds of gender discrimination. However, people have sough redress on grounds of caste and class discrimination.

Section 48(1) and the corresponding Rule 42 prohibit cooperatives from having any transactions with non-members, except if the bylaws provide for such transaction and if the approval of the Registrar has been obtained. Legally this implies that since few women are members of cooperatives in the first instance, they cannot access the services of cooperatives.

Section 20 provides for nominal or associate membership. A nominal/associate member can access some services but has neither the right of vote nor a share in the surplus, if any. Very few, if any, cooperatives have women as nominal or associate members, alongside male relatives with full fledged membership — not even housing cooperatives, which might find such an arrangement useful even though the house is usually in the name of the man. Some PACs are covered by the Public Distribution System through which subsidized food grains and other food items are channelled. Since ration cards are provided to all families in a village, women who are heads of households and who otherwise may not be eligible to be members become nominal/associate members, in order to purchase the subsidized food items.

The APSC Act appears to treat cooperatives as extension agents of the Government for the fulfilment of important public service. Therefore, women and men who are members are seen more as beneficiaries of services than as organizers-cum-users of services. Through Section 18 of the Act, the Registrar can classify cooperatives on the basis of their purpose and membership, and through Section 16, and Rule 4, the Registrar can amend the bylaws of any cooperative altering membership and purpose. This has resulted in members not identifying with a cooperative as theirs, and women and men who are members are expected to be thankful for services rendered to them, if any.

MSCS Act and Use of Cooperative Services by Women

Section 65 of the MSCS Act places some restrictions on transactions with nonmembers, and as women are, by and large, not members of cooperatives under this Act, they do not access services of cooperatives registered under this Act. Women who are members of cooperatives can of course access the services of their cooperative.

APMACS Act and Use of Cooperative Services by Women

The letter and spirit of the APMACS Act require that those who are members use the services of the cooperative and accept responsibility for its functioning, if they wish to exercise their right to vote, their right to contest, and their right to continue as members.

Section 9(2)(vi) requires the by-laws to set minimum performance standards for members in relation to use of services and participation. As women are members of cooperatives under this Act, most of them are active members and can access services. Section 19(3), too, requires that members fulfil the conditions required in the by-laws before they exercise the right of vote.

Section 19(1) specifies that any person who needs the services of a cooperative and is willing to fulfill the responsibilities of membership may be admitted as a member, provided that the cooperative is in a position to offer its services to the applicant. This effectively puts paid to membership for membership's sake, and women are admitted (as are men) only if these conditions are fulfilled. Women who are admitted as members, therefore, do access the cooperative's services.

The APMACS Act expects members through Sections 16 and 17 to share deficit just as they expect to share surpluses in any given year. As a result, the financial stake of members in their cooperative is higher, as is their sense of identity with their cooperative. Women who are members, therefore, expect good service from their cooperative, and also help design the services and their organization in a manner that is useful to them. Section 9 expects the members to define their agenda and frame their own bylaws, and this, too, results in an active membership which owns the cooperative and its actions. These sections are not particular to women, but they are key to ensuring that women and disadvantaged men who are not used to defining, designing and managing institutions think through their cooperative and control it effectively.

Women's Leadership in Cooperatives

APCS Act and Women's Leadership in Cooperatives

In 1970, a provision had been added to the APCS Act preventing a committee member from contesting elections in his/her cooperative for a third consecutive term. This provision was overcome by some PAC Presidents by putting forward their wives as candidates for the third term, and then contesting again the next term. Although some women did become presidents of cooperatives in this manner, their husbands were the actual leaders. The provision has since been deleted.

Between 1992 and 1995, the APCS Act had a provision through which the Registrar could nominate two women to the managing committees of certain "classes" of cooperatives. Although the provision had been introduced supposedly because of Government's interest in advancing the cause of women, the provision was misused to tilt election results, as the nominees could vote for the election of the President from among the committee members. All women cooperatives with all women managing committees, such as some dairy cooperatives, too, found to their dismay that the Registrar nominated two women even to their committees. This provision was later omitted and in its place Section 31(1)(b) backed by Rule 22-A(2) now provides for two seats on the managing committee to be reserved for women in certain types of cooperatives. This certainly did bring many women into elected office in cooperatives, but the provision did little to bring women to the fore in cooperative leadership. In what women perceived to be primarily male domain, two women on the committee and few on the membership could do little to mark their presence.

In all women's cooperatives, women indeed are elected to the managing committees at primary levels. However, the numbers of primaries returning women leaders is few, and as a result, at secondary and tertiary tiers, women do not get elected as leaders. Rule 22-A(2) which contains a table on reservations in various types of cooperatives, does not provide for reservation for women in secondary and tertiary tiers. Section 21-B specifies that a committee member who is absent at three consecutive committee meetings, ceases to be a committee member, but such continued absence may be overlooked once during his/her term. As a result, even where women are required to be elected to office, their absence from meetings is condoned, and it is rare that they actively participate in decision-making.

MSCS Act and Women's Leadership in Cooperatives

The MSCS Act has no provision barring women from holding elected office, as it also has no provision requiring that they be elected.

APMACS Act and Women's Leadership in Cooperatives

The APMACS Act does not either have provisions barring women from being elected, or reserving seats for women to be elected to the Boards of Directors (managing committees) of cooperatives. However, as women have not been prevented from forming cooperatives under this Act, they have formed several primary and secondary cooperatives, either by themselves, or with men, and are in positions of leadership in several cooperatives.

A number of sections in the Act require women (and men) elected to office to perform as leaders, and indeed women who are in leadership positions in cooperatives under the APMACS Act, do strive to be good leaders. For example, Section 17 requires the Board of a cooperative with an annual deficit, to explain to its general body the reasons for the deficit, and to either set it off against a deficit reserve, or to debit it to the accounts of members as patronage rebate would have been had there been a surplus. Section 21(3) requires that the Directors have staggered terms, so that even if new persons join the Board, there are enough old hands to help them settle in. This is particularly helpful when women who have never before held an elected office choose to accept leadership responsibility.

Under Section 21(5), a director who is absent from 3 consecutive Board meetings or one general meeting without leave of absence, ceases to be director. This ensures that women elected to Boards participate in decision-making processes. Section 21 (6) specifies that a director ceases to be a director if audit, elections or annual meetings are not organized in time. This places responsibility on directors to perform and puts pressure on women to learn quickly about and fulfil their responsibilities as able and accountable leaders. Section 21(7) requires that, except in the first two years of a cooperative's existence, a person wishing to contest elections should have been a voting member for at least two years, and should have attended the last two general body meetings.

These conditions help women to come into leadership positions on their own merit, and not through any reservation policy. Section 23(6) specifies that if the bylaws so permit, a person may be eligible for re-election. Where women want to be re-elected, and where a general body, too, wants them back, it becomes possible to develop leadership over lengths of time. Although these provisions apply as much to men as they do to women, they are very helpful to persons who are new to leadership (such as most women and disadvantaged men) to take their roles seriously. Women leaders of cooperatives under the new law do, by and large, take full responsibility for their cooperatives.

Conclusions

This review of the APCS Act from the viewpoint of women's presence and participation in cooperatives, and the manner in which the law is applied reveal the following:

- Women are treated as members of a family possibly headed by men, and there is an underlying assumption that if a cooperative can meet "the family's needs", the setting up of a separate cooperative by women is not warranted and may affect an existing cooperative's business.
- Women are projected as consumers, and women's consumer cooperatives have been promoted by the Government.
- In rural areas, even if the local PAC is not working, women have been denied the right to set up their own cooperatives, as have men who have wanted to set up a new cooperative.
- Especially in rural areas, the PAC is expected to be all things to all people, and other proposed cooperatives around savings, credit, agricultural inputs and agricultural produce are usually denied registration under this Act, and women have tried and been refused registration.
- Women-only cooperatives for marketing of milk have been registered under the Act.
- Women from families with male membership in a cooperative, are discouraged from also becoming members through the by-laws and through conditions of lending.

- Women who establish unregistered cooperatives and find these beneficial, want to have their cooperatives registered, but are worried to register under the APCS Act because of its innumerable restrictive provisions.
- The APCS Act is a very restrictive piece of legislation, and one which respects neither the intelligence of the members, nor the integrity of the cooperative. It is based on mistrust and an undermining of the common woman and man, and it may not be such a loss to women that they have not been active participants in cooperatives registered under this Act.

The review of the MSCS Act in regard to women's participation in cooperatives reveals that:

- The MSCS Act seems to have very little which prevents women from either forming cooperatives or obtaining membership in cooperatives.
- Since, however, only a handful of registrations have taken place anyhow since 1985 when the Act in its present form came into effect, the problem lies perhaps with the fact that registrations take place in Delhi, and that may be a deterrent to women forming cooperatives under it.
- Again, since a cooperative registered under the MSCS Act needs to have members from more than one state, and since states are organized on the basis of language spoken by the people residing there, it is probably difficult for many women to form primary cooperatives across states.
- Women could have benefited from secondary cooperatives under the MSCS Act, which is not very liberal but is not nearly as illiberal as the APCS Act. However, as women have formed few primaries under the APCS Act, they do not have the numbers needed to identify similar groups in other states to form secondary cooperatives.
- Women who have formed primaries and secondary cooperatives under the APMACS Act, could form secondary and tertiary level cooperatives under the MSCS Act, but since the APMACS Act is only 5 years old, this may take a while longer. However, it is likely that women will want the MSCS Act to give them the autonomy they have under the APMACS Act, and, they will probably be able to collaborate with cooperatives from only such other states as have liberal cooperative legislation.

The review of the APMACS Act with regard to women's participation in cooperatives reveals that:

- The Act permits multiple cooperatives even for the same purposes in any given area and, as a result, women have been able to form cooperatives quite easily under this Act.

- Women have been able to design their own cooperatives around issues of concern to them, and in a manner they find appropriate since the law expects them to frame their own bylaws.
- The Act is simple and gives full autonomy to cooperatives registered under it placing commensurate responsibility on the members and the leaders.
- As a result, women who have formed cooperatives under this Act take their role as members and as leaders very seriously.
- Women leaders of cooperatives under this Act are treated as leaders by their larger community as well, as they have not got into positions of leadership through any affirmative policy, but in their own right.

What this study revealed was that women do not need any special provisions in cooperative legislation. If they can think through their own organization, if registration is simple and free from hindrances, if they have stake in their cooperative, if the management of their cooperative is to be in accordance with cooperative principles and by them, then they want to register their cooperatives and want to and can work them effectively. Women need a law which does not prevent them from forming cooperatives for needs perceived by them, and which respects their intelligence and competence to manage their own affairs. They need a law which does not come in the way of setting up their own cooperatives, or collaborating with men to jointly set up cooperatives. Ground realities have shown that given a non-interfering law which holds cooperators accountable for their actions, women can and do form cooperatives, benefit from them, and manage them well.

Summary

- In order to have a more comprehensive understanding of the legal constraints that women face in their full and equal participation in cooperative enterprises, a brief overview of the general legal framework, in which these enterprises operate is necessary as cooperative legislation takes various forms worldwide, and as other related legislation may also seriously impair women participation.
- Moreover, even though the language used in legislation may not be outwardly discriminating, the legal system may be construed as discriminating against women in concrete terms.
- There should be a conducive legal framework or legal reforms must be to encourage women to involve more in cooperatives to make them empowered.

Self-Learning Activity

Try to answer the following questions on your own:

1. Critically discuss legal constraint in access to membership for women.
2. What does prevent women as legal constraint not to have access to decision making?

19 Suitable Cooperatives for Women and Women's Cooperatives

Reasons to Organize Separate Women's Cooperatives

Though mixed cooperatives with open membership theoretically allow women to become members, in practice in many developing countries, women are directly and indirectly prevented in becoming members. Even if they become members, they are prevented to contest for elections and to get the services of the cooperatives. One of the solutions to this issue is to organise cooperatives exclusively for women.

In Japan and Sweden women consumer cooperatives are running successfully. In India women cooperatives are formed in the fields of cooperative banking, consumer cooperatives, dairy cooperatives and handicraft cooperatives. In India, which has the largest and strongest dairy cooperative sector, 13,000 primary dairy cooperatives have been organised exclusively for women. The reasons why separate cooperatives can be organised for women are as follows:

1. Majority of the population in developing countries live in rural areas and rural women need to be emancipated through cooperatives.
2. At the village level, at present the ownership of land goes to men in the order of priority. Only widows can retain land. This prevents women to take the services of cooperatives, or they will be at the mercy men folk to get services.
3. Through exclusive women cooperatives, women can get loan and can engage in employment and income generating activities.
4. Women can exercise leadership qualities and can improve their qualities and managerial talents.
5. Through secured income they can reduce their dependence on their husbands and avoid male domination or they can substitute the income of their husbands and can take care of their family.

SUITABLE COOPERATIVES FOR WOMEN IN ETHIOPIA

Following are some of the suitable cooperatives for women:

Credit Cooperatives/Cooperative Banks

Credit cooperatives or cooperative banks will fit in to the needs of unemployed and destitute women. Through such cooperatives they can finance and engage in small business and self-employment activities. Organising exclusive women cooperative banks, though a difficult process can help the women through the following ways:

1. Cooperative banks can help women to save their small income, because women are particular in saving money.
2. Cooperative banks can teach various baking habits to women, which can be passed on to other women and their children.
3. Leadership opportunities and democratic management practices can be taught to women members.
4. Cooperative banks can recruit only women employees and provide employment opportunities.
5. Small businesses and self-employment can be encouraged by cooperative banks.

Consumer Cooperatives

Consumer cooperatives world over gained success out of the patronage and business extended by women members. The better option is to organise exclusive women consumer cooperatives. Women consumer cooperatives can be organised in urban areas, where educated women can find good outlet for consumer goods purchasing. The advantages of exclusive women consumer cooperatives are as follows:

1. Women take the responsibility to purchase consumer goods in majority of the homes and it is natural to have their own consumer cooperatives.
2. The employees of such consumer cooperatives can be women also, there employment to one section of women can be taken care.
3. They can go for quality operations and can go for quality goods.

Dairy Cooperatives

Dairy cooperatives of India have made great success only due to the active involvement of women. The same example can be followed by Ethiopia, another developing country. Through dairy cooperatives women can get regular income and can avoid the exploitation of private milk vendors. Women dairy cooperatives offer the following advantages:

1. Rural women can get regular income and can supplement the income of their husbands.
2. It will fully engage the labour of rural women, otherwise the labour is wasted at present.
3. They can combine the farm works with that of the dairying, and they need not spend additional time and labour exclusively for dairying.

Handicrafts Cooperatives

Developing countries have popular and very old handicrafts and artisan works. This industry at present is facing problems like marketing, finance etc. Bringing such industry under the fold women cooperatives can save the industry from extinction. Further, this industry can be revitalised through cooperative fold by providing better finance, marketing and export outlets.

Women SACCOs (Savings and Credit Cooperatives)

These cooperatives are micro credit institutions, which are very popular and widely organised in many countries. These cooperatives collect small amounts of deposits from the members, pool them and give them as loans to members. The purposes for which the loans are given are to set small shops, grain trading, improved stove making, setting small cloth shops etc. Many of the women members who are destitute and divorced by their husbands are helped very much by these cooperatives.

Women Employees Cooperatives

These are the cooperatives meant for women working in government and private organisations. Such cooperatives are in the form of SACCOs, consumer cooperatives and cooperative banks. Through cooperatives women get managerial and leadership training and experiences.

WOMEN'S AGRICULTURAL COOPERATIVES

Agricultural cooperatives have played an important role in rural development in mobilizing limited resources for farmers and producers. Many traditional cooperatives continue to hold governing structures not conducive to women's free participation as they are governed by a primarily male-dominated structure. For gender mainstreaming in rural development, it is important to promote women's participation in cooperative entrepreneurship. While there has been increasing awareness toward balancing the gender power structure in traditional cooperatives, the gender bias in traditional cooperatives remains difficult to overcome. Transforming in traditional cooperatives, the conditions proliferating gender inequity is a tedious process requiring dismantling entrenched male bias in the governing structure.

In many developing countries, women work individually, often isolated, in the informal economy, operating at a low level of activity and reaping marginal income. Joining forces in small-scale cooperatives can provide them with the economic, social and political leverage they need. It can be worked out in Ethiopia also.

Summary

- There are suitable types of cooperatives which can be organized for women like – cooperative banks, artisans coops, dairy coops, tailoring coops, small scale processing coops, etc.

Self-learning Activity

Try to answer the following questions on your own.

1. What are the types of cooperatives suitable for women?
2. State the reasons for organizing separate women cooperatives.

Small Scale Enterprises for Women and Cooperatives

Women entrepreneurs may be defined as "woman or a group of women who initiate, organize, and run a business enterprise". According to another definition, a woman-run enterprise is defined as "an enterprise owned and controlled by a woman having a minimum financial interest of 51 per cent of the capital and giving at least 51 per cent of the employment generated in the enterprise to women".

Cooperatives and Women Entrepreneurs

Women entrepreneurs, who promote small-scale and cottage industries, can form cooperatives to make their ventures successful. Such cooperatives can provide the following facilities:

1. Joint purchase of raw materials, on behalf of members. Such joint purchases can be made on bulk from production centers or from wholesalers, which allows price advantage to members.
2. Production facilities in the form of constructing worksheds. Such worksheds or workshops can be rented or hired to members on a long tenure basis. In such workshops all facilities like electricity, machinery, water supply, etc will be provided at concessional rates.
3. Marketing facilities for the finished products will also be arranged.
4. Training facilities, which are very important for such entrepreneurs can be arranged regularly.

Promotion of Women's Entrepreneurship in Rural Areas

Promoting micro and small businesses are increasingly seen as a means of generating meaningful and sustainable employment opportunities, particularly for those at the margins of the economy such as women, the poor and the people with disabilities. Micro, small and medium-sized enterprises have been recognized as a crucial way to promote women's economic empowerment while fighting against poverty and gender inequity. They have been identified as engines of growth by many governments, and their promotion has been adopted as a development strategy by many institutional and regional players to create new jobs for developing countries and to drive innovation and economic dynamism. By providing a source of income and increasing access to and control over resources such as land, women can obtain more control of their own lives. Economic empowerment has been shown to impact positively on women's self-confidence, their negotiating position within the household, and the involvement of women in decision-making processes. The benefits of women's increased economic empowerment through the promotion of women's entrepreneurship are multiple. Studies show that among their benefits are women's greater independence and self-assertion, their ability to stand up to abusive spouses, and increased likeliness to serve as role models in the community.

Micro, small and medium-sized businesses offer strong benefits for alleviating poverty in rural areas and for rural development. In low-income countries in the Asian and Pacific region, the rural population accounts for more than 70 per cent of the total population. Despite a decline in recent decades, agriculture still accounts for over 50 per cent of total employment in the region (United Nations, 2006a). In a number of ESCAP countries, the rural informal economy still provides the majority of employment opportunities, mostly for unskilled labour. Women's micro and small subsistence businesses play a crucial role in the rural economy and in ensuring poor households' survival.

Cooperative entrepreneurship in agricultural development contributes to the economic empowerment of poor people living in rural areas. By joining isolated and scattered resources, it can help marginalized farmers to acquire opportunities for entrepreneurship and to strengthen capacity for self-help. Cooperative enterprises have significant advantages especially for rural women faced with gendered constraints which limit their access to entrepreneurial resources (ICA, 2005b; United Nations, 2005a). The women's entrepreneurship has also led to increased mobility among women, the creation of networks of women, and the building of women's solidarity. Women entrepreneurs face unique barriers in entrepreneurship. Inequities in access to capital, resources and government support make it particularly challenging for women entrepreneurs. Women often cannot obtain loans for their businesses due to lack of status and property rights. In the agricultural sector, women farmers have scarce access to agricultural resources and services for production due to gender inequalities, the double burdens of farming and family responsibilities, and the lack of social services and government programmes to support women.

Providing effective support for women's businesses is crucial to promoting women's entrepreneurship. This includes measures to facilitate the creation of women's businesses such as training programmes providing women with essential entrepreneurship skills, mentoring programmes to give women peer support, etc. The establishment of business incubators is another important way of helping to ensure the survivability of women's businesses. It is essential that there be "gender awareness in designing and delivering support measures targeted at female entrepreneurs" (European Commission, 2004).

Women-led Cooperatives: Women's Ways in Entrepreneurship

While motivations for women and men entrepreneurs are highly individual and vary widely, it may be useful to identify if there are any general gender preferences, if any, with regard to what motivates women and men in the conduct of entrepreneurship or running of businesses. The gender dimension in entrepreneurial motives for purposes other than to obtain return in capital or to maximize profit is an area that could be needed to explored. One factor which should be noted for women's active participation in the cooperative sector to a certain extent is that many of the opportunities for new cooperatives are in traditionally women dominated sectors such as social caring. For example, as of 2000 there were approximately 4,500 new cooperatives in the welfare sector in Sweden, covering cooperative childcare run by parents, schools, care of elderly, mental care, antenatal care, physiotherapy, dental services, services for the handicapped and other forms of social cooperatives. In Sweden around 80 per cent of those who start new cooperatives are women. As the rapid growth in employment by new cooperative enterprises from 2.2 million in 1990 to 3.25 million jobs in 1996 indicates, what has been called the social economy type of cooperatives in Western Europe have been rapidly expanding (COPAC, 2000).

Studies of female entrepreneurship find gender differences between women's and men's goals. Whereas men often start a business for mainstream profit-driven motives, there appear to be greater likeliness for women's business start-ups to be related to considerations for reducing marginalized situations. Women often place meaning on entrepreneurial involvement as an instrument to redress exclusionary discrimination. For example, for men, financial gain may be motivation and primary objective. For women, on the other hand, one primary motive is to create greater flexibility for balancing work and family (Fenwick). Women's entrepreneurial involvement in the new forms of cooperatives in Western Europe has integrated objectives to overcome gendered limitations. When elected to decision-making positions, women tend to introduce positive flexibility and work sharing in the workplace. The former has contributed to better reconciliation of individual, family and working time. The latter has made it possible to create new job opportunities for women (COPAC, 2000).

Women's entrepreneurship can often be underlain by the motive to transform, and this can be seen in a number of women's efforts to create gender responsive cooperatives. For example, as described in frustrated at their lack of voice in dairy cooperatives, women in India fought hard and eventually won the right to establish their own all-women cooperatives and, after establishing their autonomy, took initiatives for meaningful participation in setting the agenda, deciding on services and actions, or participating in management and the distribution of benefits (Stephens, 1995). The promotion of women's cooperative entrepreneurship lays steppingstones for enabling a breakthrough for equality in economic empowerment between women and men. Eco-friendly agriculture is one area where the potential exists for a breakthrough.

How to Build a Network for Entrepreneurship

Networks play important roles in starting, running, developing and sustaining enterprises. Individual entrepreneurs can gain from networks such benefits as enhanced access to information and knowledge, markets, suppliers, financing and business related services. They help entrepreneurs expand business contacts, share experiences and have a feeling of belonging. Networks are also used to represent group interests and implement lobbying activities.

Women entrepreneurs usually lack access to capital, knowledge and business know-how, and experience difficulties in dealing with government bureaucracy and complicated administrative procedures. They also remain invisible in that they do not have a channel through which to reflect their special needs to policy makers. By creating and strengthening ties and networks with others in the business community, women can be empowered to overcome a lot of barriers to business, to resolve difficulties and secure the support required for the development, sustainability, and/or expansion of business. Basic information sharing on experiences and the exchange of best practices among successful women entrepreneurs has been reported by many successful business women as a crucial ingredient for their enterprises' success. The creation of a network mechanism by which to facilitate this is crucial for women entrepreneurs seeking to build green cooperatives.

Despite the necessity of networks, women tend to not be well represented in the mainstream network due to the low numbers of women entrepreneurs, relatively small size of their business compared to men-owned business, and predominantly male-dominated business culture, climate and values. In this situation, women entrepreneurs' networks or associations at both formal and informal levels should be expanded to serve as alternative networks. In light of the low level of awareness on green production as well as insufficient infrastructure for production and marketing, it is especially important that women's green enterprises in developing countries should focus on building networks not only amongst themselves but also a diversified network among many types of participants and players in the green coop business. This may include farmers' organizations, women's groups, government and international donor agencies. These networks provide mechanisms which serve multiple purposes, including the following: to increase consumer demand on green products, to attract attention and support of policy makers and donor agencies, and to expand marketing opportunities of green products at both national and international levels.

In many countries, there already exist various women-only networks that cover both general business organizations and sector-specific networks including the agriculture sector. For example, the Korean Women Entrepreneurs Association represents one of the major women's business networks in the Republic of Korea with its twelve local branches. It consists of 270 women-owned enterprises including ten agro business enterprises and most members belong to small and medium enterprises. Founded in 1977, it has implemented various activities aiming at promoting women's entrepreneurial activities and protecting the rights and interests of women entrepreneurs including: (i) business start-up service by offering space and training on financing, business management, marketing and ICT; (ii) lobbying government and the public sector to make regulations and policies favourable for women-owned businesses including government procurement and taxation; (iii) up-to-date information service on business trends, tax systems, and activities of members and their businesses through a website and newsletter.

Other examples include:

- The Korean Women Farmers' Association, with its 8,000 members and 23 local branches, works for women farmers' rights and the expansion of their role in agriculture and local communities.
- In India, the Association of Lady Entrepreneurs of Andhra Pradesh secured land and a grant by lobbying the government. They built infrastructure facilities on the land and opened a women's business cluster based on the food processing industry in 2004.
- The Women Entrepreneurs Association of Nepal (WEAN) has successfully produced and marketed its own brand of pickles that are also being sold online for Nepalese working overseas. WEAN can increase its productivity and scale up marketing through skills training and quality control, and organizes flexible and diverse production units among network members (IFC, 2004).

With the rapid development of information and communication technologies, women entrepreneurs can easily expand their networks to other women entrepreneurs, women's business associations, experts and the academic community, and representatives of governments and international support agencies via websites and internet at any time and everywhere at minimal cost. In cases where there is no individual access to ICTs, community business centres and/or community e-centres can provide networking opportunities. Business linkages refer to the commercial interaction between different profit-oriented enterprises seeking the most efficient way of producing and marketing commercial goods. In the context of business linkages, women's networks can be formed both horizontally and vertically. Horizontal networks are groups of individuals sharing similar problems and having similar enterprise profiles. Women's self-help groups and coalitions among women's green entrepreneurs belong to this category. Vertical networks focus on linking micro to small enterprises, or suppliers within the production chain to producers. They take a step forward and link women-owned enterprises to interesting commercial partners, thus offering increased market opportunities Networks between producers' cooperatives and agro-processing enterprises belong to this category. There are other types of business linkages. In particular, sub-contracts between larger companies and local SMEs can be useful for the promotion of women entrepreneurs since many women entrepreneurs lack market information and have problems gaining access to markets. Contract farming between farmers and firms or traders, and commodity chains of large supermarkets can be included.

Problems of Women Entrepreneurs

Shortage of working and investment capital resulted from gender inequalities

Due to deep rooted social norms and values, women in most of the communities lack equal rights in passing decisions on properties or resources. This condition puts women in a most difficult situation to raise sufficient money for investment either from their own savings or credit, as they cannot meet collateral requirements of lending institutions.

Work burden of women

Women are entrusted with wide range of responsibilities that include contributing labour to production activities, up keeping home, rearing children, and others. In this regard, they face shortage of time in carrying out the business activities.

Lack of basic business skills and technical knowledge

In many countries, women do not have equal access to education and training with men. As there are general shortages of such services, men seize the existing limited opportunities. Therefore, women remain losers and consequent lack of proper skill and knowledge to undertake business activities.

Other cultural barriers

Women are not encouraged or motivated to own and run income generating activities that could improve their economic conditions. Although women significantly participate in all economic and production activities, they are not accorded proper recognition for their contribution due to the cultural barriers, which consider women as weak, less reliable, and inefficient.

Scope/Steps to Encourage Women

The following steps are advocated to encourage women to undertake enterprises:

1. *Access to capital, infrastructure, and markets:* Government and related organizations like banking institutions must come forward to provide liberal capital to organize enterprises by women. Infrastructure facilities in the form of industrial estates exclusively for women can be established. Marketing facilities for the products of women entrepreneurs can also be arranged by governments.
2. *Development of managerial and production capacities:* Training and development activities can be developed especially for women entrepreneurs and such training could be given to selected target groups. Training should be made a continuous process for such women entrepreneurs.
3. *Identifying investment opportunities:* Government and NGOs must come forward to identify investment opportunities and production venture suited to women. In all regions of the country selected areas can be located and such investment opportunities can be initiated and it can be extended to other areas in future.
4. *Promotional measures:* Promotional measures like sponsoring, delegating, participation in trade fairs, exhibitions, arranging buyer-seller meets and specialized conferences, etc can help the promotion of women entrepreneurs.
5. *Seminars and workshops:* Organizing seminars, workshops, and training programmes for giving wider exposure to women entrepreneurs will be useful to develop their entrepreneurial capabilities.
6. *Tie up arrangement:* Women enterprises can be tied to medium and large scale industries for marketing their products and to make a permanent development for their enterprises.

Institutional support needed and action plan for the involvement of women in cooperatives Development

The betterment of women by cooperatives can be undertaken through the support of various ministries, government departments and NGO's. Such institutional support must be available to women members of various cooperatives as well as for special women's cooperatives.

Following are some of the forms of institutional support envisaged:

Enactment of provisions in Cooperative Legal System

The Cooperative Proclamations/Laws/Acts of countries must be amended in such a way that all types of cooperatives must be insisted to reserve one-third or one-fourth of the seats in management and other sub-committees to women members. In the case of the election of the president of a cooperative, a turn system must be arranged i.e. every two turns one women must be elected as the president of the society. As an alternative, when the president post is occupied by a male member, the post of vice-president must automatically go to a women candidate. Such arrangements will facilitate women's participation in policy-making and decision-making in various areas.

Amendment of bylaws of each cooperatives

Bylaws of all types of cooperatives except women's cooperatives, must be suitably amended to make provisions for women members to get elected to the management committees and other sub-committees. The turn system as mentioned in the above paragraph must be introduced in the bylaws and must be implemented strictly. Penalties must be imposed for the non-implementation or willful violation. If suitable women candidate is not available that post must be kept vacant till suitable women candidate is elected.

Special types of cooperatives

In special types of cooperatives like consumer cooperatives, dairy cooperatives, SACCOS and cooperative banks, the promoters must be officially informed to admit one-third of the members from women. Because women are the prime users of such cooperatives and this will help them in decision-making and giving suggestions for policy-making in the respective areas.

Joint membership

Joint membership of husband and wife must be made in cooperatives like primary agricultural cooperatives. Because in the absence of landownership, such joint membership will boost the morale of women. When a particular type of work is done jointly by men and women in a family, both of them should be made members of cooperatives.

Coordination of other women departments/agencies

As mentioned earlier, all government departments and related agencies must coordinate their activities with the concerned cooperatives. This is to dovetail the women's development programmes with the programmes of the cooperatives.

Cooperative education

Special educational programmes for women must be arranged on a routine and continuous basis. As for as possible, women trainers must be recruited for such women's training programmes. Special training funds must be created for such purposes.

Special funds by cooperatives

Every cooperative society must set forth a portion of the net profit every year towards the education and development of women members. The bylaws of each cooperative society must be suitably amended wholeheartedly by all members. Ways and means of spending such money for women's development must be clearly spelt out.

Action Plan

The participation of women in cooperatives is important for their socio-economic upliftment. A democratic and people's movement owes some responsibility towards women and in the process of national development by removing the constraints at the following levels:

At the government level

The national development schemes and planned schemes adopted by the government should include a specific provision in regard to the involvement of women in cooperatives. The cooperative law must be supportive and suitably amended by including enabling provisions for the organisation of new women cooperatives, admission of women members in the existing cooperatives, reservation of seats for women in management committees and sub-committees.

At the cooperatives level

1. Creation of women cell/bench in the proposed regional and national federations.
2. Cooperative laws and bylaws must be suitably amended to meet the financial and infrastructural needs.
3. Cooperatives should make efforts to promote the unorganised women in different sectors of the society like labour, dairy, fishery etc.
4. Cooperatives should adopt a joint strategy with other agencies to support gender issues.
5. A nexus must be built with voluntary agencies which have for the promotion of women's participation in cooperatives.
6. Cooperatives should provide financial and other supports to income generating activities of women.

7. All cooperative unions and their above level cooperatives must create women development fund.

Summary

- Women entrepreneurs may be defined as "woman or a group of women who initiate, organize, and run a business enterprise".
- Cooperative enterprises have significant advantages especially for rural women faced with gendered constraints which limit their access to entrepreneurial resources.
- The women's entrepreneurship has also led to increased mobility among women, the creation of networks of women, and the building of women's solidarity.
- The betterment of women by cooperatives can be undertaken through the support of various ministries, government departments and NGO's. Such institutional support must be available to women members of various cooperatives as well as for special women's cooperatives.

Self-Learning Activity

Try to answer the following questions on your own:

1. How to build entrepreneurship network?
2. What are the problems of women entrepreneurs?

Role of International Cooperative Alliance

Seeds of Change

The advancement of the status of women in cooperatives and in society in general has always been important to the international cooperative movement. Since the World Summit on Social Development and the Beijing Conference, however, the promotion of gender equality has been particularly high on its agenda. In 1995, the International Co-operative Alliance (ICA) passed a resolution on "Gender Equality on Cooperatives" in which the members of the ICA noted that gender equality is a global priority for the cooperative movement. ICA members declared their commitment to take action and the ICA at the global level has undertaken a series of programmes and activities for the advancement of women. Several initiatives have been undertaken in collaboration with the ILO, such as the development of training materials on gender in cooperatives in French, English and Spanish and leadership development manuals for women cooperators soon to be published. Example, that can lead to a more equal allocation of management and leadership positions through affirmative action, equal access to cooperative benefits such as credit, cooperative education and training, and removing legal obstacles to women's equal and active participation. For successful gender mainstreaming, the strengthening of gender capacities within the cooperative movement should be a priority.

Benchmarking, sharing best practice and establishing a monitoring system in cooperatives which can trace the progress in equal opportunities through agreed indicators, are necessary for cooperatives that wish to maintain a high and dynamic profile as businesses based on ethical and social standards. Capacity building is another key area that needs to be given priority as one of the main obstacles to equal opportunities is the education gap between men and women and the resulting occupational segregation. Cooperatives and their support structures should ensure that their women members are fairly and equally represented in all training and education programmes. These programmes should be sensitive to women needs, or specifically designed where necessary, and should include confidence-building measures. Identifying potential women leaders and helping them gain visibility and experience within the organization through training, coaching and mentoring has proven to be an effective strategy. Nominating, encouraging and supporting women members to stand for election in various committees, representative bodies and higher-level cooperative structures and to participate actively in meetings, is an important step towards the advancement of women in cooperatives, but special attention must often be paid to the specific gender-related obstacles that women face.

In many countries where women are particularly disadvantaged in terms of legal rights, cooperatives should form national level coalitions and alliances with gender advocacy organizations and other civil society organizations to lobby governments for equal rights (especially in property and asset ownership) and an effective legal framework and institutions that foster gender equality. Without fundamental changes in society it is, of course, difficult for cooperatives alone to alter gender disparities which affect their operations. However, since cooperatives often have the needed representation force behind them, they are in a good position to influence national level policies and should make use of this.

From the time cooperatives first emerged out of the excesses of the industrial revolution to today's market turbulence and resulting marginalization, social exclusion and denial of access of opportunities of large sectors of the population, cooperatives have always represented a valid organizational form with an important role to play. For cooperatives hold the potential to help people to help themselves, to present an alternative way of organizing and carrying out business activities, and to demonstrate that values of caring and sharing, democracy and participation do indeed work for the benefit of society.

The ICA has come to realize that the participation of women in the Co-operative Movement will be imperative if the Co-operative Movement is to respond to the present and future needs of society. Many believe this to be a revelation that will require the future attention of the Movement. Many are convinced that this new idea is a reflection of the trends in women's struggle for equality in the 1960s and today's call by women and men for gender integration and awareness. However, we should go back into ICA's history and recall that, 'the place of women in the Co-operative Movement' has been an issue that has been addressed and discussed throughout the history of the ICA starting at the first Co-operative Congress. As we celebrate our Centennial, let us critically look at our past and, before embarking into the 21st century, ask:

"Has the Co-operative Movement made efforts to increase not only quantity but more importantly the quality of women's participation"?

Many men and women would reply, "In all countries where there are co-operative organizations, it is invariably stated that the women must be won over to the co-operative idea if the movement is to attain its object. Yet very little has been done in most countries to win the women to co-operative cause..."

This observation, made by Emmy Freundlich in 1921, remains true today despite the many ICA resolutions and policies. To cite only one example, the 11th International Congress assembled in Ghent called on member organizations to make "the election of women to the management boards of co-operative Societies obligatory...". The European Region reiterated this call only last year in a more subtle and perhaps less emphatic move, calling on member organizations to include more women on their delegations to the Regional Assembly. Rhetoric has been abundant, action minimal. One hundred years after its creation, the ICA is continuing to deny itself the benefits of women's leadership by their under-representation at decision-making levels within its membership and its governing bodies.

As we move into the 21st century, the decision-makers of today will need to address the issue of gender. Each national movement will need to take concrete action. We know that co-operatives can improve the lives of women by providing them services, now let us prove that co-operatives can be leaders in addressing gender issues and improving the overall economic and social status of both men and women worldwide.

ICA Policy on Women in Cooperative Development (1993)

Co-operatives are based on the idea of democracy and the full participation of each member without regard to gender and other arbitrary forms of discrimination. Despite this fact, women have been prevented from full participation in the co-operative development process due to discriminatory legislation, traditional economic dependence and prejudice.

Policy Background

One of the primary objectives of the ICA is to act as a catalyst for co-operative development in all parts of the world. Both the ICA Policy for Co-operative Development and the ICA Policy on Human Resource Development (HRD) were formulated in order to outline strategies to guide activities in the areas of co-operative development. Although women have been included within these policies, follow-up in terms of strategies and programmes has been inconsistent.

The participation of women in co-operatives has been a concern of the ICA since 1995. The Women's Co-operative Guild which later gave rise to the

ICA Women's Committee, was and continues to be active in promoting women's full participation in co-operatives. However, in the absence of a clear ICA Global Policy providing guidelines for the formulation of viable strategies for women, existing programmes have not been able to sufficiently focus on women.

Cognizant of the fact that previous efforts to promote women's role in co-operatives have produced inadequate results, the ICA has formulated this Global Policy on Women in Co-operative Development.

Development Objectives

The aim of the ICA Policy on Women in Co-operative Development is two-fold:

(*a*) to assure the effective participation and full integration of women in co-operative development at all levels, and

(*b*) to contribute to the effective implementation of the ICA Policy for Co-operative Development in accordance with the ICA Policy on HRD in Co-operatives in the Third World.

The ICA Policy for Co-operative Development emphasizes the establishment and growth of independent, democratic and viable co-operative organizations, in which men and women participate on equal terms. These co-operative organizations must be capable of serving their members efficiently and contributing to economic and social equity in their respective communities and countries.

The ICA Policy on HRD in Co-operatives emphasises the need for intensified education and mobilization programmes for members, particularly for women, who to a great extent have been overlooked but are essential to the overall success and development of the co-operative movement.

Target Groups

Broad participation through the mobilization of the total human potential for development is a prerequisite for the achievement of our policy objective. It is therefore essential that the following institutions and groupings be involved in this process:

1. *States and Policy-makers*

In many parts of the world, especially in developing countries characterized by economic stagnation and negative growth, continued population increase, heavy debt burden and adjustment programmes with subsequent reduction of public expenditures for social programmes, the situation of women has deteriorated. In order for women's rights to be guaranteed, it is essential that:

- women's needs, skills and resources be acknowledged;
- constitutions, laws and civic and labour codes be revised in order to eliminate the legal basis for discrimination;
- legal protection be provided for women's access to landownership, credit, basic education, training, health, child-care facilities and other social services that are necessary for the full integration of women into the development process.

2. *Development Agencies*

Development agencies have for decades primarily targeted men in their projects which have been for the most part designed by men.

It is therefore essential that:

- gender planning methods be applied which take into account the different needs and roles of women in society;
- it be recognized that by ignoring women's key role in economic development, the potential for development is seriously undermined;
- loan programmes be initiated.

3. *Financial Institutions*

Restrictions in access to credit limit the productive contribution of women. Factors that inhibit women's demands are transaction costs, collateral requirements, cumbersome application procedures and cultural constraints.

It is therefore essential that:

- reforms of financial markets, development of loan programmes, intermediary institutions, advisory services and legal reforms be initiated to facilitate women's access to finance;
- promotion of thrift and credit co-operatives, which have a proven record of involving women, be encouraged.

4. *Training Institutions*

Women's co-operatives have often lacked business skills and administrative capacity due to the inadequate provision of education and training for women. It is therefore essential that:

- provision be made for specialized education and training programmes for women, aimed at developing their financial, technical and managerial skills; and
- financial support such education and training be provided.

5. *Women's Groupings*

To boost women's participation, it is essential that women's groups and individuals:

- build informal or support networks for women;
- introduce, if necessary, special measures to increase the proportion of women involved in decision-making;
- encourage women to fully exercise their rights;
- maintain rosters of qualified women.

6. *Members, Committee Members, Co-operative Leaders and Staff*

Co-operatives in which the talents and capabilities of women are given full play will enjoy great advantages in the future. It is therefore essential that gender awareness be promoted, so that:

- women be enabled to occupy positions in a complete sense as members and managers;
- women be promoted to decision-making positions at every level.

Activities

In order to translate the policy aims into affirmative action, the ICA will address issues that highlight the close linkage between gender issues and development, e.g.:

(*a*) gender analysis/awareness and sensitization;

(*b*) revision of existing policies and strategies for co-operative development;

(*c*) education and training programmes/capacity building;

(*d*) networking;

(*e*) policy dialogue;

(*f*) research;

(*g*) resource mobilization;

(*h*) information;

(*i*) advisory services,

(*j*) establishment of mechanisms to implement gender policies.

Facilitation Role of the ICA and its Development Partners

Since the establishment of the ICA Regional Office in New Delhi in 1960, efforts have consistently been made to initiate and promote programmes aimed at emancipation of women and their involvement in the organisational and business activities of cooperatives. This has been done through a long chain of seminars, discussions, conferences and technical assistance programmes which have been carried out with the collaboration of its Member-Organisations and development partners. In the agricultural cooperatives sector some of the most recent initiatives have been as follows:

- A series of technical meetings and conferences were held which had taken note of the recommendations of UN and other international conferences and initiatives on women in cooperative development.
- A series of specialised training courses for rural women leaders in agricultural cooperatives, on an yearly basis, with the financial support of the Government of Japan and in collaboration with the JA-Zenchu and the IDACA.
- Three top level Asian and African Conferences on Farm Women Leaders in Agriculture and Agricultural Cooperatives during 1997 and 1998 [one more conference is planned in 1999] in collaboration with the JA-Zenchu, AARRO and the IDACA and with the full technical support of the Government of Japan in the Ministry of Agriculture, Forestry and Fisheries-MAFF.
- Development of training manuals and other supporting materials for the use of women leaders to develop women's associations and help increase women's participation in agricultural cooperatives.

Issues Involved

In the background of the above discussion and in view of the constraints faced by women with regard to their participation in agricultural cooperatives, the following issues need to be tackled by the concerned authorities and cooperative institutions:

- Identification of an appropriate mechanism which could provide development opportunities to women in rural areas.
- Encouraging cooperatives to have special programmes and tasks for women to perform in the organisational and business affairs. It has been observed that in many of the countries of the Region more women are being taken in to undertake administrative and functional activities – they make very good, reliable and honest cashiers, sales girls, inventory controllers, secretaries, public relations officers and member contact persons.
- Review, revision and reformation of cooperative legislation and government policies which facilitate and encourage women to become members of cooperatives and participate in decision-making processes. Cooperative institutions and their federations may take the lead on their own to institute programmes for the participation of women in cooperatives. Voluntary initiatives by cooperatives themselves do not necessarily to be qualified by government approvals. Cooperatives should lobby with their governments to replace or suitably amend the restrictive laws.
- Accord due credibility to the achievements of women in agricultural cooperative development through publicity, exchange of visits,

participation in meetings and conferences. Women need a platform through which they could justify their participation in cooperative action.

- *Replication of successful experiences.* The work done by the Women's Associations of Japanese agricultural cooperatives and Han Groups has produced good results for the community and business of their cooperatives. Such experiences need a thorough study. They have a lot of good things to offer.
- *Development of Plans of Action at all levels.* Women's cooperative organisations at primary levels should try to federate themselves into higher federations or association so that their 'bargaining power' is strengthened. The cooperatives and women's associations should develop realistic plans of action to be followed for three to five years.
- Cooperatives to initiate education, training and extension programmes for women through vocational and literacy programmes [these also include home improvement activities e.g., cooking classes, handicrafts, social interactions, environment related activities etc.
- Creating conditions for women to market their products through outlets established by agricultural cooperatives. [Agricultural cooperatives in Japan set apart a space in their shopping areas exclusively for the Women's Associations and even for the individual farmers to sell their products, including organising Morning Markets etc.].

ICA Strategy for Promoting Gender Equality

1995 — Adoption of the resolution "Gender Equality in Co-operatives" which established gender equality as a global priority for the ICA and called on members to establish action plans to address the issue.

1996 — Letter from ICA President sent to members asking for information to evaluate the level of implementation of the resolution (gender disaggregate statistics on membership, information on women's participation in power structures and decision-making, and copies of any plans/policies for achieving gender equality). Gender disaggregated statistics requested from ICA membership.

1997 — Report summarizing the information collected and suggesting elements for inclusion in a strategy presented to the ICA Board. The Board tabled the report and agreed to re-examine ways of implementing the resolution. ICA Board reviewed proposals to the ICA General Assembly for changes to the ICA Rules and Standing Orders from a gender perspective. General Assembly approved adding promoting "...equality between men and women in all decision-making and activities within the co-operative movement..." as an objective to the ICA and revised the standing orders to allow equal opportunity for qualified women and men to participate in ICA decision-making structures.

1998 — Draft Gender Strategy discussed by ICA Board (Tokyo). No specific action with regard to the strategy was taken.

1999 — ICA Board (Quebec) approved "ICA 2005" and implementation plan for 2000 which included developing an ICA Gender Strategy.

PRIORITY AND PROPOSALS

1. Genuine and clear statement of commitment from top leadership and visibility of competent women and men leaders

Statements

- Draft a statement from the ICA President, ICA Director-General, ICA Board and disseminate with the adopted ICA Strategy on Gender Equality.

Demonstration of Commitment at ICA level

- Adopt Policy on ICA Statutory Meetings to include directives on ensuring:
  - ❖ gender balanced speakers at meetings at the global and regional levels and strongly encourage SBs to do the same.
  - ❖ gender balanced delegations (encourage member organizations to send gender balanced delegations and reward compliance — public recognition, certificates or reduction in meeting fees.
- Better communicate activities undertaken by the ICA at all levels to promote gender equality especially regional activities in electronic and print formats.
- Issue annual statement from ICA President for International Women's Day (8 March) as a means of disseminating information to promote progress in the advancement of women and gender equality.

In order for genuine commitment to exist at the senior level of management whether in individual co-operatives or within the ICA structure, people must understand the issue. It is essential that gender training be provided at all levels of an organization, but beginning at the very top.

2. Capacity-building Gender training

- ICA Board Members (extend the meeting to allow for a one/two-day session by an gender training specialist — and include in the ICA budget an allocation for new Board members to benefit from gender training)

- ICA staff including regional directors
- ICA specialized body Chairs and Secretaries

(Organize gender training for the Chair and Secretaries as an additional day/s to the annual consultation meeting)

ILO has noted that almost universally, women have failed to reach leading positions in major corporations or private sector organizations irrespective of their abilities. Yet, it has been proven that "women possess qualities which could contribute significantly to improved communication, co-operation, team-spirit and commitment within organizations — qualities which today are essential for achieving excellence and maintaining the necessary networks of contacts and relationships."

3. Gender balance of elected officials and staff

Enabling environment for increased participation of women in power and decision-making.

- Achieve target of at least 30 per cent of ICA decision-making positions to be held by women at global, regional and sectoral levels (ICA Board, Regional Executive Committees or Council, SB Executive Committee or Boards) by 2005.
- Promote public awareness on the positive role and contribution of women in decision-making positions in co-operatives.
- Review ICA staff and personnel policy and encourage MOs to review their employment policies and rules to enable women to reach decision-making positions.
- Include in all management programmes an element of gender awareness and studies demonstrating the business savy of gender diverse management. Address issues such as the glass ceiling.

In order for gender issues to be considered a real priority of work, responsibility and accountability must be assigned and progress must be measurable both in qualitative terms and quantitative terms. As it is difficult to strike the balance between the marginalization and the mainstreaming of gender activities, real efforts must be made to evaluate progress. "Good data, well used is essential to good policy."

More consistent documentation and dissemination of experiences, collection of data — disaggregated by sex, will assist in identify progress — or the lack of — and allow the ICA to develop appropriate policy or operational activities.

4. Accountability and Monitoring Structure

- Appoint individuals who will be responsible for ensuring that gender issues are addressed (gender focal points).

- ❖ Ensure that a gender focal point is appointed in each regional office who is able to regularly report on activities undertaken to promote gender equality. (Note: ROAP has a gender advisor. Gender in all other offices is 'integrated' in programme, but no specific responsibility for gender has been assigned.)
- ❖ Request SBs to appoint individual to be responsible for following up on gender equality promotion and providing information regarding their activities dealing with gender issues.
- ❖ Prepare Regional Gender Strategies by 2002 which include a detailed plan of action to improve gender balance in ICA regional structures including regional specialized bodies and member organizations.

Information for monitoring

Collection or qualitative and quantitative evidence of progress.

- Collect gender disaggregate statistics for membership and employees.
- Collect and share positive experience and replicable models for achieving gender equality from member organizations in their capacity as employers and within their institutional structures (elected officials).
- Evaluate and prepare on annual basis a report from ICA Development on the impact of its programmes on promoting gender equality not only for internal reporting purposes, but also for wider dissemination.
- Provide support for initiative to map the participation of women in the ICA as a tool to identify progress or the lack of progress. Although the allocation of new resources to carry out a number of the activities to promote gender equality will be needed, many can be implemented by the reallocation of existing resources. However, reallocation will require real commitment to making gender equality a real priority.

5. Human and financial resources

- Assess budget to see what proportion of financial resources are allocated to activities to promote gender equality especially with regard to development programmes, but also with regard to communication and staff training and present this on annual basis to the ICA Board and to MOs.
- Seek new resources for new and existing programmes with gender issues.
- Keep gender balance in mind when recruiting for new ICA staff.

Summary

- In 1995, the International Co-operative Alliance (ICA) passed a resolution on "Gender Equality on Cooperatives" in which the members of the ICA noted that gender equality is a global priority for the cooperative movement.

- The ICA has come to realize that the participation of women in the Co-operative Movement will be imperative if the Co-operative Movement is to respond to the present and future needs of society.
- ICA has designed strategy for promoting gender equality in cooperatives.

Self-Learning Activity

Try to answer the following questions on your own:

1. What are the priorities of ICA to encourage women in cooperatives?
2. What are the major gender issues, which ICA does address?

References

Chen, M.A., *Beyond Credit: A Sub-sector Approach to Promoting Women's Enterprises*, Agha Khan Foundation Canada, 1996.

ESCAP, (2004), "Partnerships Moving Beijing Forward; Gender Equality and Empowerment: A Statistical Profile of the ESCAP Region", paper prepared for high-level intergovernmental Meeting on the Review and Implementation of the Beijing Platform for Action, 7-10 September 2004, Bangkok, Thailand.

European Commission (2004), *Promoting Entrepreneurship Among Women* (Best Report No. 2).

FAO, (2001), *Agricultural Cooperative Development: A Manual for Trainers*, Rome, Italy.

Hafkin N. and Nancy Taggart, (2001), *Gender, Information Technology and Developing Countries: An Analytic Study* (Education Resources Information Center).

Hashemi, Syed, Sidney Schuler and Ann Riley (1996), "Rural Credit Programmes and Women's Empowerment in Bangladesh", *World Development*, Vol. 24, No. 4, pp. 635-653.

ICAc. Regional Women's Committee for Asia and the Pacific (2005). *Report on the Activities of ICA Regional Women's Committee 2002 to 2004.*

ICA, *Women in Decision-Making in Cooperatives*. Issued jointly by the International Cooperative Alliance Regional Office, New Delhi, and the Asian Women in Cooperative Development Forum, Philippines.

ILO: *Legal Constraints to Women's Participation in Cooperatives*, Compilation of 11 Country Studies in Asia, Africa and Latin America, Cooperative Branch, 2002.

ILO: *Promotion of Cooperatives*, Report V (1), ILC 2001.

ILO: *Gender Issues in Cooperatives: An ILO ICA Perspective*, Gender Sensitization Package for Cooperative Leaders, Cooperative Branch, Geneva, 1995.

Johnson S and Rogaly B, *Microfinance and Poverty Reduction*, Oxfam: Oxford 1997.

Marcucci, Pamela (2001). "Jobs, Gender and Small Enterprises in Africa and Asia: Lessons drawn from Bangladesh, the Philippines, Tunisia and Zimbabwe", ILO-SEED Working Paper No. 18.

Mayoux, L., "Microfinance and Women's Empowerment: Approaches, Evidence and Ways Forward", Open University Development Policy and Practice Discussion Paper No. 41, August 1998.

Mumtaz, Khawar (1995), *Gender Issues in Agricultural and Rural Development*, Gender Issues in Agricultural Development Policy in Asia and the Pacific, FAORAP. Bangkok.

Nakkiran. S., *Cooperative Management-Principles and Issues*, Deep & Deep, Delhi, 2006.

Report of Co-operative Commission, UK: *The Co-operative Advantage: Creating a Successful Family of Co-operative Businesses*, January 2001.

Maithili Vishwanathan, *Women in Agriculture and Rural Development*, Rupa Books Private Limited, New Delhi.

Daman Prakash, *Women Farm Leaders of Agricultural Cooperatives* – Third Asian Conference Report and its Documentation, Tokyo, Japan, 1998.

Sinha, Shalini (2005), *Developing Women's Entrepreneurs in South Asia: Issues, Initiatives and Experiences*, UNESCAP, Bangkok.

Smyth I and March C., *A Guide to Gender Analysis Frameworks*, Oxfam, 1999.

SDC (2003), *Gender-Oriented Entrepreneurship Promotion: Strategies and Tools along the Project Cycle*. (Bern, Switzerland, Swiss Agency for Development and Cooperation (SDC).

Stephens, A. (1995), *Gender Issues in Agricultural and Rural Development Policy in Asia and the Pacific*, FAORAP, Bangkok.

Taimni, K.K. (1998), *Challenges before Cooperatives in South Asia: Building a Comparative Advantage*, Extracted from the Study, Cooperatives in the New Environment: Role of the Registrar of Cooperative Societies in South Asia, FAO, 1997.

Tuladhar, Jyoti (1996), *Factors Affecting Women Entrepreneurship in Small and Cottage Industries in Nepal: Opportunities and Constraints*. ILO and SIDA.

United Nations (1999), *Convention on the Elimination of All Forms of Discrimination against Women*, initial report of States Parties, Myanmar.

—(2002), *Supportive Environment for Cooperatives: A Stakeholder Dialogue on Definitions, Prerequisites and Process of Creation*, Report of an Expert Group Meeting held in Ulaanbaatar.

—(2003), *Social Safety Nets for Women: Studies on Gender and Development*, New York.

—(2005a), *Cooperatives in Social Development,* report of the Secretary-General A/60/150.

—(2005b), *Improvement of the Situation of Women in Rural Areas,* report of the Secretary-General A/60/165.

— (2006a), *Full Employment and decent work for all: regional highlights,* (ECE/INF/2006/5) Regional Commissions, New York Office.

—(2006b), *Improvement of the Situation of Women in Rural Areas.* Resolution Adopted by the General Assembly: 60/138.

Index

❑❑❑